C Loc Ref

The West Country Writers' Association

THE FIRST FIFTY YEARS OF THE

WEST COUNTRY WRITERS' ASSOCIATION

by
ANNE DOUBLE

With a **Foreword by Christopher Fry**
and **Preface by Margaret Drabble**

First published in Great Britain in 2001

The West Country Writers' Association

Text © 2001 Anne Double

The moral right of Anne Double to be identified as the author of this work has been asserted by her in accordance with the Copyright, Design and Patents Act 1988

All rights reserved

Except for use in a review, no part of this book may be reproduced, stored in a retrieval system or transmitted in any form or by any means, electronic, mechanical, photocopying, recording or otherwise, without prior permission of the publisher

Designed by Marina Oliver, Tudor House
Jacket design by Julie Fairless, Design Ink

Printed in Great Britain by Antony Rowe Ltd
Chippenham, Wilts

CIP Catalogue entry for this book is available from the British Library

ISBN 0-9540120-0-3

Published 2001 by West Country Writers' Association
Half Hidden, West Lane, Bledlow, Princes Risborough, Bucks. HP27 9PF
website: www.westcountrywriters.co.uk

The West Country Writers' Association

What they say about the book

'I took part in all the early Congresses, including the first one at Bath. I have always believed that the WCWA contributed strongly to the concept of regional literature, which includes work (fiction and non-fiction) about the region as well as writers (on any subject) identified with the area by living there for all or part of their lives. The WCWA has a fine record, and long may it continue in this over-centralised country that Britain has become.' *(Victor Bonham-Carter)*

'An essential book for all interested in writing and the West Country.' *(Anita Burgh)*

'The West Country has been the inspiration for many different kinds of writing. Inevitably, half a century of the West Country Writers' Association merits a tale of its own. This book does justice to that story.' *(Janet Green)*

'Our literary associations are very lively affairs, as this History shows.' *(Richard Lee)*

'It is important that the history of the West Country Writers' Association should be chronicled. This is a deeply researched book about a unique organisation that for fifty years has enabled its members to exchange ideas, learn about many aspects of writing, and hear talks given by the great names of contemporary literature.' *(Peter Macdonald)*

'My most memorable moment connected with the WCWA was first meeting Laurie Lee. Here was the man who had written *'I walked out one Midsummer Morning'* and *'Cider with Rosie'*. I was totally entranced!' *(Eileen Stafford)*

'We in the West Country have been privileged to be associated with many famous writers. Indeed, a Cornwall County Council booklet lists more than a hundred in Cornwall alone and many of these have been members of the WCWA.
However, the Association was not formed to boost the images of the famous few, but to encourage and support all who have a passionate love of writing and the West Country. Their contribution to our literary heritage is acknowledged in Anne Double's account of the first 50 years of the WCWA.' *(E. V. Thompson)*

'It is a grave mistake to think real distinction only exists in big things rather than small things. The story of the West Country Writers' Association is proof of this.' *(Joanna Trollope)*

The West Country Writers' Association

About the Book

Anne Double has succeeded in writing a wonderfully evocative account of a very special organization. It is an informative and highly entertaining book of the first half century of the WCWA. The inauguration came triumphantly, when the idea was supported and sponsored by the Bath Assembly. It went through tribulations and near-extinction, to a triumphant revival and steady progress. All are faithfully recorded.

The book has been thoroughly researched from original documents and the personal recollections of members. It brings alive the various personalities involved. The roll-call of members, past and present, resembles a biographical dictionary of prestigious writers from all sorts of literary backgrounds.

The West Country has adjustable boundaries, and members of the WCWA join for a variety of reasons: they live there, were born there, write about the area, and without exception love it. They may be journalists, poets, novelists, cartoonists - at some time the WCWA will have included any type of writer you can think of. It is not just for writers - editors, agents, booksellers and librarians belong too.

Not only members will want to read this book, however. It is a unique slice of literary history, a fascinating account of how people with a common interest have worked together for mutual benefit and companionship.

The West Country Writers' Association

The Author

Anne Double was born precisely two weeks earlier than the WCWA and spent her childhood in Liverpool. Her attachment to the West Country began at the age of thirteen when she started reading *The Mayor of Casterbridge* on a wet caravan holiday in Wales and fell instantly in love with Dorset. After winning the WCWA short story competition in 1987 she found that the prize was a long stint as the Association's secretary. She now lives at the top of a hill in Herefordshire with her husband Anthony and five children.

Dr. Robert Cooper, Vice-President, writes:

Eleven years ago, the West Country Writers' Association ran a short story competition for young writers. There was a clear winner, 'The WCWA'. Anne Double won the prize, but in her the WCWA won an outstanding secretary, and the author of this book. Anne's contribution to the WCWA has been immense. She, supported by her husband Anthony, has been tireless in her work for us. She has enabled our yearly congress to run like clockwork. She is a superb organizer. She is charming and ever-smiling, nothing is too much trouble for her. I know this book of the first fifty years of the WCWA will be a success as Anne has written it. It will tell us about all the most distinguished members of our Association, and not the least of these will be our Secretary Anne Double.

The West Country Writers' Association

Contents

Acknowledgements...11
Author's Textual Notes...13
Foreword...15
Preface..17
Part I: Prehistory: 1946-51......................................19
Part II: The Early Days: 1950-64.................................39
Part III: The Middle Years: 1964-77..............................95
Part IV: The Information Age: 1978-2000.........................161
Part V: The New Millennium......................................207
Appendices
I   Officers over the Years..................................217
II   Congress Venues and Speakers.............................222
III   Members 2001...224
Notes...226
Index of Names 230
Subscription List...236

Acknowledgments

How long is a piece of string? This book could have been every bit as long. Over fifty years there have been so many interesting writers attached to the WCWA that I shudder to think how many I must have missed out. Frank Littlewood ended the 1969 Newsletter by proclaiming FORGIVENESS WANTED for his efforts: I, too, ask forgiveness of all those members to whose role I have done scant justice or whom I have not mentioned at all.

I am deeply grateful to the WCWA Committee under the Chairmanship of Frances Brown who entrusted me with the project of producing this history, something I had long wanted to do. I have grateful memories too of Bryan Little, who first took me to the WCWA archives in 1991 and more or less handed them over as a sacred charge. I hope I have done what he wished, though I suspect he would have preferred more scholastic facts and less story-telling!

Any research which involves frequent trips to the West Country is bound to be enjoyable and I am indebted to those people who have made it more so by helping with the research, making documents available, and accommodating me during my many visits: John and Joan Paxton have been particularly hospitable, as were Victor and Cynthia Bonham-Carter when I was in Somerset. Victor also allowed me to borrow his full set of *The West Country Magazine*, which is an invaluable reference work as well as an excellent publication. Chronologically, the next important source of information was the WCWA Newsletter, and I am grateful to David Keep who provided me with copies of all the issues I did not have as well as with some other useful books of West Country interest. Many people contributed their memories, letters and other material: my thanks to Joan Lowry, Meryl Macdonald Bendle, Bob Cooper, Geraldine Kaye, and especially Dorothy Stiffe, who sent me the full set of scrapbooks she compiled about congresses from 1951-1990. The Literary Estate of Henry Williamson has allowed us the privilege of using the Owl Colophon, and Anne Williamson has been unfailingly helpful, not only supplying me with unpublished diary material and the very photograph of Waveney Girvan that Henry referred to in his letter of November 1964, but doing all this with such alacrity and enthusiasm. The other major source of original material has been the Bath Records Office where the WCWA archive is housed, and I must thank the staff there for their helpfulness and good humour - even when I wanted one last thing fetched from the archive at five minutes to closing time on a Friday afternoon.

It has been an honour to have a foreword and preface provided by two such writers as Christopher Fry and Margaret Drabble; I am deeply conscious of their kindness, and thank them both for endorsing the work.

On the production side, my thanks are due to the editorial subcommittee - John Harcup, Jane Tatam, Margaret Bacon and Marina Oliver - who have worked on the practical details of costing and publishing. Bob Cooper has kindly taken on distribution, and Julie Fairless has done wonders with design. Margaret Bacon and Marina Oliver have been a most supportive copy-editing and proof-reading team, always generous with their time and always willing to share their vast experience of the writing profession. Marina's technical skills, supported by those of her husband Chris, in preparing the text on disk, have been invaluable. Without her expertise and patience this book would not have appeared - or at least, not on time.

And finally, many thanks to my family for all their support and assistance, and for learning to live with the WCWA over the last couple of years.

Textual notes

Throughout this book, no attempt has been made to be politically correct about the use of the term 'Chairman', simply because the holder of the WCWA Chair has always been known as the Chairman, regardless of gender. My apologies to anyone who might find this offensive.

Every attempt has been made to observe consistency in the use of capital or lower case letters for various titles (such as chairman, congress, newsletter) but wide variations of usage occur in the quoted material which has been recorded faithfully, leading to many apparent inconsistencies of usage.

The founders of *The West Country Magazine* very carefully styled it so, to distinguish it from the *West Country Magazine* which it had superseded. After some time they became less particular and began to refer to their publication as the *West Country Magazine* or *WCM*. Having started with the original form, I have maintained that usage throughout.

Several members' poems are included in the text, because I wanted there to be some examples of genuine West Country writing in the book and a short poem can stand alone more easily than out-of-context prose. Obviously I have been spoilt for choice, so one simple rule has prevailed. With the single exception of our President (one poem by him and one poem about him) I have only used poems by members who are no longer alive. I am sorry that space did not allow there to be more.

I am indebted to Victor Bonham-Carter, Christopher Fry, Bob Cooper, Meryl Macdonald Bendle, Geraldine Kaye, Janet Green, Joan Lowry, Harry Guest, Michael Hartland, Bill Pickard, David Keep and Simon Rocksborough Smith for permission to use their words; to Ion Trewin for permission to use extracts from the writings of his father, J.C. Trewin; to Anne Williamson and the Literary Estate of Henry Williamson for permission to use extracts from the writings of Henry Williamson; to the *Times Literary Supplement* for permission to use the extract 'Regional Pride', first published on 1 June 1951.

Photographs

I am indebted to the many people who have allowed me to use their photographs in this book: to the *Western Daily Press* for permission to reprint the picture from the first luncheon in 1950; to Lois Lamplugh for the photograph of the annual luncheon at Bath in 1956; to Anne Williamson and the Henry Williamson Literary Estate for the Ox's Cross photographs and the photograph of Waveney Girvan with Henry Williamson, as well as for permission to reproduce the owl colophon; to Meryl Macdonald Bendle for the photograph of Henry Williamson at Torre Abbey; to the *Western Morning News* for permission to reproduce the cutting from May 1968; to Janet Green for the photographs of the Fortieth Anniversary Congress and of St. Michael's Mount; to Christopher Fry for supplying the portrait of himself in the 1960s; to John Harcup for all other photographs of Christopher Fry and of Laurie Lee, as well as those of Victor Bonham-Carter, the 1995 committee, Bob with Meryl and Geraldine at Bristol, the Weymouth Civic Reception, Adele Ziolkowska and Harvey's Wine Cellars; to Dorothy Stiffe for the photographs of Leslie Grinsell and Charles Causley; and to Frida Harris for the photographs of John Paxton, Raymond Allen and George Baker. Other photographs were taken by myself or my husband Anthony Double, who also provided the photograph on the inside cover.

Every effort has been made to trace all copyright holders. In some cases, dealing with long-dead authors from the earliest days of *The West Country Magazine*, this has so far proved impossible. If any of these come to light, and if any others have been inadvertently overlooked, I will be pleased to make the necessary arrangements at the first opportunity.

Every effort has likewise been made by both myself and the editorial committee to observe factual accuracy, but any errors which may have crept in remain my own responsibility and not that of the WCWA.

Anne Double
Garway Hill, Herefordshire
February 2001

Foreword

When John Trewin invited me to put my feet into Henry Williamson's shoes as President of the West Country Writers' Association I hadn't a notion that I should be getting thirty-five years of such pleasure from it. I'm even surprised that I said yes. At that time I didn't take easily to official occasions. In the after-the-War years I could reasonably have been called a lalophobic opsimath. Besides, what right had I to call myself a West Countryman? True, I had been born in Bristol, though taken away to Kent when I was three. But then there was half of my ancestry, I thought, which had peopled Somerset for centuries. And an uncle (on the "other side") who had been the mayor of Penryn. There was a working-holiday with Robert Gittings in 1932 at Thorne St. Margaret, near Wellington, when I had started to write a play - and my honeymoon in Cornwall, not far from Fowey, the Cutty Sark moored in the river below our windows. So I could feel easy about my credentials, perhaps. And each year as the weekend in early May came round I felt part of a family reunion - a far happier one than the Monchenseys could manage. The history of the Association makes a wonderfully heartening story of Fellowship. And how sensible to have been born in Bristol.

Christopher Fry   November 2000

Preface

This history is the ideal introduction to The West Country Writers' Association. It tells you all the things you wanted to know and never dared to ask - what it is, how it began, who was involved, who quarrelled with whom, and why it continues to flourish. Anne Double has done a fine and scholarly job, and produced a lively and entertaining narrative from what must at times have seemed like a mass of confusing records and minutes. From her opening pages on the mysterious founder Waveney Girvan she grabs our attention. She brings him and his idiosyncrasies brilliantly to life, and goes on to provide vivid pen sketches of a host of eccentrics. She introduces us to the passionately pedantic Bryan Little of Bath, to the 'explosively genial' Shavian St John Ervine, to the distinguished, gentlemanly and wealthy H. A. Vachell, and to a host of other personalities both obscure and famous. The accounts of Henry Williamson alone are a treasure-trove of reminiscence, and Laurie Lee steps out from the pages as though he were still faithfully attending the WCWA meetings. This is a piece of literary history, not just a useful public record.

The account of the Association's changing aims and evolution is detailed and informative, and everywhere enlivened with anecdotes and illustrated by poems. But what more would one expect, in a description of a group of such diverse, interesting and gifted writers, united in their love of such an inspiring landscape? The magnificent West Country broods over and lights up squabbles about membership and difficulties about what we now call 'venues', and Anne Double has found some memorable quotations to brighten her story. She brings us Compton Mackenzie's rapturous prose and Christopher Fry's elegant verses, as well as a touching and entertaining first-hand description of the heroic Ascent of St Michael's Mount in the early nineties.

Recent members will meet here genial hosts and familiar friends, and learn much about the past decades of this distinguished and at times touchy and difficult conglomeration of talents. It is hard to organise a group of spirited and independent authors who do not wish to wear badges or labels, and who find it hard to agree even on a definition of the West Country. So we must all be impressed by the hard work of the officers of the committee, who over the decades have kept the association alive. It went through bad patches, and had to face hard choices, but there was nearly always somebody willing to be coerced into taking responsibility. This very readable account catches the spirit of the whole enterprise - friendly, helpful, and at once professional and informal.

Margaret Drabble   February 2001

PART I

PRE-HISTORY: 1946 - 1951

Who, Why, When, What, Where...?

> *The West Country Writers' Association was founded in 1951 by Waveney Girvan to foster, by the interchange of ideas, the love of literature in the West Country.*

With these words we have traditionally begun the information sheet which is sent out to prospective new members or anyone who enquires about the West Country Writers' Association. Probably very few, if any, of them have the slightest clue who Waveney Girvan was. Probably relatively few of our established members have the faintest idea who Waveney Girvan was either. The trouble is that the statement has such an authoritative ring to it that few like to admit their ignorance: the name sounds so literary - Waveney/Waverley, well they *sound* alike! - that we all nod sagely at the mention of our founder while wondering privately who on earth he was. His full name was Ian Waveney Girvan but he never used the first forename, leaving subsequent generations of members a little unsure as to whether 'Waveney' was his forename or part of an unhyphenated surname. Consequently nobody ever has the confidence to refer to him as plain 'Girvan' and he always gets his full five syllables, redolent with literary possibilities.

In fact it is quite difficult to unearth anything he did write, apart from a bibliography of Henry Williamson, an out-of-print appreciation of Eden Phillpotts and some articles and reviews for *The West Country Magazine* which he helped set up in 1946. Waveney Girvan was not principally a writer at all: he was - eventually - a small publisher who found himself among like-minded literary friends at a particular time and place, the West Country of the immediate post-war years.

Nor was he even a West Countryman. He was a Scot, whose father was a military doctor, and he lived wherever his father's military postings took him. One of these places just happened to be Bodmin and he fell in love with it, so he came to regard himself in adult life as 'an honorary Cornishman'.

And was he even really our sole founder or, as we shall see in subsequent chapters, just one of several figures who worked together to bring the WCWA to life? His first importance lies in his foundation of *The West Country Magazine*, for this periodical, which ran for twenty-six issues from 1946 - 1952, provided the seed from which the Association sprang, and it is impossible to talk about one without the other.

Our founder was neither a writer nor a West Countryman, and he was not the sole founder: the attempt to define or explain the WCWA is always fraught with such contradictions. Rather like Lawrence's famous dictum about the novel, if you try to nail anything down in the WCWA, the Association gets up and walks away with the nail. So it is with the brave, dogmatic mission statement: yes, the WCWA was founded in 1951, and Waveney Girvan played a leading role, and it existed to foster the love of literature, specifically the literature of the West Country - but who was Waveney Girvan? Why did he want to start a writers' association? And why then? What constituted a 'West Country Writer'? Where, indeed, is the West Country?

Who?...When and Why?

To take the first question first: Waveney Girvan describes himself, in the 'notes on our contributors' of *The West Country Magazine*, as 'born 1908; author of *A Bibliography of Henry Williamson (1931)*; student of

Cornish and Devon literature.' Victor Bonham-Carter, who probably remembers him better than anyone these days, fleshed out that brief portrait in a talk he wrote for the annual luncheon of the WCWA at Torquay in 1995. I say 'wrote' rather than 'gave' because Victor was unfortunately incapacitated by a broken leg on that occasion, and the talk which he had thoughtfully prepared in advance had to be read to the luncheon in his absence by Bob Cooper. Waveney, he tells us, was an accountant by profession but did not practise much because 'as a young man, he was principally and surprisingly an inventor':

> In 1935 he invented a device that tightened, locked and cut the steel strapping that one used to see on packing cases on railway platforms. It was called Security Steel Strapping, and Waveney sold it to a firm in Sheffield, which paid him a salary to run that side of their business. This he did from 1935 - 1946; and as steel was a 'reserved occupation', that was his job during the Second World War.
> When peace came, the firm stopped Steel Strapping, and Waveney found a new job, more to his taste and talents possibly, as production manager for the publishers T. Werner Laurie, where he stayed some 16 years - until shortly before his death in 1964.[1]

During this time with T. Werner Laurie he ran two London publishing houses of his own, Carroll & Nicholson and Westaway Books: the first had a general list and the second was confined to the West Country, and it launched a number of new books and authors with West Country connections. His own writings, apart from the Henry Williamson bibliography, were confined to articles for periodicals including *Truth, The Patriot* and *New English Review*, as well as *The West Country Magazine*, which grew out of Westaway Books and the friendship with other writers that this brought him.

At this point, the questions 'When?' and 'Why?' become inextricably linked with the question 'Who?' Fiftieth anniversaries have proliferated in recent years as we have remembered the stages by which war ended and peace was established - Dunkirk, VE Day, VJ Day. It is no accident that *The West Country Magazine* began in the immediate postwar years, and the fifty-year-old WCWA too was a child of its times. David Keep, a recent chairman, was once heard to remark that Waveney Girvan started *The West Country Magazine* because it was the only way he could get his hands on paper supplies during rationing. There was obviously more to it than that, but the remark does have an element of truth. Postwar austerity certainly had an influence on the foundation of *The West Country Magazine*. Henry Williamson, being President of the WCWA in the year when Waveney Girvan died, wrote an open letter to all members in November 1964 to announce the death of the founder and pay tribute to his work, and he makes much the same point about the prosaic beginnings of *The West Country Magazine*:

> Ian and I were together when he decided to buy the *West Country Magazine,* towards the end of the Hitlerian war. It was the day of the 'little magazines'. Denys Val Baker was one of the pioneers. No new periodicals were allowed at that time of dearth owing to paper and other shortages - Europe prostrate, the cousin nations bled white - but magazines which had been published previously were permitted revival. Ian and I met at the house above the woods of Lee Bay in North Devon, where Malcolm Elwin was then living, and talked about the revival. Elwin accepted the editorship.[2]

Malcolm Elwin was a thoroughly literary man who had worked as critic, publisher's reviewer and literary journalist as well as being a respected biographer with books about Byron's family, Thackeray and Charles Reade to his credit. He and Waveney Girvan had become friends in the days of Westaway Press and in 1944 they thought about setting up a regional magazine devoted to the West. As Victor Bonham-Carter tells us, it was agreed that Malcolm Elwin, the established man of letters with a wide circle of literary friends, should be the first editor, while Waveney Girvan the ex-accountant would see to production, distribution and finance. Because of the embargo on starting new periodicals, they both looked at a defunct periodical published at Dawlish and called *West Country Magazine* which, according to Victor Bonham-Carter, they both considered 'a very poor thing', and decided to buy it just as Henry Williamson describes. Even so, it was 1946 before they were able to start production of *The West Country Magazine* and as Malcolm Elwin says in his first editor's preface:

> There was formerly a WEST COUNTRY MAGAZINE published at Dawlish. From its proprietor we have acquired the right to the title of THE WEST COUNTRY MAGAZINE, but we have otherwise no connection with that periodical. We are not 'an old friend with a new face', but an entirely new magazine, independent of any commercial combine and of any social, religious, or political organization.[3]

He goes on to remark that '...the size of the magazine and the quality of the paper are not as we could wish; they will be improved as soon as conditions permit' and indeed the first few issues of the magazine, printed by the *Somerset County Gazette* at Taunton, display an intriguing variety of paper types, qualities and shades according to whatever was available. 'RETURNING TO NORMAL - BUT SLOWLY!' proclaims the advert for Winel Office Equipment Products (Proprietor: Henry Elwin) in the first edition of *The West Country Magazine*. 'Our proud job of supplying the needs of the armed forces is complete; now we can concentrate on producing the famous Winel Office Filing Equipment. For some time the supply will fall short of demand... we want to be fair, so orders are entered in sequence of receipt for delivery'. The advertisements throughout this amazing periodical are a period piece in themselves, with everything from Aertex for shirts to Calor Gas for cooking announcing 'Your turn will come!' as they strive to keep up the public interest in goods that they cannot supply.

Possibly with the help of Winel Office Products, the magazine managed to keep going, but Malcolm Elwin soon dropped out of the story when his partnership with Waveney Girvan broke down. Henry Williamson's letter mentions the problem:

> Elwin had made it a literary magazine, and published a fine first number, with Powys and other good writers. Ian suggested the magazine should be of general interest, thus to get advertising from hotels in Devon and Cornwall, etc. Elwin felt that he could not continue as editor, and Ian did the job himself.[4]

This is not the whole story. A more weighty reason for the break-up was another symptom of the times in which they lived: fascism. It is well known that Henry Williamson's right-wing politics probably cost him the OM which he so dearly wished for on his 80th birthday and which his friends felt that he deserved, but in Victor Bonham-Carter's opinion, 'Henry Williamson was a political innocent to say the least, whereas Waveney Girvan was well aware of what he was doing'.[5] His extreme right-wing politics brought him into contact with the 12th Duke of Bedford and his agent John Becket, a close supporter of Oswald Moseley and William Joyce. It was from the 12th Duke of Bedford that Waveney Girvan raised the financial backing to get *The West Country Magazine* off the ground. Malcolm Elwin found Waveney Girvan's politics offensive, and although they had been brought together by a mutual love of the West Country and an admiration for the works of Henry Williamson, Elwin could not go along with the politics. Malcolm Elwin's name appeared on just two issues of *The West Country Magazine*, and then the publication had the great good fortune to secure J. C. Trewin, esteemed theatre critic and Cornish man of letters, as editor for the rest of its existence.

But the history of *The West Country Magazine* is another story except insofar as it led to the formation of the WCWA. The times were right: the war was over, creativity was springing up again, and despite the shortages there was probably no more auspicious time for trying to get into print. Henry Williamson's letter gives us a flavour of those optimistic days:

> New publishers were springing up, there was a shortage of books. It was the time of 'the sellers' market'. A current phrase was 'one can sell old rope', such was the scarcity of all commodities.[6]

For writers it must have been the best of times and the worst of times: you could get your work published, but you couldn't get the paper. In an age when it is so difficult for an unknown author to get into print, it sounds like heaven. Certainly many works were published then which would never see the light of day in these commercialised times and it was just the right moment for a regional magazine, and then an association dedicated to regional writing, to spring up. In his open letter, Henry Williamson paints an idyllic picture:

I met Waveney Girvan in the valley of the Bray in the early thirties. He had proposed a visit to us at Shallowford, a thatched house beside the river, to ask me if he might publish a bibliography of my writings. I have a photograph of him sitting beside me on a timber waggon in the shallows of another river, the Barle, by Dulverton. We had gone there to buy fish from the trout farm, to put into my beat on the Bray. We are hatless, and sitting with my eldest son, then a small boy. The water ripples in the May sunshine, around the great wheels of the timber waggon. We are holding up pint pots of beer, toasting the photographer.[7]

Henry meant to look out the photograph to have it blown up and copied but he never did: however, his biographer and daughter-in-law Anne Williamson has done so, and thanks to her we are able to reproduce it in this book.

But the main object of Henry's open letter was to let members know of the founder's death, and he explains that Waveney Girvan had gone into hospital for observation, had an operation which found him to be fatally ill, and died in the early hours of Thursday 22 October 1964. He then drops in the most extraordinary throwaway line - '...he had an outstanding interest in "Flying Saucers", being editor of *The Flying Saucer Review'*. No explanation, no expansion - but what a new dimension this lends to Waveney Girvan. The man who at first sight appeared to be simply a minor publisher with a dark line in politics turns out to have an intriguing touch of singularity. And it's not just flying saucers and steel strapping: Anne Williamson tells us of a night in 1934 when the two men sat up all night drinking beer in the Biltmore Hotel after Henry came across Waveney in New York - selling champagne! Henry's diary for 1934 is full of insights of what Waveney Girvan got up to in New York.

> Sat 10 March: Party at Biltmore...dined in a drugstore. Afterwards with W. Girvan to a movie palace. He says his million bottle deals with champagne and cognac almost concluded, & he will make £20,000 without having risked a penny of his own. Queer business: people talking to him all the 24 hours, all chaos, only 1% of contacts of any use. Home [HW was staying at the Brevoort Hotel] at 3 am, very white & lovely streets in the snow and

coloured lights.
Mon 12 March: ...went to theatre 'As Thousands Cheer' with Girvan & afterwards to 'Hollywood' nightclub, Rudy Vallee & scores of extraordinarily beautiful girls...I enjoyed myself with Girvan. To bed at 3 am...[8]

John Trewin, too, describes an unforgettable character:

> One of the last messages I had from him before his death in the autumn of 1965 [sic] was from North Cornwall. Wherever he went, in London or elsewhere, it was of Cornwall that he talked, and he talked with an extraordinary grace and mercurial wit that made me wish for a concealed tape recorder. Something of the art of conversation died with Waveney Girvan.
> Of middle height, he had close-brushed, shining black hair and intensely dark eyes that were usually full of laughter. So was his voice. Little could repress Waveney's sense of humour. As Chairman of any committee he must have been unmatched, though graver folk were worried sometimes by his irreverent way with notices of motion, seconders, and votes of thanks. 'Why not call it all "Any other business"?' he said.
> I don't imagine anyone who was there has forgotten the morning of a West Country Writers' annual meeting at Falmouth in May 1961. For some reason, neither the then Hon. Secretary or the minutes had appeared. Delighted to be left without any papers at all, Waveney conducted the meeting like a conjuror pulling whole families of rabbits out of a surprising variety of hats. No man enjoyed himself more than he did that morning while he was evolving an agenda, improvising the minutes, and holding a conversation with an unseen secretary, or with himself in various capacities. The manner at times was positively Gilbertian. I told him so afterwards, and he said: 'I take that as a compliment. We'd have had Gilbert as a member on the strength of *The Pirates*.[9]

Waveney Girvan was clearly a character. He had that same touch of singularity which marks out so many West Country writers, and which marks the spirit of the region as a whole. When he died, his character inspired a sonnet from one West Country writer to another:

WAVENEY GIRVAN

That mind was quick along a dozen paths,
So much to stimulate, engage, amuse,
So many speculations to be followed...
The fourteen years I knew him passed too swiftly.
How many pubs we drank and argued in! -
Enlivened always by his springing wit,
His love of talk that never was exhausted,
Nor we exhausted by this rare companion.
I call the roll of some who valued him:
Charles Petrie, Wilson Midgley, John Trewin,
Jan Stewer, Eden Phillpotts, I not least,
And Henry Williamson and Leonard Strong.
To have lost him leaves his friends always the poorer,
To have known him leaves them lastingly enriched.
Kenneth Hopkins.[10]

What...?

So what is a 'West Country Writer'? In what way does he or she differ from any other writer, and what is it that qualifies a writer to be considered part of this august body? When Malcolm Elwin and Waveney Girvan put together the Editorial Preface for the first issue of *The West Country Magazine*, they had a clear idea of what they expected. 'We shall willingly omit nothing calculated to contribute to the essential quality of a magazine intended for all lovers of the West Country,'[11] they announced, and they cited stories, essays, travel, letters, observations from naturalists and archaeologists, 'instructive' views on town and country planning - any 'good writing' - as being welcome in their pages.

That variety of discipline continues to this day. At a meeting of the Romantic Novelists' Association, Crime Writers' Association or Science

Fiction Association, one can be fairly confident of rubbing shoulders with romantic novelists, crime writers or sci-fi buffs respectively. At a WCWA assembly, no such assumptions can be made. It embraces the whole range of writing, creative and factual, in all its branches. There are poets, novelists of every genre, and playwrights; there are critics, reviewers, biographers, essayists, academic authorities, compilers of textbooks and technical manuals; there are children's writers, journalists, lexicographers, travel writers and theologians. As the years have passed the definition of 'writer' has been expanded to include scriptwriters and broadcasters on radio and TV; and those engaged in professions peripheral to the writing trade - publishers, agents, booksellers, librarians - have also been welcomed into the fold, in accordance with the founder's original idea that it might one day become an association for all arts in the West Country.

That West Country quality of singularity sparkles through the list of members and their works. Though there are probably no longer any authorities on flying saucers, the Association once included the compiler of the rulebook for Archery at the Olympic Games,[12] and we can still boast an expert on public monuments, several steam train buffs, the author of the definitive guide to jumble sales, and members with such diverse specialisms as seaside postcards, aphorisms, Gilbert & Sullivan, and travelling fairground folk.[13]

The list of members' titles is just as curious: volumes called

How to Buy and Run a Small Hotel
Advice to Aspiring Writers in the Merchant Marine
Hysterectomy and the Alternatives
Passenger Steamers of the Bristol Channel[14]

nestle in the files alongside the romances, thrillers and books of topography. Add a handful of Cornish Bards and some household names like Daphne du Maurier, Christopher Fry and Laurie Lee, who have all been members in their turn, and the mix is bewilderingly various. It is almost as difficult to define a 'West Country Writer' as it is to pin down the Association, but always there are two factors which unite them: the fact that they *are* writers, or professionally engaged in the business of writing, and some connection - whether birth, residence or subject matter - with the West Country.

Where...?

And that immediately begs the question of what, precisely, constitutes 'the West Country'. Waveney Girvan thought he had the answer. The scene was the first annual luncheon of the newly formed Association in 1951, where Compton Mackenzie, the very first guest of honour, proposed the toast 'To the West Country' as every guest of honour does to this very day, adding that he had 'never given a toast from deeper in my heart'.[15] Rising to Compton Mackenzie's challenge to define what was the West Country, Waveney Girvan 'rashly' declared:

> Draw a line starting slightly East of Gloucester in the North and ending slightly West of Southampton in the South. All the land westward of that line, and all the islands adjacent to its coasts, that is the West Country. If any part of Wiltshire is left out by this delineation, then the eastern line must be slightly bent so as to include the whole of that fair county. Otherwise we have no further territorial ambitions in England.[16]

So 'the Six Counties' were established: Cornwall, Devon, Dorset, Somerset, Wiltshire and Gloucestershire. But what about the Isle of Wight and Bournemouth, which had historically belonged to Dorset? Bits of Hampshire had to be included. And if Gloucestershire was in, what about neighbouring Worcestershire? And Herefordshire, where it is impossible to get any further west without being in Wales and where you look *eastward*s to Laurie Lee's home in the Cotswolds? Our president, though born in Bristol, is most closely associated with Chichester, and recent officers have had addresses in Swansea and the Lake District. Many of the founder members were based in London, and early committee meetings were regularly held in the capital. The West Country is clearly an elastic concept.

Waveney Girvan was happy to concede the point, cheerfully

proclaiming in *The West Country Magazine*:

> One of the day's major accomplishments was undoubtedly in arriving at a definition of the West Country. In addition to the six usually recognised counties, Hampshire was added to conform with the boundaries of the BBC's West Region. Elsewhere, Kenneth Hopkins persuasively pleads for the inclusion of this delightful county, and as we wish to keep on friendly terms both with Mr. Hopkins and the BBC, Hampshire is in. Next year we hope to welcome other representatives of the county: "I've cum up from Aldershot" may sound odd at first, but we'll get used to it.[17]

Perhaps this demonstrates not just his lively character, but a much easier attitude than is sometimes attributed to the founding fathers when they were defining their territory. Purists may look to 'the Six Counties' as a dictum set in stone, but Waveney Girvan was quite relaxed about stretching the point. Kenneth Hopkins answered him in the same edition of *The West Country Magazine* with a humorous three-page discursion on why Hampshire *had* to be included for, as he says,

> Well! With the South and the East, Hampshire obviously has little to do; and I will take no space discussing the self-evident fact that Hampshire is not in the North. What then is Hampshire?
> Hampshire is a splendid beginning to the admirable West.
> Hampshire is an integral part of the ancient kingdom of Wessex, and has imperishable associations with the great Kings of the West, with Arthur, whose very Table is preserved at Winchester, and with Alfred, whose statue very solidly set in the middle of a main street affords to the traveller tangible evidence that Winchester is a stronghold of the West. Winchester, with her thousand years and more of recorded history, and her cathedral full of buried kings. I will say no more in a geographical way except that two of the most beautiful rivers of the West, the Stour, making its way through the quiet fields of Dorset, and the Avon, carrying to the sea a reflection of Salisbury's slender spire, are both Hampshire rivers, too... I am proud of the West, and love it. And I know that my county stands four-square as the first bastion

and strong defender of the West against people and influences from "Lunnon, other side of Lunnon, up-country and forren parts".[18]

As Kenneth Hopkins rightly points out, the true origin of the concept of 'West Country' lies with the ancient kingdom of Wessex, and Alfred its heroic, human giant of a King, but 'Wessex' as a name is now most closely associated in literary minds with Thomas Hardy, the most famous West Country writer of them all - although sadly he died twenty-five years too soon to be recruited to the WCWA. Hardy was responsible for the revival of the term 'Wessex' to describe that area in which he set his created world, and even went so far as to produce a map of Wessex, with his fictional names for towns and natural features set alongside real names like Stonehenge, Stour Head and Southampton. Hampshire was definitely in - it was 'Upper Wessex' - but Gloucestershire was too far north for his range, and Cornwall, a county wreathed in personal associations for Hardy since the day he 'set out for Lyonesse' and met his future wife, becomes 'Off Wessex'.

Hardy may subsequently have come to regret this map because it led people to relate his fictional settings (and characters) too rigidly to their corresponding real locations (and inhabitants). He noted in a late preface (1912) to his 1895 novel *The Woodlanders* that, in response to readers' queries about the exact location of 'Little Hintock', he once set out on his bicycle to try to find it, but failed to identify any one exact spot. His readers, however, were constantly reassuring him not only that they knew precisely the place he was thinking of, but that he had described it perfectly. Precise identification of settings had become a nuisance, and Hardy tells us in his *Life*[19] that whereas his friend Barnes was exclusively a Dorset writer, he was feeling after a more general sense of the whole Wessex area and never one particular place. Wessex, so Hardy the archetypal Wessex Man would have us believe, was not a real place so much as a country of the heart and mind, where he was able to set his protagonists against a timeless landscape: but Tess's *Cross-in-Hand* is real enough, as are the physical features of the Mayor's Dorchester.

As with Wessex, 'the West Country' is rooted in a real region, but can be carried anywhere in the hearts and minds of those who love it. It is both Waveney Girvan's six-and-a-bit counties, real and physical, and it is the sum of the values and idiosyncratic qualities that have inspired creative artists for generations. It is to do with a real place, and it is a way of life - or of looking at life.

Wessex was important to Hardy not just because it was a beautiful area but because it was the setting for his grandmother's tales and the world they opened up to him - a world just out of reach in the past. She gave him his fascination with stories of odd and eccentric ways of rural life, of strange events played out against an apparently tranquil landscape, of a life that seemed so colourful, set a generation back before the coming of machinery in the Agricultural Revolution. Hardy was a storyteller, in the rural tradition of story-telling, and although we have great diversity in the interests of our membership today, there is no denying that the earliest members of WCWA were, principally, storytellers too. The first issues of *The West Country Magazine* contain some topographical articles, some poetry, some essays on modern manners; but the short story is their staple. And Hardy always held it a truth that any teller of short stories must grab and hold on to his audience like the Ancient Mariner, that '...a story must be exceptional enough to justify its telling'.[20] Wessex for him was an unfailing source of such exceptional material.

Something of that flavour of life in the West Country is conveyed by a small volume which David Keep rescued from a jumble sale and donated to the Association. Called simply *West Country Short Stories*, it embodies the West Country delight not just in traditional storytelling, but in telling stories of strange and exceptional events. It was published in 1949 and shows the same spirit of region that inspired the founding of the WCWA. Its editor, Lewis Wilshire, was a founder member, as were no fewer than thirteen of the contributors, including Eden Phillpotts, A. L. Rowse, Lady Vyvyan, L. A. G. Strong, John Moore, and Henry Williamson whose story *'Billy Goldsworthy's Cow'* reveals a depth of understanding of the rural people of his village, laced with an unusual sense of humour. Wilshire included stories by Hardy, Q, Baring-Gould, R. D. Blackmore, Jefferies, Defoe and several other well-known authors who were already dead, but whose work represented for him, '...stories that could not possibly have come from anywhere else!'[21] He arranges the stories under six headings, the six counties of Waveney Girvan's definitive West Country, because he wanted to illustrate the differences in habit, custom and speech between county and county even within the region. Many of the stories are told in local dialect, many have a strong supernatural element, all are tales of rural people and all celebrate idiosyncrasy. Not all his authors, he says, have spent all their lives in the West, but all

> ...have contrived to penetrate to the heart of the place and its people, to pin down in words the unique spirit and quality of the West.[22]

This is the spirit in which *The West Country Magazine* was founded, and which Malcolm Elwin invokes in the first editorial preface:

> We do not suggest that the West Country, rather than any other part of England, pretends to a more general appreciation of true values. But the West Country is especially blessed in the possession of unspoilt natural beauty, and many of its inhabitants are still fortunately engaged in simple rustic pursuits more conducive to happiness than grim servitude to urban industrialism. For this reason annually come thousands of visitors from industrial areas, seeking recreative strength from the beauty of the West Country, its rustic charm, and the fresh winds on its hills and beaches. We address ourselves to these visitors as well as to West Countrymen - indeed those who see the West only during too short holiday visits are the more likely to delight in reading, in homes remote from well-loved scenes, the writings of West Country authors about West Country settings.[23]

In these days of 'creeping sameness' when it is a common complaint that *every* town now looks the same, with the same chains of the same stores in the same style of shopping mall, it is easy to see why people become so attached to the West Country which is, as Elwin says, outstandingly beautiful but which also has a distinctiveness of character in its twisty lanes, smugglers' coves, inconvenient parking, regional dialects and old stories. It is an exceptional region - exceptional enough to be worth writing about.

Malcolm Elwin may not have suggested that the West Country had a monopoly in the 'appreciation of true values', but Bryan Little was not shy about making sweeping claims for the region when he gave a lecture on 'Bath and Literature' at the first luncheon for West Country writers in 1950, the year before the Association was launched:

> The West Country's contribution to literature has been specially and disproportionately large, and [it is] an area where an unusual author-density per head of the population exists now, in spite of the London draw. There seems to be something literary in the Western air and in the romantic outlines of Western hills and combes...[24]

Other early members were equally fulsome in their claims, for example A. L. Rowse writing in *The West Country Magazine*:

> No region has exerted such a pull on the imagination, on mind and heart, as the West does...[25]

John Trewin tempered this florid tendency when he set out his mission statement for the magazine as 'simply to express the spirit of the Western Counties without affectation or fuss':

> The West is not what vulgarisers would have it be, a welter of pixy whimsies, Devon-heaven rhyming, Mummerset folk-weave, the arch and the coy, the sham rural and the consciously quaint... The idea is intolerable. So, too, are the Cold Comfort melodramatics of writers who come to the West... to 'do most of their cursing there'. It is hard to say which is worse - to go West and woolly or West and wild. Either way madness lies. Here at least we shall hope to keep the heart warm and the head cool.[26]

Eccentrically enough, it took a Yorkshireman to sum up this spirit of the West most poetically. At the 1950 luncheon in Bath, J. B. Priestley was the guest speaker who caught it precisely:

> I believe that in the West the Saxon of the Anglo-Saxon

foundation is still haunted by the Celtic imagination. It is like the brandy still burning on the Christmas pudding. I think it is a country of knights and enchantresses: it is as if Merlin were still alive.[27]

Listening to this speech was an 'old novice', Sam Uglow, who described himself in this way because he had only recently taken up writing after retiring as a schoolmaster. He wrote a perceptive article for *The West Country Magazine* summing up his thoughts on all that he had heard at the Bath meeting about this concept of 'regional writing'. His description of the gradual stages by which environment goes into writing is illuminating:

> An embryo writer begins with an urge to express himself on paper. From the very beginning, he has a vague ambition to make a name for himself in the literary world, and he realizes that the first step up the ladder has been attained when his efforts appear in print for the first time. Before he settles on a particular medium he has to have the necessary materials. It is very simple really. He finds the materials on his own doorstep; automatically they are ready for use, and use them he does. He is one with his upbringing and his environment and, in both, he has the proper stuff for his work and the basic elements for his literary development. It is regionalism, pure and simple. To be more specific, if his locality is the West, a wealth of material lies at his disposal. If his malady takes the form of a poetic frenzy (which it often does), he raves of the glittering pathway of the setting sun on the western sea. He moralizes on the fate of the fly in the sundew on the Cornish moors. He rhapsodizes on the lush foliage of the hedgerows, the cricket on the hearth, the churring of the nightjar. He senses tragedy and mystery in the jagged rocks of the coasts, the mists shrouding the tors, the loneliness and barrenness of the moorlands.
>
> Eventually, in a more settled prosaic frame of mind, he writes of the everyday scene - an eminently satisfying theme for his self-expression. It is this very point of self-expression which clinches the argument for regional writing. The writer is so attuned to the spirit of the place that his interpretation becomes spontaneous.

Most likely he turns to his real mother tongue, the dialect which he hears spoken daily and in which, in truth, he regularly utters his thoughts. The wonderful lore of the countryside is at his disposal, and in it are possibilities for fun and humour, sincere characterisation and description. Later he may discard dialect as a vehicle, but he retains the wealth of simile and allegory which it holds; even though he loses something when a plover is substituted for a 'horniwink' or a wasp for an 'apple-drain', and utter dejection takes the place of a 'dying duck in a thunderstorm'. But the whole substance of his more finished work is permeated by his early associations of language and locale and enriched thereby.

To give particular instances... I could quote many pertinent examples from the coterie of West Country writers assembled for that special gathering; they brought their own home atmosphere with them... and if there is still any doubt as to the virtue of regionalism as a stepping stone to literary fame, it is only necessary to add that J. B. Priestley was the chief guest at the luncheon, and I ask you! What is good enough for Yorkshire is good enough for the West Country.[28]

So here we have the WCWA, its feet very firmly planted in the six counties of the real south-west of England, but embracing all writers who carry that spirit of the West - 'the brandy still burning on the Christmas pudding' - in their creative imagination. But that still does not answer the question which secretaries are so frequently asked by potential recruits: what is the WCWA *for*? what does it *do*?

The replies offered are generally a string of negatives. It is not a writers' circle (no disrespect to writers' circles, but it just cannot offer the sort of practical support and advice that a writers' circle is designed to give), it is not a useful 'trade union' like the Society of Authors, and it is not an altruistic campaigning body like PEN. It does not (at least, not directly) advance writers' careers or promote their books. It has a simple mission statement about promoting the love of literature in the West Country, but turns out these days to be a mixture of authors - some not at all 'literary' - who live all over the country, founded by a Scot who produced more gadgets than books, with a strong sense of regional identity that was best summed up by a Yorkshireman. When you pin a label to it, it walks away with the pin. As past chairman David Keep said on his retirement, 'I am still not quite sure what the WCWA *does:* it is sufficient that it *is*'.[29]

In as much as it *does*, we can say that it has around three hundred members, who have the opportunity to keep in touch through a newsletter, an annual congress, and smaller informal regional gatherings throughout the year. These local meetings happen more in some areas than others: they have proved remarkably resistant to organization. Some members, renowned for their hospitality, give regular lunches in their own homes, with or without a speaker or special event to enhance the occasion: elsewhere a co-ordinator sets up a meeting or lunch at a local pub. Some are one-off events: others happen at the same time every year. Some areas of the West Country enjoy several such events: other areas miss out. Because they happen spontaneously it is difficult to get an even coverage, though this is an area of activity which is often requested by new members who want to get to know their writing neighbours or who perhaps cannot get to the annual congress.

The congress is, and always has been, the central activity of the Association at which members are brought together for 'the interchange of ideas'. Starting from a one-day event in 1950 it has evolved over the half-century and changed its format from time to time, but it has always been held in a West Country town at a weekend date, usually early in May, and it has always centred on the formal annual luncheon flanked by an exhibition of members' publications and at least one literary lecture.

The newsletter does not have such a consistent history. It first appeared in 1968 and continued rather spasmodically in its early years, taking a variety of different styles and formats. Since the 1980s, however, it has appeared regularly twice a year, conveying booking information for the congress and reports on the doings therein as well as book reviews, profiles of prominent members, notes on new members and other snippets of West Country information according to the tastes and interests of the many editors who have looked after it. Some members, especially in their later years when their outings have been curtailed, have kept in touch only through the newsletter and have written to express their pleasure at reading about old friends and familiar places with each edition. One elderly member, Phyllis Hinton (who, in her nineties, described herself as 'blind and legless'!) took great pleasure in having it read to her by a carer. More than one elderly member has described the Association as an extended family, increasingly valued as the years take their toll of other family and friends.

'What does one get out of the WCWA?' asked the first woman chairman, Jacynth Hope-Simpson, in 1981.

> 'Speaking personally, I have been a member for eight years, and what I have valued most has been the chance to get to know people quickly and to exchange ideas with them, without spending a lot of time on social preliminaries. In a way, this is more like the friendships one had as a student, than many later relationships. Certainly, at a time when I moved house twice in twelve months, I realised how much I appreciated the WCWA as a source of friends with whom I could always take up where I left off.'[30]

The WCWA is, ideally, a source of great friendships, an opportunity for expanding horizons, a chance to meet and converse with all sorts of interesting people. For the author whose lot is a lonely one it offers a chance to meet people who understand the feeling; over the years it has undoubtedly assisted many a writing career in an indirect way. Like the novel it may be difficult to define, but as E. M. Forster said, 'The final test of a novel will be our affection for it, as it is the test of our friends, and of anything else which we cannot define'.[31] That the WCWA has survived fifty years of ups and downs is a testimony to the affection in which it is held.

PART II

THE EARLY DAYS: 1950 - 1964

> *The West Country Writers' Association was founded, in effect, by one man: Waveney Girvan.*
> John Trewin

This was how John Trewin described the origins of the West Country Writers' Association in a letter to Meryl Macdonald Bendle when, around the time of its twenty-fifth anniversary, he was asked about its history. As far as he was concerned, Waveney Girvan founded the Association.

Well, yes, but there was more to it than that. The WCWA grew out of a partnership between two bodies:

▶ *The West Country Magazine*

Published from 1946-1952; founded by Waveney Girvan of Westaway Books and edited first by Malcolm Elwin (two editions) and then by John Trewin, who underplays his own enormous contribution in attributing all the credit to Waveney Girvan.

▶ *The Bath Assembly: a Festival of the Arts*

Honorary Administrative Director: J. E. Boddington MA, from headquarters at the Pump Room, Bath.

The link between the two was another eminent West Country writer who is not so well remembered but who has an equally worthy claim to be recognized as one of the founders: Bryan Little.

Bryan Little was so obsessed with the West Country that it is surprising to find that he was actually born in Kent, with maternal grandparents of Liverpool and Isle of Man extraction. His school years at Cheltenham College were the source of his abiding passion for West Country towns and their architecture, and after a brilliant First at Cambridge and war service at the Admiralty he was able to settle down to the work he loved best - writing and teaching about architecture and topography, particularly in the West Country. Bath, Bristol and Cheltenham were his particular loves, and by the time the WCWA was founded he had already published his first major book, *The Building of Bath* (1947), which was to be followed by studies of Bristol, Exeter, Cheltenham, the Three Choirs Cities and Cambridge, as well as countless other reference books on civic and ecclesiastical architecture. Not surprisingly, he was an early contributor to *The West Country Magazine*, with his first piece - a descriptive history of Bruton in Somerset - published in 1948.

There cannot have been anybody to rival Bryan Little's knowledge of Bath. A small, slight man, towards the end of his life he looked so frail that a puff of wind might have blown him over, and on his legendary guided tours of Bath there were always very anxious American tourists when his tiny figure leapt into the road to point to the original extent of some seventeenth century foundations - entirely oblivious of the twentieth century Bath traffic bearing down on him. His knowledge of his subject was vast, and he had powers of total recall. Without any notes or preparation he could reel off the facts and figures of any West Country edifice: sadly, as an erudite academic, he lacked the creative ability to make those facts and figures come alive for his audience. His enthusiasm for the history of a given locus was so great he could not see how other people might need a little light relief occasionally - or that their respect for total accuracy was not as strict as his own. I remember sitting with him in a Bath tea-room while, much to the wrath of the management, he discoursed loudly on the inaccuracy of their olde worlde image: 'I've written and *proved* to them that their advertising is quite wrong', he would say, 'but they don't seem to take any notice...'

At that special time when the arts began to revive again after the Second World War, the fathers of the Bath Assembly began to feel they could stretch their wings a bit and expand their festival to include more literary input. Bryan Little, as a doyen of Bath and by now a regular contributor to *The West Country Magazine*, had the idea of bringing the two bodies together. It was he who wrote to John Trewin at *The West Country Magazine* and suggested the next Bath Assembly - ie 1950 - should be encouraged to include a 'Congress' of West Country writers. So began the 'triangular correspondence' between *The West Country Magazine*, the Bath Assembly and Bryan Little, out of which the WCWA eventually evolved.

On 6 July 1949 Waveney Girvan replied, as from *The West Country Magazine*, to Bryan Little:

> Mr. J. C. Trewin has told me of your very good idea concerning next year's Bath Assembly. I have accordingly written to Mr. Boddington, putting forward in broad terms your suggestion and when I hear from him I will certainly write to you again. *The West Country Magazine* would, of course, be very pleased to assist in any way within its powers.[1]

The Bath Assembly liked the idea, and J. E. Boddington replied to Waveney Girvan requesting a meeting to discuss it further. The post obviously moved faster in those days than it does today, because it was only two days later, on 8 July 1949, that Waveney Girvan was in touch with Bryan Little again:

> Further to my recent letter, I have now heard from Mr. Boddington and he seems to like your idea.
> Would you agree to call and see him for a preliminary talk some time in the near future? If you would then be good enough to let me know of any concrete proposals or the need for further

talks, I should be very pleased to come down to Bath or Bristol as the case may be and see what I can do to help.[2]

In both these letters, Waveney Girvan quite clearly speaks of 'your idea'. Bryan Little thought of it first - though there is an amusing postscript to the second letter:

> Yours was a most attractive idea and one that had been at the back of my mind for some time, though I could not quite see the peg to hang it on.[3]

Waveney Girvan is keen to record that he had thought of it too - but, tellingly, he could not 'see the peg to hang it on'. Bryan Little could, and did. He did all the practical work, calling in on Boddington 'in the near future' as bidden. By 9 July 1949 he had arranged the meeting, and the successful outcome was relayed back to Waveney Girvan on 27 July 1949: the Bath Assembly liked 'the idea' very much indeed and by 15 August the same year they had formally agreed to hold 'a Congress of Writers' during the Bath Assembly of 7-20 May 1950. Today we are often asked why we call our main event a 'Congress' rather than a 'Conference', and it is interesting to see that the word was used from the very beginning, was in fact what Bryan Little had first proposed to the Bath Assembly.

J. E. Boddington supplied Bryan Little with a selection of dates in September 1949 when he could meet Waveney Girvan for the first time, and Bryan duly acted as the go-between again and set up a meeting which was very fruitful indeed. Not only was a Congress of West Country Writers confirmed for 9 May 1950, but a list of over a hundred writers, culled from the contacts of both *The West Country Magazine* and the Bath Assembly, was drawn up. These writers were circulated with an invitation, on Bath Assembly headed paper and at the Assembly's expense, to a literary lunch and to what Waveney Girvan later called 'our Parish Council'[4], the first informal get-together of the as yet unnamed West Country Writers' Association.

The proposed programme for 9 May 1950 went as shown opposite.

After ten years as secretary of the Association I think I can be permitted to smile at the thought that PROBLEMS were the first ever item on the West Country writers' agenda. And they crop up not once but twice on the first draft programme.

> 11.30-12.45 Private meeting of West Country writers to discuss their own problems
>
> 12.45 Guests of the Bath Assembly at Luncheon in the Pump Room
>
> 2.30 Talk by one of these writers on some such subject as 'Bath and Literature'
>
> 3.15 General discussion on problems connected with the arts (patrons of Bath Assembly limited to 200 to submit questions for discussion)
>
> 4 pm Entertained to Tea in the Pump Room by Bath Assembly Ltd.
>
> Before 11.30 am it is hoped to arrange some official opening of a Book Exhibition dealing entirely with books of the West Country.

Not a lot about the programme has changed since 1950: the basic ingredients of talks, discussion groups, luncheon, book exhibition and the all-important 'tea' are just as familiar to congress-goers of 2000. Secretaries have occasionally been known to ask, at more jaundiced moments, whether they are really doing anything more valuable than running a glorified luncheon club, because the annual congress dominates so much of the committee's business and the secretary's time. It is clear, though, that this is how the WCWA began: it started from the idea of an annual coming-together for lunch - and how else, after all, is

The West Country Writers' Association

'the interchange of ideas' to be effected except by *getting* people together? With some adaptations, this draft programme set the pattern for congresses for the next fifty years and established the congress as the heart of the Association's activities.

The actual programme for the day follows.

WRITERS' CONGRESS

Tuesday May 9th 1950

11.30 am	Assemble at Pump Room. Coffee. Lady Mander will act as hostess. Writers introduced to each other. Private discussion on writers' problems.
12.30 pm	Private meeting finishes.
12.45 pm	Reception to writers by Directors of Bath Assembly.
1 pm	Lunch at the Pump Room.
	Toasts:
	a) The King
	b) The Bath Assembly, proposed by Lady Mander or Adelaide Phillpotts - replied to by the Chairman.
	c) The West Country, proposed by Wilfred Pickles - replied to by Jan Stewer (both speeches in dialect).
2.30 pm	Conference continues and there will be present specially invited patrons of the Bath Assembly. The total number to be present being about 250. Paper to be read by Bryan Little on Bath & Literature about 45 minutes. Wives of writers would be admitted to the afternoon session but applications should be made beforehand for tickets. Discussion on Bryan Little's talk.
3 pm[sic]	Questions on art in its various forms to which the following people will be invited to act as a Brains Trust: Bryan Little, F. H. Grisewood, Anne Treneer, Jan Stewer, Reg Arkell with perhaps Wilfred Pickles.
4.30 pm	Tea.

Somewhat predictably, the 'one of those writers' who gave the talk on 'some such subject as "Bath & Literature"' turned out to be Bryan Little, who was never slow to spot an opportunity to speak. In the event, Wilfred Pickles cried off as guest of honour - the last minute dropping-out of speakers is another feature all too familiar to secretaries - and was replaced by J. B. Priestley, and that was a stroke of luck because at that lunch Priestley gave us his classic description of the West Country spirit as 'the brandy still burning on the Christmas pudding'.

The Prelude

A press photograph preserved in our archives shows J. B. Priestley, Lady Mander and H. A. Vachell taking the waters at the Pump Room on the auspicious occasion of this first luncheon. It is a period piece. Carefully posed with the lady to the one side and the two gentlemen to the other, it shows the three writers raising their glasses - not actually *tasting* the spa waters, as the caption suggests - to the new venture. Lady Mander was also the Cornish writer Rosalie Glynn Grylls who was an early contributor to *The West Country Magazine*. She wrote passionately of her native county (spelling 'Keltic' with a 'K') and knowledgeably of the literature of the West. She also wrote a history of Queen's College for Girls in Harley Street, London, to mark their centenary in 1948. In the early days there was a sense of balance between the West Country and London, between the countryside and society life, with many of the founder members living and working in town.

This first photograph could be a scene from early black and white cinema. Lady Mander's costume, hat, handbag and eager expression mark her out as the romantic heroine; H. A. Vachell - 'the personification of Bath' according to Waveney Girvan[5] - with wing-collar and watch chain, the perfect elderly gentleman; J. B. Priestley, with his slightly quizzical expression (perhaps it was the spa water that put thoughts of brandy in his head when he came to give the toast) and silky tie the roguish outsider destined to charm them both.

Horace Annesley Vachell was famous for his distinguished appearance

- the high, stiff collar, stock and morning coat - all set off in his later years by the silvery hair and clipped old-Harrovian tones. In his writing career he had produced fifty novels, fourteen plays, and several volumes of short stories as well as essays and autobiographical works, but though he was loved for his rambling, kindly commentaries on upper-middle class life, he was never seen as a great writer. Writing was more in the nature of a hobby for him as he had vast independent resources, and his work consequently lacked urgency. His well-loved home was Widcombe Manor near Bath, so he definitely qualified as a West Country writer, and at the time of the founding he was just the sort of 'grand old man' ('He says he is eighty-nine', remarked John Trewin, 'And we must take his word for it!'[6]) to front the Bath Luncheon.

In the early days the WCWA certainly seemed to have one foot in the rural West and one in London literary high society. It was also something of a gentlemen's club. In the photograph of the 1956 luncheon in the Pump Room, ladies' hats are far outnumbered by the sober suits of men. The invitation list drawn up by J. C. Boddington numbered one hundred and eighteen writers, of whom only twenty-seven were women - and three of those carried the title 'Lady' - though this probably says as much about the nature of postwar society as about intentional prejudice.

A few years after the WCWA was created, the overall proportion had risen to fifty-two women out of one hundred and sixty-seven members, though the first vice-presidents were predominantly male by a ratio of twelve to two, and only seven females made it on to the prestigious list of thirty-four officers, honorary members, and committee. Announcing the first congress of West Country writers within the 1950 Bath Assembly, John Trewin proudly announced, with not a whiff of political correctness, 'During the two weeks of the Festival there will... be an exhibition of West Country books. On May 9 itself you can find... the men and their works together.'[7]

As the climate of society changed and women writers became more numerous, so the proportion of women quickly increased until, nowadays, the odd lone male on the committee has been known to make a special plea for some gentlemen to keep him company. All the same, the Association only elected its first female chairman in 1980 when Jacynth

Hope-Simpson took office, and at its fiftieth anniversary six out of the nine vice-presidents are male - and the three ladies were only created vice-president two years ago.

At the 1950 Bath Luncheon, despite Lady Mander 'acting as hostess', women were very definitely shown their place: 'wives of writers would be admitted to the afternoon session but applications should be made beforehand for tickets'.[8] Presumably *husbands* of writers didn't get in at all.

Not surprisingly, all three engineers of this 'prelude to the West Country Writers' Association, still not yet named'[9] recorded their impressions of the day. What is surprising is the different value they lay on each other's roles. Bryan Little's diary goes into great detail:

> About 50 of us gathered, and in many ways the private morning session was the most helpful of all, with Lady Mander (nee Rosalie Glynn Grylls) a most charming hostess and looking not a day older than when I last saw her as Mrs. Mander at Cambridge. I was particularly pleased to meet Trewin at last, and also a great many others whose names are familiar to me as Westcountry magazine [sic] contributors & in other ways. We ended by a meeting of ourselves at which many points were discussed & from which I think we may form a Westcountry Writers' Assn. & perpetuate the Exhibition of books in greatly improved form. Very good that Vachell was there & in fine fettle. Then to lunch in the Pump Room which was well done but where the speeches made things drag on beyond the timetable, though J. B. Priestley was admirably brief in proposing The Westcountry and the Mayor was felicitous, but Jan Stewer far too prolonged with pointless Devon dialect matter. The result was that our public session started very late. Lady Mander chaired me during my talk on "Bath and Literature" and then we improvised an authors' Brains Trust with Lady Mander, Trewin, Kenneth Hare, Geoffrey Grigson and myself with Girvan in the chair. Then tea and some of us across to the Book Exhibition.[10]

It comes as quite a shock to realize that John Trewin and Bryan Little had not met until that day, although they had been in contact for years.

Reading between the lines there are other little gems of significance here - the famous Priestley speech was 'admirably brief', the morning meeting of writers was 'the most helpful' part of the day, the mayor was 'felicitous', but the Devon dialect sessions, to Bryan Little's mind, 'too prolonged and pointless'. The dialects of the West Country, prized by Lewis Wilshire in his collection of stories and championed frequently in *The West Country Magazine*, were regarded as one of the region's distinctive features that helped keep the brandy burning on the Christmas pudding. Already, though, we see the first niggles between those who were rooted in the rural traditions of the West and those more academic minds who found dialect, frankly, tedious.

Perhaps more surprising is Bryan Little's lack of reference to Waveney Girvan. He only merits a mention once, when it comes to the Brains Trust 'with Girvan in the chair'. Who, then, was at that 'meeting of ourselves... from which I think we may form a Westcountry Writers' Assn'? Trewin 'and others whose names are familiar to me as Westcountry magazine contributors' are cited, but he does not name that stalwart of *The West Country Magazine*, Waveney Girvan, who was actually elected chairman on the occasion. Possibly the two did not get on.

At this point it has to be remembered that Bryan Little became the self-appointed archivist of the WCWA, seeing that the Association's papers were safely stowed at the Records Office in Bath and assuming sole jurisdiction over which correspondence went into the records. There is, not unnaturally, a preponderance of Bryan Little material. The impression given that Bryan Little had far more to do with the founding of the Association than anyone else may have been the result of his own conscious or unconscious bias in choosing what to preserve - or it may just have been that he obviously had more access to his own letters than to any others. It does seem clear that Bryan Little thought of the Bath idea first, or at least was first to do something to bring it to reality, and for that he has had scant acknowledgement. But it remains a fact that John Trewin continued energetically to maintain that Waveney Girvan was the true and only founder - Waveney Girvan who scarcely merits a mention by Bryan Little.

Waveney Girvan's account of the day is understandably different. It appears in *The West Country Magazine*: John Trewin, as editor, had given a very brief description of the occasion in the Summer 1950 edition, holding over the detailed reports until the next issue in Autumn 1950. There were three reports in all. Kenneth Hopkins wrote the amusing plea for the inclusion of Hampshire and Sam Uglow contributed his thoughts on regionalism, both previously quoted, but the official report was written by Waveney Girvan, announced by John Trewin with a dramatic flourish: 'Attention, then, for the Chairman, who holds the gorgeous West in fee'.

> The West Country Writers' Congress, as part of the 1950 Bath Assembly, was, I felt, voted a success. Having helped in the organization for some time before the event, and having had the honour of being elected Chairman in the morning, it is difficult for me, even now, to view the occasion objectively. But I do believe it was memorable in many ways. It was the first regional gathering of its kind ever to be held in England. I would go even further with the claim: no other region could possibly have mustered such a distinguished company in a city with comparable literary associations. And we still have a number of aces in reserve; I hope that A. L. Rowse, L. A. G. Strong, A. G. Street, Frederick Grisewood and several others will not be prevented next year from attending, as they were this.
>
> The Congress was memorable, too, for its friendliness. Most of the writers to whom I spoke said they had enjoyed meeting each other for the first time. The warmth and courtesy of the West infected the day, and all professional and local jealousies (if ever they existed) were dropped... after the glitter of the luncheon and the speeches, it was the impromptu and informal meetings which were the most appreciated features of the day.
>
> The Brains Trust was, perhaps, enjoyed by the audience, but I have to agree with those who find this form of entertainment an outmoded act of condescension from the half-educated to the wholly ignorant. On the other hand, it may be as well to explain that it was arranged to give a chance to the public to see the lions perform. (The public were kept well away during feeding time.) ...Perhaps it would be possible for the public to meet the writers informally at an afternoon session. This was, indeed, what did happen immediately after the Brains Trust, when members of the

audience climbed up on the platform to continue the questioning at close range. Geoffrey Grigson seemed to be the centre - almost the Sinatra - of public attention.

This leads to another consideration. I thought that the authorities at Bath had under-estimated the publicity value of the Congress. With J. B. Priestley as the guest of honour, with H. A. Vachell as the personification of Bath, with Jan Stewer articulating for Devon, with a host of others whose names make news - why was not more news made? This is a feature which will have to be considerably improved next year. And so will the book exhibition. But for the untiring efforts of Herbert Howarth, now Director of the National Book League, the exhibition would have looked even more like a quiet day in the remainder market than it did. Mr. Howarth worked a miracle in the time, but space and facilities, alas, were not his to command...

With all the delights enumerated, it was a crowded day - too crowded, it was felt by many. The suggestion was often heard that next year the Congress should have two days at its disposal, and this has been put forward to the Directors at the Bath Assembly. It is not that more functions are urged, merely that they should be better spaced to give greater time to social meetings and to visiting the delights of Bath.[11]

Not a mention of Bryan Little. There is plenty that a modern committee member would recognize: anxieties about the space available for the book exhibition, complaints about an overcrowded programme, hand-wringing about publicity - and also that positive point '...it was the impromptu and informal meetings which were the most appreciated features of the day'. And somehow it all sounds much more fun than in the diary of Bryan Little. Waveney Girvan's wit shines through the account ('the exhibition would have looked even more like a quiet day in the remainder market than it did') and gives us the clue to John Trewin's obviously sincere esteem for the man.

Trewin's account of the day was written in 1977 in response to a request for information from Meryl Macdonald Bendle, and in an accompanying letter to Meryl he makes his point about Waveney Girvan even more strongly:

-50-

Yes: it's odd how records disappear. It should be made quite clear that the WCWA was the idea of one man, Waveney Girvan. He talked it over with me often before any plans were made, but the conception was entirely his, and without his early work nothing would have been done. I wish his name, as Founder, could appear on the Association's note paper. I have never known any organization to be so entirely the achievement of one man... Without some idea of Waveney no stranger to the West Country Writers will realise how the Association was formed. He could be very serious when the time called for it; he could speak in public and write with a quiet, disciplined eloquence, and it was very hard for anyone to refuse him anything.[12]

And yet we have it in Waveney Girvan's own hand that the idea was Bryan Little's! Trewin's letter is long and rhapsodic in his praise for Waveney Girvan, and ends with the point reinforced - '...that [*The West Country Magazine*] too, like the WCWA, owed its birth to Waveney Girvan'.[13] He had his wish about the headed note paper, but his official account of 9 May 1950 is diplomatically balanced, giving full measure to both Waveney Girvan and Bryan Little:

> I have written elsewhere that the principal rival of the Bath Assembly is the city of Bath itself. Certainly, in the warm flood of sunlight on the morning of May 9, it took much resolution to go indoors, even to the first West Country Writers' Congress. Once inside, all was well. It was a pleasure to meet in person some of the writers whose manuscript and typescript I knew so well, down to the last loop and hanging 'e'. I found it very hard, I admit, to scrap a few preconceived ideas. For example, on discovering that X., who in mind's eye had always been a tall veteran of seventy-five with a neat silver beard and a slight stoop, was actually of middle height, ruddy, and with a genial fiftyish briskness. I felt like telling him to go home and remove the disguise.
>
> Still, all the shocks were cheerful. By luncheon, after meeting in both an informal get-together and a private business session, we knew each other fairly well and no longer wanted the identity labels which Lady Mander, as hostess, had thoughtfully suggested... I remember Waveney Girvan sparkling wittily from

the Chair - the day owed much of its success to him - the sight of Bath's 'special possession' Horace Annesley Vachell... beaming beside Reginald Arkell in the front row, and the sound of a variety of West Country accents that would have cheered Shaw's Professor Higgins. Later, as some of us reached the Pump Room for luncheon - our hosts were the directors of the Assembly - the first face we saw was that of J. B. Priestley, surrounded by photographers presenting arms. In proposing the toast of 'The West Country', he used phrases that will be much quoted... A. J. Coles-cum-Jan Stewer, 'two gentlemen at once', as Mrs. Malaprop very nearly remarked in an older Bath, replied with Devonian warmth and refrained kindly from describing the work of his colleagues as a parcel of ol' crams. But I jump ahead. The luncheon had begun with the toast of 'The Bath Assembly'. Lady Mander, proposing this (Alderman Berry replied to it), called Bath the cultural centre of the West... That afternoon, after Bryan Little had spoken eloquently of the Bath he chronicles, we had a Brains Trust... Tea ended the official day, though many of the writers went across to view their colleagues' work (nicely put, I think) in the Exhibition of West Country Books. This should be more prominent at any future Congress. Some of the Bath Assembly officials may have been surprised to find it was there. While people were exchanging addresses, half-a-dozen of us went with Robert Waller and Rupert Annand, of the BBC, to record a broadcast symposium at Widcombe Manor, the home of H. A. Vachell. He calls it the golden house. It is an extraordinarily gracious place; it looked almost unreal that evening in light that the honey-coloured stone absorbed like a sponge... Mr. Vachell himself made a suitably mellow contribution to the recording which was broadcast from Bristol on the following night. I remember, too, the charming fantasy of the Launceston poet and story-writer, Charles Causley, when he spoke of his awe at meeting those 'fabulous monsters', his fellow-writers. Many of us felt as he did.[14]

How lovely to think that the great Charles Causley, one of the literary giants at the turn of our own new millennium, was once an awe-stricken junior at the beginning of the WCWA's existence and how satisfying to know that many of his first poems were published by *The West Country Magazine*.

It is tempting to think that the brisk fifty-year-old whom John Trewin had always pictured as a silver-haired seventy-five might have been Bryan Little, or to wonder whether - despite Waveney Girvan's doubts that there were any literary jealousies at large - Bryan Little's academic seriousness might have been anathema to the mercurial Waveney Girvan and vice versa: such ideas can only be speculation. John Trewin makes no claims for himself, but it is clear that his wise and guiding presence also helped shape many of the events of that first day. The foundation of the WCWA is, in the end, a matter of balance: no doubt the Association would never have got off the ground if it had not been for the energetic character and entrepreneurial flair of Waveney Girvan, but he in turn depended upon both the influential literary reputation of John Trewin and the background administrative work of Bryan Little - and all three of them would have been lost without the generous patronage of the Bath Assembly.

Bath itself has always played an enormous role in the history of the WCWA. Its Assembly was another sign of the re-emergence of the arts after the days of wartime austerity, and a notice appears in the Spring 1948 edition of *The West Country Magazine*:

> The Bath Assembly, a new Festival of the Arts, will last this year from April 21 until May 1. Its programme includes a notable series of concerts; a performance of Mozart's *Il Seraglio*, in English... a play - presented by Sherak Players to alternate with the opera... a festival of children's films... Professor Skupa's Czech puppets; and a Georgian Ball in the Pump Room on April 23. On two nights historic buildings will be floodlit between 10 and 11 pm.
>
> The Bath Assembly Ltd., is a non-profit-making company to promote Festivals of the Arts in Bath; it works in full association with the Arts Council. The Bath Corporation has agreed to offer a guarantee of up to £3,000, and the Arts Council has agreed to guarantee the first £750 of any deficit.[15]

Music was dominant at first, but John Trewin, as a good theatre critic, picked out the play for his review of the first Assembly:

> Bath... is the right city for a festival of the arts: at the end of April its first Assembly, with spring sunshine to warm the honeyed stone, gave hope of much to come. Strangers found it hard to choose between the city - where square and crescent, silver-gold, rose tier by tier above the Roman core of Aquae Sulis - and the brimming programme of the Festival itself: more rivalry than Sheridan's Bath. Glyndebourne, which had the artistic direction of the Festival, can be proud of its musical events. No doubt next year's chief dramatic performance will be better. *The School for Scandal* needs style above all things, and it was just this style and flourish that Basil Dean's recent production lacked. Still, Evelyn Laye's Lady Teazle had some spirit; in appearance she was a true Gainsborough; and it was pleasant to meet Sheridan in the period piece of the Theatre Royal.[16]

It was a natural progress for the Bath Assembly, in its third year, to spread its literary wings and work in symbiotic partnership with *The West Country Magazine*, with which it was of an age. Without the Bath Assembly that first lunch would never have taken place, and Waveney Girvan's (or Bryan Little's) idea might never have found a peg to hang itself upon. The WCWA was born in Bath and owes its existence as much to the Assembly as to the founders.

Bath continued to play a part in the Association's development. The first congress and lunch of the WCWA proper, in 1951, was also at the Pump Room, and the Association came home to observe its twenty-first anniversary at Bath. It came very close to being buried at Bath too, for that twenty-first congress was close to being its last - but that still lay in the future.

It was fitting that the first lecture given at a congress of West Country writers should have been on the subject of 'Bath and Literature'. Bryan Little's original manuscript is preserved in the archives in Bath, and it is fascinating to observe his tidy mind at work. The text is carefully written out in longhand, with the key words underlined in a variety of different coloured pencils. His opening remarks repay generously the debt owed to the Bath Assembly - and make some sweeping claims for the West in general and Bath in particular:

> BA seems now to have settled down as the chief <u>Western</u> cultural event of the year, though by no means incapable of making itself felt in the national and international plane. Partly a matter of musical, dramatic, etc. art <u>performed</u> (though not originating in the West), partly to focus attention on what the <u>West</u> has done and can do... Nowhere more distinguished in this respect than <u>Bath</u>. In fact its place in <u>literature</u> is the real meaning of Bath's world-wide fame, great as are the achievements of Bath's architects [names] and the renown of her healing waters. But many who have never had recourse to the one nor seen the other feel that they <u>know and love</u> Bath through the medium of her social life as described by various authors and through various literary works that are largely written round or about Bath.[17]

In the margin is a somewhat apocalyptic note, '<u>Renown</u> will <u>outlast</u> buildings'. From one whose life was so dedicated to architecture, this is praise indeed. He goes on to compare Bath to Athens as 'a shining city of the spirit' and, great as his attachment was to Cheltenham, quotes *Gentleman's Magazine* of 1828 in contrasting the two spas: 'One [Bath] is an Olympus of Gods, heroes and men, and the other a menagerie of monkeys, parrots and owls'. No wonder that the Bath Assembly responded with an offer of even more generous support.

By the evening of 9 May 1950 the WCWA had been born and given a name, but the event had only been planned as a one-off writers' day. Where was it to go from here? The success of the day ensured that it would certainly go somewhere, that the congress would at the very least become an established feature of the Bath Assembly. In fact it could quite easily have remained just that: an annual Bath Assembly Writers' Day. That 'private meeting of ourselves' described by Bryan Little had decided, however, that there would be more to it than a regular programme slot at Bath. A chairman had been elected and a provisional committee formed to give the WCWA a life of its own, still heavily subsidised by the Bath Assembly and backed up by *The West Country Magazine*, but ultimately independent of both.

The formal inauguration of the WCWA was planned for the next year, 1951. J. E. Boddington suggested to Waveney Girvan not only that the Bath Assembly should again host a West Country Writers' Congress, but also that the Assembly should run a series of literary competitions open only to those residing in the West of England, or who could claim to be West of England men or women. The suggested classes were:

1) Literature
   a) Poetry
   b) Descriptive articles
   c) Short Stories

2) Drama (One act plays)

Waveney Girvan passed the suggestion on to Bryan Little, and he approved of the idea - appending to the list of suggested classes, 'Best book of the year on a West Country subject?' It was, however, no longer a question of a triangular correspondence between Waveney Girvan, Bryan Little and J. E. Boddington: now it was 'The Provisional Committee of West Country Writers' - Lady Mander, Mrs M. H. McClintock, Aubrey de Selincourt, John Garrett, Kenneth Hopkins, Bryan Little, Gilbert Phelps, L. A. G. Strong, and J. C. Trewin, under the chairmanship of Waveney Girvan - who consulted the board of directors at the Bath Assembly to work on the plans for the competition and for the second 'Congress of West Country Writers' which was to launch the WCWA.

The provisional committee came out of these discussions well, persuading the board of directors to bear all the expenses of the competition, including the provision of prizes. In a letter of 14 December 1950, Waveney Girvan reported to Bryan Little, who seems not to have been privy to these discussions, on the conditions agreed for the literary competition:

> The Committee then discussed the offer received from the Directors of the Bath Assembly to award literary prizes. These were to be for a short story, a descriptive article, a one-act play

and for poetry. Mr. L. A. G. Strong advised that the prizes should not be less than £25 each, preferably £50 for the longer compositions, and that the competition should be conducted in co-operation with the Society of Authors. It was also suggested that the story and descriptive article should not exceed 5,000 words each, the one-act drama should not exceed 40 minutes in playing time, and the poem should be not more than 50 lines. The poetry should not, however, have any other restrictions placed upon its form. Manuscripts need not be typewritten. It was further suggested that the judges should be:

Mr. L. A. G. Strong
Mr. J. C. Trewin
Mr. John Garrett

and an ex officio member of some body such as the National Book League. Although it might not be possible to insist that the poetry should reflect, in theme, spirit or setting the West Country, it was felt that this should be a condition imposed upon the other compositions. It was suggested, but not decided, that the entrants should either be resident in the West Country or West Country people by birth.

The Chairman reported that he would be seeing Mr. Boddington shortly after the meeting and that these and other matters would be discussed. Arising out of our meeting, I met Mr. Boddington and informed him of our decisions and recommendations. He appeared to be agreeable on all points and told me that he would let me know about the size of the prizes. He also asked if the committee would have any objections to adding one of the Directors of the Bath Assembly to the body of the judges. I said I would seek your views and now invite them. Mr. Boddington suggested 31 March 1950 [sic] should be the closing date and that the decision should be available by the middle of April.[18]

In the event prizes were awarded, of £25 and £5 for the short story of no more than 5,000 words; £10 and £5 for a descriptive article of no more than 1,000 words; £10 and £5 for a poem of no more than 50 lines, and

£30 and £10 for a one act play of not more than 40 minutes playing time. For the poem, preference was to be given to poets resident or born in the West Country, and the other classes should reflect 'the theme, spirit or setting' of the West Country.

Two things are notable here: Bryan Little does seem to be very out of the swim of things, and the Bath Assembly was expected to be exceedingly generous - to the point of asking permission to have a representative among the judges. In view of their kindness it is even more of a surprise when Waveney Girvan goes on to pull another rabbit triumphantly from the hat: the WCWA was already outgrowing the Bath Assembly and had had a better offer.

> The Chairman informed the Committee that he had received a tentative invitation from the City of Plymouth to hold its Congress there in 1952. It was unanimously decided that, if and when the official invitation arrived, it should be accepted with great pleasure. It arrived yesterday and was so accepted. It would appear that the City of Plymouth will be more alive to the publicity value of the Congress than was the City of Bath this year, for publicity has already appeared in *The Western Independent* of 10 December.[19]

After this last information Bryan Little has sagely pencilled in the comment 'too soon unless constantly followed up', a sentiment which all press officers of the Association will endorse. But the origins of the civic reception at congress are clear: the early fathers expected much in the way of sponsorship from the authorities of the city in which they met, and the cities saw the congress as good publicity for their attractions. In many cases this hard-headed business link has all but disappeared, but it is still the case that in venues with a big tourism industry - Torquay, for example, or Bournemouth - the civic reception and the mayor's attendance at our annual luncheon are handled by the Tourist Office rather than the Council.

Meanwhile the 1951 Congress was taking shape as a much grander affair than the first, a two-day event with far more writers invited to attend. The provisional committee had held a meeting at Westaway Books in London on 29 November 1950 with the task of forming and launching the WCWA during that congress. They had quickly struck a familiar problem, as Waveney Girvan reported to Bryan Little, 'The first discussion was on the definition of a West Country Writer...'[20] In fact the definitions they arrived at were surprisingly relaxed, and might disappoint those purists who in subsequent years have insisted on strict adherence to the 'Six Counties' Waveney Girvan was later to cite:

> In suggesting new names, the members of the Provisional Committee should be guided by the following qualifications:
>
> 1 Birth or residence in the West Country, the West Country comprising the counties of Cornwall, Devon, Somerset, Dorset, Wiltshire, Gloucestershire and Hampshire.
> 2 Authorship of a book produced at publisher's risk.
> 3 Authorship of a book dealing with the West Country, although the author may himself not be West Country by birth or by residence.
> 4 The rendering of some service to West Country letters.
> 5 Notwithstanding any of the above qualifications, the members of the Provisional Committee shall have the power of nominating a new member if in his or her opinion the writer is a West Country man or woman and who, in their opinion, deserves to be encouraged in the profession of letters.[21]

What would horrify the elitists even more is the next paragraph:

> It will be seen that Clause 4 & 5 are somewhat elastic, but the general opinion appeared to be that this was unavoidable. With regard to Clause 5, it was felt that one of the objects of the West Country Writers' Association should be to encourage the literary aspirant and, therefore, discretion was to be granted to waive Clause 2 from time to time.[22]

Clause 2, it should be noted, even when implemented fully, only asked for *one* published book; the demand for three did not come from the provisional committee who drew up the ground rules. It is probably true that the rich mix of the WCWA, the reason for its strength and continuance, lies partly in this open-minded approach to qualification. Yes, the twin criteria of authorship and West Country affiliation are the bedrock of the Association, but a certain lenience in admitting some of the less well-qualified, in encouraging people who have not 'made it' yet, in being a little woolly about the edges, has brought about a balanced membership that keeps the Association alive and gives it its friendly character. It is pleasing to see that this was the intention of the founders.

The Launch

All the stops were pulled out for the 1951 launch. The editorial of *The West Country Magazine* for Spring 1951 announced the event with a flourish, saying:

> Let me quote:
> 'And then westward to Blandford and Dorchester, and westward again to Exeter and Plymouth, and, with the west wind blowing now, on through Launceston and across the Bodmin Moors where the mist was curling round Brown Willy, and westward still to Helston, the mist vanquished, and the great white October clouds sailing across the rich blue sky of the west, of the life-giving west from which love and music shall come until the day of the seven whirlwinds and the crack of doom.'
> And again:
> 'Praa Sands saw them, and Landewednack and the lonely Ruans. There was not a cave to which they did not scramble down, nor a winding cliff-path by which they did not wander above the ocean. The magic of the west that haunts the air from Biscay to the Hebrides is nowhere more potent than in the Meneage, where, as in the north-west the basalt, the serpentine breaks into the granite dark and strange as the Phoenician traffickers of long ago.'
> Those are two extracts from *The West Wind of Love*, by Compton Mackenzie, who will speak at the Writers' Luncheon at

Bath. Mackenzie, a romantic and a wit, knows and loves the West. He has lived in Cornwall, and though at Bath he will be representing the Rest of England, he will be able - most happily - to speak for both sides of the fence.

We are hoping (if matters of printing and paper allow) that the Summer issue of West Country, with a full Bath programme, will appear towards the end of May. The Provisional Committee of the Writers' Congress has been at work on details. On page 20 of this issue you will find an announcement of the Bath Assembly literary competitions... The Congress is on May 29th and 30th.[23]

The National Book League was asked, and agreed, to run the book exhibition; the Society of Authors was notified about the proposed formation of the new Association and asked to be kept informed; the *Times Literary Supplement* reviewed the occasion, which it called 'an arts festival with the West Country as its theme' in a piece which gives a strong flavour of the day: 'The Association's hope is to be of service to the West in many ways beyond the fields of literature...' - these words were echoed by John Trewin when he said that '...the general bond was love of the West Country; though the Association was intended for writers... Girvan hoped that in time all the lively arts might be represented'.[24] As is the case with their leniency on membership qualifications, the founding fathers are done a disservice by those who complain about the extension of membership to booksellers, agents, illustrators and other adjuncts to the literary profession. Waveney Girvan originally wanted the Association to be extended to all the arts, and he would have hoped to embrace musicians, actors and visual artists in the membership eventually. When, exactly, was never quite clarified - '...those larger projects are expected to develop as the new organization gains in strength and prestige' - but the spirit of these early days was clearly more open and welcoming than we tend to think, just as the early rules were positively liberal. The elitism crept in later.

So, on 29 and 30 May 1951, the WCWA was officially launched, and Compton Mackenzie proposed the toast 'To the West Country' as guests of honour have done at forty-eight annual luncheons since, and Waveney Girvan gave his famous reply attempting to define the region. The Object of the Association was set out:

'To foster the love of literature in the West Country as a contribution to the national life.'

The last phrase (as a contribution...) was dropped when John Trewin was chairman in 1970
According to Waveney Girvan, sixty or so writers attended, and

> ...apart from the official junketings, the memorable lectures by L. A. G. Strong on the poets of Devon and Cornwall, the Brains Trust with Lady Mander, John Moore, St. John Ervine (explosively genial), Christopher Hollis, John Garrett, John Nance, and the two co-opted members, H. A. Vachell and Compton Mackenzie, a great deal of our time, particularly on the first of the two days, was devoted to the formation of the West Country Writers' Association... The object of the Association is to 'foster the love of literature in the West Country as a contribution to the national life'. It has been felt that men and women of letters, owing allegiance to their region, should be able, when united, to serve the West Country in many ways, either by the pen or through the force of their personalities. Their means may be literary, though the ends sought could reach into many other fields of activity. The West needs no popularisers, but it may need friends and protectors. As one member pointed out, who better equipped than the Writers to protest against the current spoliation of the countryside by the indiscriminate felling of trees in the West Country? And if Cornish voices in the West speak in unison with those of Gloucestershire in the East, then authority, wherever it lies, may listen more intently than if a single county had complained.
> Another writer pointed out that if only the West had been united its representation at the Festival of Britain could have been as strong and effective as that of Wales or Northern Ireland. I hope to see the day when the West Country can have a Centre in London where the region's interests can be represented in the metropolis, where exiles can meet, and where West Country exhibitions, lectures and social gatherings can be held. Ambitious,

perhaps, but possible and profitable I am sure, if well enough organized. Our Association is still young, but it does, I think, provide for the first time an organization representing the whole of the West Country in its widest interpretation, and I hope it will soon be recognized as such and used to its fullest possible extent.

My Committee's first move was to plead for the restoration of the title 'Great Western Railway'. The Association is, of course, non-political (or should I say non-party?), and it is committed to no views on nationalisation. It was felt that on the grounds of efficiency alone our plea was justified, and that the sentimental argument - never to be ignored - was very strong indeed. The West Country papers gave us encouraging support, and our plea was reported in several other journals, notably *The Manchester Guardian, The Daily Mail, The Spectator, Time and Tide, Truth* and *Country Life*. As a result, a very large number of postcards have been received, and are continuing to arrive, with the sender's name and address, echoing the plea 'Give us back our Great Western Railway'. Ultimately, these postcards will be sent in the form of a petition to the quarter where it is most likely to have effect.[25]

This is an interesting glimpse of the ways in which Waveney Girvan would have liked the Association to give service to the West. 'Give us back our Great Western Railway' is a cry that must have echoed down the years - and we have always had our fair share of railway enthusiasts - but it is not quite what new members are looking for when they join. A network of exiles' clubs in London did advertise their meetings through *The West Country Magazine* for some time, but the more ambitious of Waveney Girvan's dreams - though the efficiency of the railways and the role of regional government are still contentious topical issues fifty years on - never did take off as serious areas of activity for the Association.

Waveney Girvan finished his report in dashing style:

> I hope the West Country Writers' Association will have a long and vigorous life. At the end of the Bath Congress, several of the members were invited to give their views over the air. When I had the temerity to express my own, I was promptly called 'a confounded liar' by our valued vice-president, Mr. St. John

Ervine. Although as Chairman I rule him completely out of order, I felt that our Association had got off to a very happy and auspicious start.[26]

One is never quite sure how to take him! John Trewin, in his report, remarks on 'Waveney Girvan keeping his flock (even Mr. Ervine) wittily in order...', so presumably it was all in jest. As Trewin also said, 'The main thing was, and is, that the Association is in being.'

Eden Phillpotts, by then the Grand Old Man of Devonshire writers at nearly ninety years of age, was invited to become the first president, and duly accepted. He was a very suitable figure to head this unpredictable organization, being himself, like Waveney Girvan, neither a West Countryman by birth nor initially a writer. Despite his name being synonymous with Devon, and the Dartmoor area in particular, he was actually born in India; and although he had published well over a hundred books by the time he became WCWA president, he had started out as an insurance clerk whose great ambition was to be an actor but whose mother had hoped he would enter the Church. Brought back from Rajputana to Plymouth on the death of his mother, he went to London to seek his fortune when he was only seventeen, and he studied at a drama school in the evenings after working all day in the Sun Fire Office. It became apparent that he did not have much of a future treading the boards - but it also became obvious that he could write. Once he was earning £400 a year from his writings, he left the insurance office to edit *Black and White* magazine, and his long career began. Novels, poems, stories and a string of successful plays - including *The Farmer's Wife* which was a huge success on the London stage - filled the next sixty years. At the height of his powers he could turn out three or four novels a year, usually with a brooding Dartmoor setting and a common-sense philosophy: his admirers today describe him as being the Thomas Hardy of Dartmoor. His most productive years were spent in Torquay and in 1921 he was made a Freeman of the Borough of Torbay - thirty years before he was to assume the presidency of the WCWA.

Ten vice-presidents were selected from among the well-known authors of the day. They, too, are an intriguing collection of characters:

▶ A. J. Coles - the 'two gentlemen at once' Jan Stewer, whose dialect

talk had been tedious to Bryan Little
- St. John Greer Ervine - the definitive biographer of G. B. Shaw, and an explosive character by all accounts
- Christopher Fry - who needs no introduction. At that time he had completed *Venus Observed* for Laurence Olivier, and was just seeing *A Sleep of Prisoners* through its first performances
- Frederick Grisewood - who worked for the BBC
- John Moore - of 'crack-brained Brensham' fame
- A. L. Rowse - Cornish poet, historian and academic
- Marguerite Steen - now remembered as a prolific novelist, but she had previously been on the stage and actually started out as a dancing mistress
- H. A. Vachell - the writer 'out of the top drawer' of upper middle class life
- Brian Vesey-Fitzgerald - a naturalist whose books were mainly about wildlife and rivers, but who also published on gypsy lore, traditional fairs and, somewhat surprisingly, the official rules of boxing
- Lady Vyvyan - born in Australia, brought up in Cornwall, a graduate of the LSE, and an intrepid traveller who wrote up her experiences in the Klondike as C. C. Rogers, later C. C. Vyvyan

The provisional committee which had been responsible for arranging the congress formed the first committee of the WCWA with Waveney Girvan confirmed as the first chairman. John Nance became the first honorary secretary, and Mr. A. G. Findlay (the initials stood for Archibald Garrioch), who came from a firm of chartered accountants with the familiar name of 'Girvan and Nicholson', was the first treasurer.

To assist the committee, ten members volunteered to be 'Regional Correspondents' for Cornwall, Devon, Somerset, Dorset, Gloucestershire, Bristol, Wiltshire and - of course - Hampshire. There were ninety-four founder members: the original list will be found at the end of Part II.

A different list appeared in the booklet prepared for WCWA's fortieth anniversary. It is referred to as 'the first membership page' and many people take this to have been the list of founder members, but it is of a much later date. Quite apart from the expansion of the membership - it stands at one hundred and sixty-seven in the later list compared with the ninety-four founder members - the name of the secretary/treasurer shows the difference. John Nance remained honorary secretary for only a very short time before being replaced by John Keast, who also took on the treasurership. The list of ninety-four members is clearly the list of founder members as it shows John Nance as secretary, his name crossed out and manually replaced by John Keast in the handwriting of Bryan Little.

By the time of the later list, Brian Vesey-Fitzgerald had disappeared from the vice-presidents, but they had gained H. M. Tomlinson and Henry Williamson, and eleven honorary members (such as Compton Mackenzie) had been added. Of the original list of ninety-four members, just six are still members fifty years on - Christopher Fry, Victor Bonham-Carter, Charles Causley, Lois Lamplugh, Winston Graham and John Bayliss.

It is sobering to compare the first membership list with the invitation list (also reprinted at the end of Part II) and see which writers failed to take the bait - T. S. Eliot, Sean O'Casey, C. Day Lewis, Edith Sitwell and Sylvia Townsend Warner were all, sadly, among the ones who got away. Of those eminent members who were invited to become a vice-president, only two declined the honour - A. G. Street and J. C. Powys. A. L. Rowse omitted to reply (thus establishing the habit of a lifetime) but a phone call from the chairman soon elicited his acceptance.

John Trewin summed up the new Association gracefully:

> One of the things I like about the Association is its lack of pomp, its refusal to hide under a cloud of verbiage. Its objects are condensed into one sentence. And, as John Nance has said, many of us feel that something is ahead 'much larger than a mere gathering together of a few people united by a common love of a particular part of the English countryside or a particular way of life'.[27]

John Whitley Nance is an intriguing character because little is known of him - except that he had the tiniest handwriting. His appearances in *The West Country Magazine* had been numerous; he wrote poems that revealed a delightfully humorous approach to both poetry and life - such as this ditty from 1951:

SUMMER SONG

Hush, Muse! and doe nott clammer soe,
Butt tayke ye playce along ye queue,
   I muste awaye
   On holidaye
As evenn poetts sometymes doe.

Awaye to Cornewal in ye busse -
I cannot paye ye traine doune -
   And wyth mie packe
   Uponn mie backe
Forget civilisacioune.

Forgett ye fumey fire, forgett
Ye kychenn synck of dysshes fulle,
   Ye holey bynne
   For tynnes inne,
And mowe ye lawne, and weedes pulle,

But pytch ytente inn ye sonne,
And lye ye thyssle meadowe inne,
   And shayre mie house
   With woode-louse
Lyke anye wylde Bedowinne.

And heare ye gulle above ye cliffe,
Ybreakynge wayv along ye shore,
   Ybeere drynk,
   And doe nott thynk,
And soe remaine for evermore.[28]
John Nance

Quite why John Nance should have ceased being secretary so soon after his acceptance of office is a mystery. He was a great enthusiast for the newly formed Association and even recorded its birth with a sidelong glance in:

ASSEMBLY: BATH

The geraniums are crimson in the gardens
Where the orange-peel and the ice-cream wrappers float lazily by
The literati ingeniously inspect Bath's falling angels
Part worn with time (or climbing, as am I).

Over the down-platform at the railway-station
A hill, like a green wave, draws itself up to curve down
In a welter of leaves and grass spume-flecked with blossom
Leisurely onto the beaches of the town.

There are poets in the Pump Room. There are concerts -
Bassoons contradict the serious statements of the strings,
Shakespeare plays out the past in a mist of midges.
History dodges the buses. Words need wings!

Circus and Crescent clutch convenient contours.
Exhausted, I sip in a Bar my Scotch and Polly
Whilst high afloat and aflame on the cheek of the evening
Hang Prior Park, Sham Castle, and - is it the Beckford Folly?[29]

John Nance

His greatest flight of fancy, however, was the amazing letter circulated to all members in June 1951.

How do you start a literary association? Simple - just hold a literary lunch and tell everyone who accepted the invitation that they are now founder members!

> This letter is being sent to every Writer who received an invitation to attend the Luncheon of West Country Writers at Bath this year... If you were NOT present at the Meetings in Bath, we would like you to consider this letter as an official invitation to become a member of the Association. We feel sure you will accept.

If you WERE present, you will already consider yourself a member - or at least we hope you do.[30]

The text of this lengthy letter is reproduced at the end of this section, but the last two paragraphs deserve close attention.

> Those are the bare bones of a number of decisions which may one day become a literary landmark. As I said very briefly over the Radio at the conclusion of the Congress, and hope to be allowed to elaborate at some later date, a quite unexpected excitement livened all our deliberations, as though there had been some spontaneous uprising of the Human spirit. Everybody present, your Committee feel, was conscious of that atmosphere.
>
> Now, whilst your Committee gets down to its side of the business, which is, with the assistance of its Regional Correspondents, to put the Association on the map, there is a task for you to do. That task is to fan into a flame the spark of regional enthusiasm which so unexpectedly yet so unquestionably was lit at the Congress. Many of us have the feeling that something immensely important and significant may come out of our Association, something much larger than a mere gathering together of a few people united by a common love of a particular part of the English countryside or a particular way of life. We have in the Association a living thing; we want it to be courted and respected, but above all we want it to lead. We have stumbled upon a great opportunity to be of service not only to ourselves but equally to the communities we represent. Do not let us pass it by.[31]

Secretaries don't write letters like that any more! This is missionary zeal indeed - and it makes one feel quite inadequate today to measure our down-to-earth writers' get-togethers against 'some spontaneous uprising of the Human spirit'.

But for all that, in less than a year John Nance was gone. In his notes on the 1952 Congress John Trewin mentions '...the regretted resignation of John Nance (with professional cares growing)...' and that is all we know of his sudden disappearance until he briefly re-emerges in 1959 to hold the line when John Keast had to step down. *The West Country Magazine* itself did not survive beyond 1952, but no more of John Nance's regular poetic contributions appeared in its last two editions.

His replacement, John Keast - 'Cornish historian and author of the standard work on his native borough, Fowey' according to John Trewin,[32] - took on the treasurership as well. He remained in both posts until illness forced his resignation in 1959, and thus saw the Association through its crucial formative years.

That the Association became 'a living thing' as John Nance predicted is certainly true and has accounted for its fifty years of survival, but whether we are 'courted and respected' is questionable, and could we be said 'to lead'? The 1952 Congress at Plymouth certainly thought so. The programme is described in *The West Country Magazine* for Summer 1952:

> On June 3 the conference begins with St. John Ervine's talk on Bernard Shaw (3pm, Central Library, Tavistock Road). Mr. Ervine is working on the definitive life of Shaw... Shaw stayed with him at Seaton... Mr. Ervine's chairman on June 3 will be the Rt. Hon. Isaac Foot, a former Lord Mayor of the city, and one of the famous orators of his day...
>
> The annual general meeting of the Association, with Waveney Girvan presiding, will take place at the Library between 5 and 7pm. Next morning (June 4), at 10 o'clock, J. C. Trewin opens the West Country book exhibition and bookshop at Hatchard's in Dingle's store, Royal Parade. Most of the visitors to the conference will attend; at 10.30 they will leave Royal Parade on a tour of Plymouth arranged by the City Corporation.
>
> Later, there is to be a civic luncheon at Buckland Abbey, Drake's former home, ten miles from Plymouth. Frank Swinnerton, novelist and essayist (and present 'John O'London'), proposes the toast of the West Country, to which L. A. G. Strong, novelist, poet, dramatist and publisher (and native of Plymouth) will reply. Finally, a cast assembled from the local amateur societies, and produced by Sadie Speight - once of the Plymouth Repertory Theatre - will stage Hugh Ross Williamson's *Queen Elizabeth* in the Abbey Tithe Barn.[33]

After the event John Trewin reminisced:

> As I look back to those events of seven weeks ago, I remember St. John Ervine's warm voice in the most eloquent tribute to Bernard Shaw I have ever heard; the Lord Mayor of Plymouth's readiness, Frank Swinnerton's phrasing, and L. A. G. Strong's relished swoop into Devon dialect, at the Buckland Abbey luncheon; the scene in the honey-coloured cathedral-nave Tithe Barn during *Queen Elizabeth;* and the wit and tact with which Waveney Girvan presided over the writers at all times.[34]

It seems the AGM was full of crusading ideas, though none of them were, perhaps, world-shattering:

> The gathering brought one suggestion (from 'Jan Stewer') that the name of Dartmoor Prison should be changed to Princetown; and another that Plymouth should offer its Freedom to Eden Phillpotts, President of the WCWA and most renowned of living West Country writers. The Association renewed its support for a proposal that the former GWR should revert to its true name...[35]

Only six years previously, Malcolm Elwin had been calling upon friends to 'boycott GWR's delicious sandwiches' as they had refused to take out advertising in his fledgling magazine.[36]

For 1953 the Association was off to Salisbury, where they heard Angela Thirkell and Eric Linklater, and lunched in the Guildhall on Cream of Tomato or Mock Turtle Soup, Roast Chicken or Wiltshire Ham, and Raspberry Melba or Apricot Conde.

WCWA was now well set on its path of moving the congress to different venues around the region year by year. The Bath Assembly was left behind, its sponsorship no longer required. In fact the 1952 Bath Assembly was reported rather dismissively in *The West Country Magazine* by 'a correspondent' -

> Before it began, the Bath Assembly of 1952 had undergone some unconstructive and over-perfectionist criticism from Bathonians and others who seemed to have got themselves into an attitude of

mind that condemned, unseen, unheard, and without much discrimination much of the programme. There was, indeed, a somewhat awkward quality in the plan of the Assembly between Roman civilisation and Haydn-Mozart, and some of the printed publicity had created an avoidably bad impression by some unlucky betises. But in the upshot the Assembly turned out far better than many of its critics expected. The weather was excellent; the incongruous and tasteless Roman water pageant aroused, at its rehearsal climax, the combined wrath of Jupiter Pluvius and the river nymphs of the Avon, and had to be cancelled.[37]

- though he does admit that the Assembly was firmly established as '...the West Country's leading cultural opportunity of the year'.[38]

In 1952 *The West Country Magazine* disappeared suddenly, silently, just one edition after mourning the demise of Denys Val Baker's *Cornish Review*:

Mr. Denys Val Baker fought gallantly for ten issues; and he has accepted the decision with true and wise philosophy.[39]

John Trewin and his contributors presumably had to accept with equal philosophy that times were changing for the small regional magazine, though Victor Bonham-Carter always regretted that the flourishing WCWA did not retain the magazine and include its price in subscriptions. Certainly it was an excellent magazine, and its loss was sad.

The WCWA however, newly independent of both the Assembly and the magazine that had nurtured it, was settled and established with continuity of office holders and a flair for publicity: the 1953 Salisbury Congress was not only reported in *The Western Morning News, The Western Evening Herald,* and *The Western Independent,* but was given a double page of photographs in *The Sketch* and a Sunday afternoon feature on BBC radio. Edna Manning, an early member who contributed many congress reports to the useful scrapbooks put together by Dorothy Stiffe over the years, has left us a detailed description of Angela Thirkell's lecture on Trollope and memories of the writers present. She ends with an amusing picture:

My last memory of this delightful Congress was Mr. Hughes, the Salisbury librarian, waving us together to take a photograph when we were walking in The Close. He knelt down on the sward to get a good picture, and someone shouted, 'That's where we want to see the librarian - on his knees to us!'[40]

Certainly by 1953 the WCWA was well and truly launched, established and independent, and for the next ten years seemed set for a flourishing future with the world of books at its feet.

The West Country Writers' Association

The following are letters sent from Waveney Girvan to Bryan Little regarding the first Congress in 1950.

THE WESTAWAY PRESS LTD.
PUBLISHERS OF

THE WEST COUNTRY MAGAZINE

Directors:
I. WAVENEY GIRVAN
B. N. GIRVAN

TUDOR HOUSE,
PRINCETON ST.,
BEDFORD ROW,
LONDON, W.C.1
(Tel.: Holborn 0753)

IWG/VEB/WCM

6th July, 1949.

Bryan Little Esq.,
114 Pembroke Road,
Clifton,
Bristol, 8.

Dear Mr. Little,

   Mr. J. C. Trewin has told me of your very good idea concerning the next years Bath Assembly. I have accordingly written to Mr. Boddington, putting forward in broad terms your suggestion and when I hear from him I will certainly write to you again. THE WEST COUNTRY MAGAZINE would, of course, be very pleased to assist in any way within its powers.

Yours sincerely,

Waveney Girvan

The West Country Writers' Association

THE WESTAWAY PRESS LTD.
PUBLISHERS OF

THE WEST COUNTRY MAGAZINE

Directors:
I. WAVENEY GIRVAN
B. N. GIRVAN

TUDOR HOUSE,
PRINCETON ST.,
BEDFORD ROW,
LONDON, W.C.1
(Tel.: Holborn 0753)

8th July, 1949.

IWG/VEB/WCM

Bryan Little Esq.,
114 Pembroke Road,
Clifton,
Bristol 8.

Dear Mr. Little,

    Further to my recent letter, I have now heard from Mr. Boddington and he seems to like your idea.

    Would you agree to call and see him for a preliminary talk sometime in the near future? If you would then be good enough to let me know of any concrete proposals or the need for further talks, I should be very pleased to come donw to Bath or Bristol as the case may be and see what I can do to help.

    Yours was a most attractive idea and one that had been at the back of my mind for some time, though I could not quite see the peg to hang it on.

        Yours sincerely,

        Waveney Girvan

The West Country Writers' Association

Letter from Mr Boddington to Bryan Little, March 1950

Hon. Secretary: JARED E. DIXON *Hon. Treasurer:* FRANK W. PAYNE *Chairman:* Ald. A. W. S. BERRY	*The Bath Assembly* A Festival of the Arts 7th May to 20th May, 1950	*Hon. Administrative Director:* J. E. BODDINGTON, M.A. THE PUMP ROOM BATH TEL. 5481/5

Bryan Little, Esq.,
114 Pembroke Road,
Clifton, Bristol 8.

1 0 MAR 1950

Dear Sir,

    Mr. Waveney Girvan, a Director of the West Country Magazine has indicated to me that you are interested in the proposal to arrange in Bath on Tuesday, May 9th, 1950, a Congress of West Country Writers.

    On behalf of the Board of Directors of the Bath Assembly I ask whether it will be possible for you to come to Bath on that occasion. The programme as at present contemplated is as follows:

11.30 a.m. - 12.45 p.m. Private meeting of West Country Writers to discuss their own problems.

12.45 p.m. Guests of the Bath Assembly at Luncheon in the Pump Room.

2.30 p.m. Talk by one of these Writers on some such subject as "Bath and Literature".

3.15 p.m. General discussion on problems connected with the arts (patrons of the Bath Assembly to a limited number of about 200 would be invited to be present at these two afternoon meetings, and to submit questions for discussion).

4.0 p.m. Entertained to tea in Pump Room by Bath Assembly Limited.

    It is hoped, during the morning before 11.30 a.m. to arrange the official opening of a Book Exhibition dealing entirely with books of the West Country.

    Will you kindly let me know, as soon as possible, whether you can accept this invitation to be present.
                      Yours sincerely,

                        Hon. Administrative Director.

The West Country Writers' Association

Programme as agreed for the First Writers' Congress 1950

WRITERS' CONGRESS.

Tuesday, May 9th, 1950.

11.30 a.m.   Assemble at Pump Room - coffee served. Lady Mander will act as Hostess. Writers introduced to each other. Private discussion on writers problems.

12.30 p.m.   Private meeting finishes.

12.45 p.m.   Reception to writers by Directors of the Bath Assembly.

1 p.m.   Lunch at the Pump Room.   Toasts. -

         (a) The King,

         (b) The Bath Assembly, proposed by Lady Mander or Adelaide Philpotts - Replied to by the Chairman.

         (c) West Country, proposed by Wilfred Pickles - Replied to by Jan Stewer (both speeches in dialect).

2.30 p.m.   Conference continues and there will be present specially invited patrons of the Bath Assembly, in. The total number to be present being about 250. Paper to be read by Bryan Little on Bath and Literature about 45 minutes. Wives of Writers would be admitted to the afternoon session but applications sho ld be made before hand for tickets. Discussion on Bryan Little's talk.

3 p.m.   Questions on art in its various forms to which the following people will be invited to act as a Brains Trust: - Bryan Little F.d. Grisewood, Anne Treneer, Jan Stewer, Reginald Arkell with perhaps Wilfred Pickles.

4.30 p.m.   Tea.

The West Country Writers' Association

INVITATIONS LIST 1950

The following 120 writers were invited to the Congress of West Country Writers at the Bath Assembly on 9 May 1950. Surprisingly, Christopher Fry is not among them. Perhaps it was not generally known that his birthplace was Bristol.

Reginald Arkell
John Arlott
Lady Cynthia Asquith
John Atkins
Robin Atthill
Mrs. Frances Bellerby
Claude Berry
John Betjeman
Miss Eilen Bigland
Sean O'Casey
Charles Causley
Agatha Christie
Jack R. Clemo
A.J. Coles (Jan Stewer)
R.F. Delderfield
Miss Freda Derrick
Annan Dickson
Giles Dugdale
Ralph Dutton
Ronald Duncan
T.S. Eliot
Malcolm Elwin
Rt.Hon. Sir Isaac Foot
John Garrett
Daniel George
I.W. Girvan
R.C. Robertson Glasgow
Douglas Gordon
Mr. Winston Graham
Geoffrey Grigson
F.H. Grisewood
Kenneth Hare

Wilson Harris
Miss Muriel Hawkey
E.W. Hendy
Kenneth Hopkins
Mrs. Phyllis Hinton
Lorna Horstmann
Miss Monica Hutchins
Y. Ison
A.K. Hamilton-Jenkin
John Keast
W.F. Jackson Knight
G. Wilson Knight
J.W. Lambert
Miss Lois Lamplugh
Charles Landstone
Ralph Lawrence
Charles Lee
Miss Margaret Leigh
Cecil Day Lewis
Bryan Little
S.R. Littlewood
W. Macqueen-Pope
Mrs. Mary Howard McClintock
S.P.B. Mais
Lady Mander
H.A. Manhood
Mrs. Ruth Manning-Saunders
H.J. Marshall
E.W. Martin
Daphne du Maurier

The West Country Writers' Association

Cyril Maude
Miss Angela Milne
Miss Wendy Monk
Bruce Montgomery
Bernard Moore
John Moore
Dr. John Murray
R. Morton Nance
Gale Pedrick
Richard Perry
Gilbert Phelps
Richard Phibbs
Miss Adelaide Eden Phillpotts
Eden Phillpotts
Miss Peggy Pollard
Miss D.A. Ponsonby
Littleton C. Powys
T.F. Powys
J.C. Powys
S. Gorley Putt
Miss Hilda M. Quick
Hugh Redwood
Major Arbold Riley
A.L. Rowse
John Rowland
Ashley Rowe
Lt. Col. B.H. Ryves
St. John Ervine
Aubrey de Selincourt

Professor Jack Simmons
Miss Edith Sitwell
Miss C. Fox Smith
Thos. Sharp
Howard Spring
A.G. Street
L.A.G. Strong
Marguerite Steen
Sir William Beach Thomas
Gilbert Thomas
H.W. Timperley
Ben Travers
Miss Anne Treneer
John Trevena
J.C. Trewin
Horace Annesley Vachell
Brian Vesey-Fitzgerald
C.E. Vulliamy
Lady Vyvyan
Miss Sylvia Townsend-Warner
C. Henry Warren
E.L. Grant Watson
Ralph Whitlock
Henry Williamson
H.J. Willmott
Lewis Wilshire
G.M. Young

The West Country Writers' Association

FOUNDER MEMBERS OF THE WCWA
May 1951 - 94 Members

PRESIDENT
Eden Phillpotts

VICE PRESIDENTS
A.J. Coles (Jan Stewer)
St. John Ervine
Christopher Fry
Frederick Grisewood
John Moore
A.L. Rowse
Marguerite Steen
H.A. Vachell
Brian Vesey-Fitzgerald
Lady Vyvyan

COMMITTEE

Waveney Girvan (Chairman)
John Garrett
Kenneth Hopkins
Bryan Little
Mrs. Mary Howard
   McClintock
Lady Mander
Gilbert Phelps
Aubrey de Selincourt
L.A.G. Strong
J.C. Trewin
A.G. Findlay (Hon.
   Treasurer)
John Nance (Hon. Secretary)

REGIONAL CORRESPONDENTS

Ashley Rowe
Denys Val Baker (Cornwall)
Gilbert Thomas
E.W. Martin (Devon)
W. Kean Seymour (Somerset)
Giles Dugdale (Dorset)
Mrs. Ursula Roseveare
   (Gloucestershire)
Paul Woodhouse
   (Hampshire)
Lewis Wilshire (Bristol)
H.W. Timperley (Wiltshire)

MEMBERS

Robin Atthill
Ben Travers
Mrs. Frances Bellerby
Claud Berry
John Betjeman
Victor Bonham-Carter
John Bayliss
Alec Brown
S.H. Burton
Charles Causley
Mrs. M.C.S. Cruwys
Miss Gwendoline Courtenay
Annan Dickson
Ralph Dutton
Ronald Duncan
Miss Lois Deacon
Rt. Hon. Isaac Foot
Douglas St. Leger Gordon
Winston Graham
Kenneth Hare
Miss Muriel Hawkey
Mrs. Phyllis Hinton
L.P. Hartley
Mrs. Lorna Horstmann
John Keast
W.F. Jackson Knight
J. Lambert
Ralph Lawrence
S.R. Littlewood
Miss Lois Lamplugh
Mrs. Berta Lawrence
Laurie Lee
H.A. Manhood
W. Maqueen Pope
Miss Wendy Monk
Bruce Montgomery (Edmund Crispin)
Richard Phibbs
Miss D.A. Ponsonby
Littleton Powys
Miss Hilda M. Quick
Hugh Redwood
Mrs. Adelaide Ross (Adelaide Eden Phillpotts)
Nicholas Ross
R.C. Robertson-Glasgow
Prof. Jack Simmons
Miss C. Fox Smith
Miss M.S. Fox Smith
Miss Marjorie Stace
Miss Anne Treneer
Harry Trethowan
Mrs. Kathleen Thomas
E.W. Vernall
E.L. Grant Watson
Ralph Whitlock
Ralph Wightman
Henry Williamson
H.J. Willmott
Miss Rosalind Wade
Col. J.H. Williams
Miss June Wilson
C. Wrey Gardiner

Competition Rules for the 1950 Bath Assembly

WEST COUNTRY COMPETITION

THE DIRECTORS of the Bath Assembly (which will be held this year from May 20 to June 2) are offering prizes for new creative work originating in or dealing with the West Country. Work submitted must be hitherto unpublished.
The classes for which entries are invited are :—
(1) *A Short Story* not exceeding 5.000 words. Prizes of £30 and £5.
(2) A *Descriptive Article*, not exceeding 1,000 words. Prizes of £10 and £5.
(3) A *Poem* of not more than 50 lines. Prizes of £10 and £5.
(4) A *One Act Play*, of not more than 40 minutes performing time. Prizes of £30 and £5.

Entries in Classes 1, 2, and 4, should, in theme, spirit, or setting, reflect the West Country. In Class 3, preference will be given to poets resident in the West Country or born there.
A panel of judges, among whom are Mr. L. A. G. Strong, Mr. J. C. Trewin, and Mr. John Garrett, has been appointed.

Competitors may obtain entry forms from the Information Bureau, Abbey Churchyard, Bath, by sending a stamped addressed envelope; or public libraries may have copies of the form for distribution.

The last date for entries to reach Bath is March 31. 1951.

The West Country Writers' Association

Notes of Bryan Little's Talk to the first Writers' Congress

Talk by Bryan Little —

<u>Bath Writers' Congress. 9/5/50.</u>

"<u>Bath and Literature</u>"

Introduction. BA seems now to have settled down as the chief <u>Western</u> cultural event of the year. Though by no means incapable of making itself felt in the national and international plane. Partly a matter of musical, dramatic, etc. art performed (though not originating in the West), partly to focus attention on what the <u>West</u> has done + can do. Also leitmotif of the <u>15th _____</u>

Therefore desirable to bring <u>literature</u> into the forefront of the proceedings as soon as possible, as this is an art (like architecture) where the Westcountry has a pre-eminent place, both by achievement and association/, and literary folk are those who can keep West on the map. An attempt made at first BA.

The Westcountry's <u>contribution</u> to <u>literature</u> has been specially and <u>disproportionately</u> large, and an area where an unusal author-density per head of the population exists now. (in spite of London draw) / There seems to be something literary in the Western air + in the romantic outlines of <u>Western</u> hills and combes, and the Bath waters may perhaps vie with the Castalian spring in their literary effect. Associations and allusions <u>very rich</u>.

Camelot — Casterbridge
St Mary Redcliffe — Alfoxden (Nether Stowey)
Ivy Town — Barchester.
Scenes + personalities depicted by living <u>Western</u>
authors — vide Book Exhibn. Wiltshire. Clemo

nowhere more distinguished in this respect than Bath. In fact its place in literature is the real making of Bath's world-wide fame, great as are the achievements of Bath's architects and the renown of her healing waters. But many who have never had recourse to the one nor seen the other feel that they know and love Bath through the medium of her social life as described by various authors and through various literary works that are largely written round or about Bath.

names

renown will outlast buildings.

Curious that I, etc. but I proceed to recall the most famous of the works that give point to what I say.

Chaucer Wife of Bath — "literary accident", 'inverted anticipation of H VIII' (except that they all had to die — bedtime stories.

<u>18th century and later</u>

a) Associations with authors in general and resort of cultured people. Prior Park

Bath a place that inevitably attracted all the talent of its time, even though the same people also went to TW, Bristol Hotwells. (mention ~~for~~ Clinker + Evelina en passant). Everyone went there, hence numerous chance mentions, links, associations etc. Si monumentum requiris, circumspice tabellas muris affixas. (TS-C) Bath became part and parcel of Georgian literary + cultural life.

Propp Accounts in diaries, letters etc. Goldsmith on Nash

The West Country Writers' Association

6) Work done in and on the subject of Bath. Some of these works, e.g. Anstey's New Guide" comparatively little read now, others, being by great authors and being read all over the world, have made Bath immortal, an immortality reinforced by such factors as Swinburne's poem and Landor's comparison to Florence.

Largely narrows down to Fielding, Smollett, Goldsmith, Sheridan (his life, romance, and works), Jane Austen, Dickens (the name Pickwick), and modern authors like H. A. Vachell and Edith Sitwell. Bath also the chosen residence of several other modern authors and has given much recreation, spiritual replenishment and inspiration to others who do not live there. This a factor likely to (unpredictable). cf Nether Stowey 1790)   <u>continue</u>

The great authors, particularly perhaps Sheridan, Jane Austen and Dickens, are those who have made Bath a household world as far away as the Antipodes. They have long been the ones who have won for Bath a fame that not even architectural beauties could gain on their own, and who have made it so obvious a place for a cultural festival. Even in late Georgian days it was true that Bath, more than other Spas, was a resort of literature + culture. Gent's Mag. 1828.   c.f. also Athens "shining city of the spirit". per contra Geragas + Paestum in spite of their remains.   Enlarge on this

P.T.O.

-85-

lead up, with reference to the debt owed by Bath to authors, to the paraphrase of Horace etc.
(Odes III, 30)

αἵ τε λιπαραὶ καὶ ἰοστέφανοι καὶ ἀοίδιμοι Ἑλλάδος
ἔρεισμα, κλειναὶ Ἀθῆναι.
                           Pindar. Frag. 76.
cf. Pump Room architrave.

The West Country Writers' Association

Times Literary Supplement Report

Regional Pride

The ancient kingdom of Wessex had long lost a clear significance, except to historians, when it was revived by a great novelist and made familiar to a world of readers as a living element of the United Kingdom, as individualized as Wales or Scotland. The writer who resurrected the name grew to forget the crossing of county boundaries within the old kingdom; Dorset became only the centre piece. The inhabitants, particularly the intellectuals who are native or who have settled there, are now Wessex conscious and proud of their land. A public demonstration of this regional pride was made at the Congress of West Country Writers, which was held, for the second successive year, as part of the Bath Assembly. At a civic luncheon MR. COMPTON MACKENZIE proposed the toast of "The West," and among the west country writers present were MR. A. L. ROWSE, MR. H. A. VACHELL (now a veteran of Bath), MR. J. C. TREWIN and MR. L. A. G. STRONG. An arts festival, with "The West Country" as its theme, was held, well-known writers as a Brains Trust submitted themselves to questions, MR. STRONG gave a talk on the poets of Devon and Cornwall, and there was an exhibition of west country books.

The proposal was made at a meeting of authors who had gathered for the Assembly to constitute an Association of West Country Writers. It is believed that this is the first time such an association has been formed on a regional basis for the purpose of encouraging the art of letters in a defined area. The "West Country" is considered as that part within the B.B.C. west region—roughly, west of a diagonal line from Southampton Water to the Severn in the area of Gloucester. The association's hope is to be of service to the West in many ways beyond the field of literature; but these larger projects are expected to develop as the new organization gains in strength and prestige. Samuel Johnson, Fanny Burney, the Thrales, Thomas Hardy and many other familiar ghosts of Bath must have given the idea their blessing.

TLS ══════════ 11|6|51.

Next page - Letter from John Nance recruiting members for the WCWA

-87-

The West Country Writers' Association

WEST COUNTRY WRITERS' ASSOCIATION /951/

Tudor House
Princeton Street
London W.C.1

June 1951

For information

Dear

This letter is being sent to every Writer who received an invitation to attend the Luncheon of West Country Writers in Bath this year. It is in part a recapitulation of what took place during the Congress there, and in part an appeal for the future.

It was decided by those present at several very representative gatherings, to form an Association of West Country Writers, with Mr Eden Phillpotts as our first President. The names of other well-known authors were put forward as Vice-Presidents, and most of those approached have now accepted. It was further decided that the present Committee, which was responsible for organising this year's Congress, should form the first Committee of the proposed Association, under the Chairmanship of Mr Waveney Girvan. To assist the Committee, Regional Correspondents were nominated from amongst those present at the meetings, with certain gaps which were to be filled later. The writer of this letter was appointed Honorary Secretary, and Mr A.G. Findlay, who is associated with the firm of Girvan and Nicholson, Chartered Accountants, was appointed Honorary Treasurer.

All the appointments will come up for review at the General Meeting which will take place during next year's Congress. We have been invited to hold this at Plymouth, and Mr L.A.G. Strong will be our spokesman there.

The subscription was fixed at Ten shillings per annum, and it was decided that all those who were invited to attend the Luncheon at Bath this year should be invited to form the first members of the proposed Association. The admission of further members was left in the absolute discretion of the Committee which, it was felt, was representative not only of all Regions but also of all branches of the Writer's craft.

A set of Rules for the Association has now been prepared by the Committee, and a copy accompanies this letter. These will remain the Rules until the next General Meeting, when, in accordance with the procedure laid down in them, they may be brought up for review.

1

The West Country Writers' Association

Those are the bare bones of a number of decisions which may one day become a literary landmark. As I said very briefly over the Radio at the conclusion of the Congress, and hope to be allowed to elaborate at some later date, a quite unexpected excitement livened all our deliberations, as though there had been some spontaneous uprising of the Human spirit. Everybody present, your Committee feel, was conscious of that atmosphere.

Now, whilst your Committee gets down to its side of the business, which is, with the assistance of its Regional Correspondents, to put the Association on the map, there is a task for you to do. That task is to fan into a flame the spark of regional enthusiasm which so unexpectedly yet so unquestionably was lit at the Congress. Many of us have the feeling that something immensely important and significant may come out of our Association, something much larger than a mere gathering together of a few people united by a common love of a particular part of the English countryside or a particular way of life. We have in the Association a living thing; we want it to be courted and respected, but above all we want it to lead. We have stumbled upon a great opportunity to be of service not only to ourselves but equally to the communities we represent. Do not let us pass it by.

         Yours sincerely,

         (John Nance)

         Honorary Secretary.

NOTE.

If you were NOT present at the Meetings in Bath, we would like you to consider this letter as an official invitation to become a member of the Association. We feel sure you will accept.

If you WERE present, you will already consider yourself to be a member - or at least we hope you do.

In either case, it would be of great service to the Association if you would slip your subscription, Ten Shillings, into an envelope, together with your name and address, and send it to the Hon.Treasurer, West Country Writers' Association, Tudor House, Princeton Street, London, W.C.1. (Unless, of course, you have already done so).

The West Country Writers' Association

Notice of WCWA first AGM

President
Eden Phillpotts

Vice-Presidents
A. J. Coles ('Jan Stewer')
St. John Ervine
Christopher Fry
Frederick Grisewood
John Moore
A. L. Rowse
Marguerite Steen
H. A. Vachell
Brian Vesey-FitzGerald
Lady Vyvyan

THE
WEST COUNTRY
WRITERS' ASSOCIATION
TUDOR HOUSE, PRINCETON STREET
LONDON, W.C.1
Tel. HOLBORN 0753-4

Chairman
Waveney Girvan

Hon. Secretary
John Nance

Hon. Treasurer
A. G. Findlay

JN/GH/WCA

1st May, 1952.

The first formal Annual General Meeting of the West Country Writers' Association will be held at 5 p.m. on Tuesday June 3rd, at the Central Public Library, Plymouth.

The Agenda will be:-

1. Reading and consideration of the Rules.

2. Chairman's report.

3. Policy for election of new members.

4. Plans for 1953.

5. Accounts for year to 31st May, 1952, and election of Hon. Auditor.

You are reminded that if in accordance with Rule 17 you wish (in conjunction with another member) to nominate someone to be a member of the Committee, you must let me know immediately. If no nominations are made, the present Committee will continue in office under Rule 22.

John Nance

Hon. Secretary.

WCWA Objects

The object of the Association is *To foster the love of literature in the West Country as a contribution to the national life.*

The first headquarters are in London, at Tudor House, Princeton Street, W.C.1., and the first officers are as follows:

President   Eden Phillpotts

Vice-Presidents: A. J. Coles (Jan Stewer)
St. John Ervine
Christopher Fry
Frederick Grisewood
John Moore
A. L. Rowse
Marguerite Steen
H. A. Vachell
Brian Vesey-FitzGerald
Lady Vyvyan

Committee: Waveney Girvan (Chairman)
John Garrett
Kenneth Hopkins
Bryan Little
Mary Howard McClintock
Lady Mander (R. Glynn Grylls)
Gilbert Phelps
Aubrey de Selincourt
L. A. G. Strong
J. C. Trewin
A. G. Findlay (Hon. Treasurer)
John Nance (Hon. Secretary)

Regional Correspondents so far appointed: Ashley Rowe, Denys Val Baker (Cornwall); Gilbert Thomas, E. W. Martin (Devon); William Kean Seymour (Somerset); Giles Dugdale (Dorset); H. W. Timperley (Wiltshire)

The founder-members of the Association are the President, Vice-Presidents, Committee, Regional Correspondents, and those writers invited by the Board of the Directors of the Bath Assembly to the luncheon on May 30.

Admission to future membership of the Association will be by invitation of the Committee; and the subscription is ten shillings a year.

Next year's meeting, at which L. A. G. Strong will be spokesman of the Association, takes place at Plymouth.

The West Country Writers' Association

1953 Congress Programme

THE WEST COUNTRY WRITERS' ASSOCIATION - ANNUAL CONGRESS
SALISBURY - JUNE 18TH and 19TH, 1953

PROGRAMME.

Thursday 18th June.

4 p.m.	Reception by the Mayor and Mayoress of Salisbury in the Guildhall, followed by Tea.
5 p.m.	Lecture by Mrs. Angela Thirkell. Chairman Mr. William Hughes (Salisbury Public Librarian)
6.30 to 7.30 p.m.	Visit to the Cathedral Library.

Friday 19th June.

10.30 a.m.	Lady Mander will open the West Country Book Exhibition at Messrs. W.H. Smith & Son Ltd, 7-9, High Street, Salisbury.
11 a.m.	Committee
11.15 a.m.	Annual General Meeting of the Association in the Guildhall.
1.0 p.m.	LUNCHEON in the Guildhall.
	Guest of Honour - Mr. Eric Linklater
	Responder - Mr. John Moore
3.30 p.m.	Visit to Wilton House. *Dep. Dep. Mayor.*
5.0 p.m.	Tea at Wilton.

. . . .

First WCWA Letterhead

	THE WEST COUNTRY WRITERS' ASSOCIATION	
President Eden Phillpotts		*Chairman* Waveney Girvan

Vice-Presidents
A. J. Coles ('Jan Stewer')
St. John Ervine
Christopher Fry
Frederick
   Grisewood
John Moore
A. L. Rowse
Marguerite Steen
H. A. Vachell
Brian Vesey-
   FitzGerald
Lady Vyvyan
	TUDOR HOUSE, PRINCETON STREET
	LONDON, W.C.1
	Tel. HOLBORN 0753-4
		Hon. Secretary
		John Nance
		
		Hon. Treasurer
		A. G. Findlay

Second Letterhead late 1950s

	THE WEST COUNTRY WRITERS' ASSOCIATION	
President Eden Phillpotts		*Chairman* Waveney Girvan

Vice-Presidents
A. J. Coles ('Jan Stewer')
St. John Ervine
Christopher Fry
Frederick
   Grisewood
John Moore
A. L. Rowse
Marguerite Steen
H. M. Tomlinson
H. A. Vachell
Brian Vesey-
   FitzGerald
Lady Vyvyan
	1 DOUGHTY STREET
	LONDON, W.C.1
	Tel: CHAncery 3668
		Committee
		John Garrett
		Kenneth Hopkins
		Bryan Little
		Lady Mander
		Mrs. Mary Howard
		   McClintock
		John Nance
		Gilbert Phelps
		Aubrey de Selincourt
		L. A. G. Strong
		J. C. Trewin
		
		Hon. Secretary
		John Keast

PART III

THE MIDDLE YEARS: 1964-1977

> *I joined the WCWA in 1968. It was quite a difficult process.*
> Geraldine Kaye

The Small Brown Cardboard Box

Just twenty years later, by the time of its twenty-first anniversary, plans were being made to wind up the West Country Writers' Association.

How did it get from John Nance's brave new world to this parlous state?

Setting up a new organization is one thing: maintaining it long-term in good working order is quite another. From 1951 to 1964 things seemed to have been going on swimmingly. The congress had gone from strength to strength with Salisbury, Weymouth, Torquay, Exeter, Bournemouth, Bristol, Barnstaple, Falmouth, Taunton and Lyme Regis added to its original two venues of Bath and Plymouth. In fact Bath was the only venue to have been used more than once, and of Waveney Girvan's 'six counties' only Gloucestershire had not been visited (Cheltenham's turn was to come in 1967). The Association had drawn heavily upon its own talent for speakers - A. L. Rowse, L. P. Hartley and L. A. G. Strong were among the star names - and it had attracted guests of the calibre of Eric Linklater, C. S. Forester, Val Gielgud and Vera Brittain, with J. B. Priestley coming along again when the Association made a return to Bath in 1964.

Waveney Girvan had remained in the Chair for that whole period with Lady Mander as his vice-chairman, and the only change at the top had been necessitated by the death of Eden Phillpotts in 1960, just two years short of his century (his near contemporary, H. A. Vachell, had died five years previously). Fortunately the Association was able to replace him as president with another giant of West Country literature, Henry Williamson. Otherwise, only the offices of secretary and treasurer had undergone some changes, with John Keast assuming both roles in 1952 after John Nance had to resign 'with professional cares growing' and A. G. Findlay disappeared from the scene. In 1959 roles were reversed when John Keast became ill and John Nance returned for a short period before handing over to Honor Carr in 1960. It was a difficult handover: because of John Keast's illness there were no records of payments or bankers' orders, and Waveney Girvan had to write an open letter from the Chair explaining that the 'chaotic nature of financial records' meant that the committee had no choice but to take all subscriptions as paid and start afresh under Honor Carr.

Honor was to remain secretary and treasurer for six years, and some flavour of the committee meetings of her time was given in a recollection by Frank Littlewood:

> The first committee meetings I attended were at Honor Carr's flat at Putney not far from the bridge, and, to get to her flat, one had to go up in the smallest and slowest lift in the world, I feel quite sure. If two people got in - and only the slimmest were possible - they had to breathe in and hold their breath. Honor provided a delightfully prepared tea, with cake stand, but I can remember little of the business because Honor ran everything. The principal, if not the only, item handed over was a small brown cardboard box about eight inches by five, and say perhaps five wide. It was full of cards with all the members' names and addresses and the state of their subscriptions. It was all very neat and up to date - alas, not all the subscriptions were![1]

The Annual luncheon of the WCWA at the Pump Room, Bath, in May 1956. Lois Lamplugh, who donated the photograph, is seated at the left of the table in the foreground

PHOTO: WDP

Lady Mander, J.B. Priestley and H.A. Vachell at the first luncheon of West Country writers at the Pump Rooms, Bath, on 9 May 1950

PHOTO: WDP

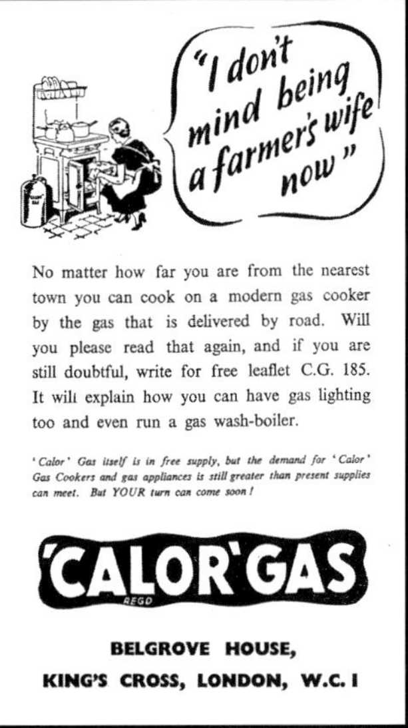

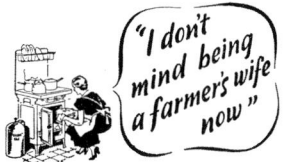

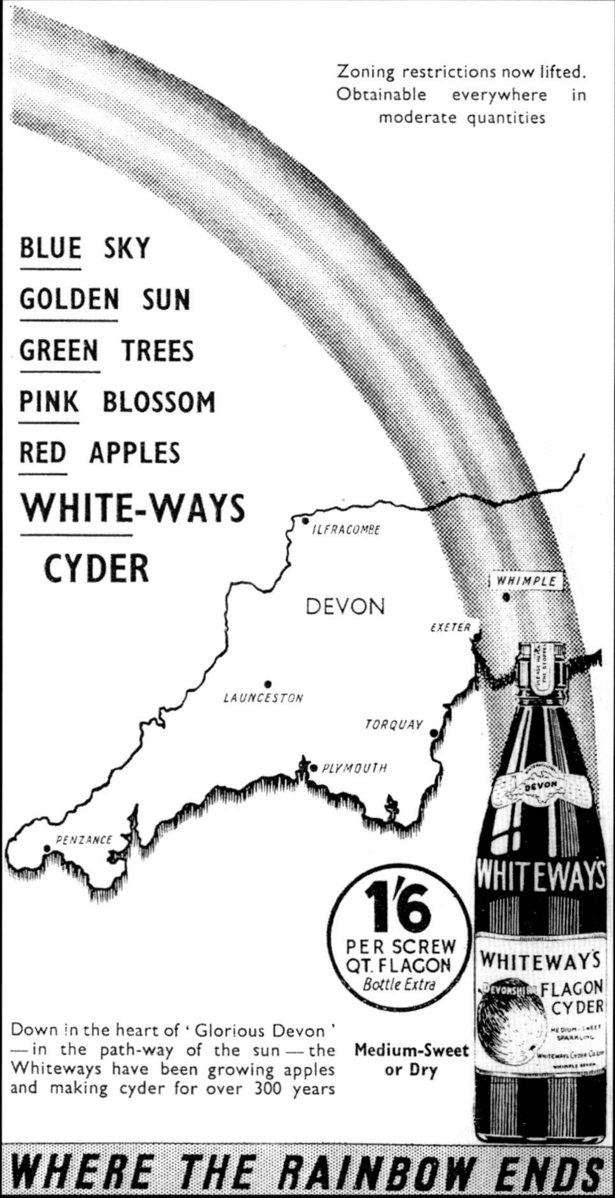

"I don't mind being a farmer's wife now"
No matter how far you are from the nearest town you can cook on a modern gas cooker by the gas that is delivered by road. Will you please read that again, and if you are still doubtful, write for free leaflet C.G. 185. It will explain how you can have gas lighting too and even run a gas wash-boiler.
'Calor' Gas itself is in free supply, but the demand for 'Calor' Gas Cookers and gas appliances is still greater than present supplies can meet. But YOUR turn can come soon!
'CALOR' GAS
REGD
BELGROVE HOUSE,
KING'S CROSS, LONDON, W.C. I

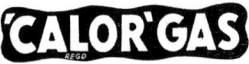

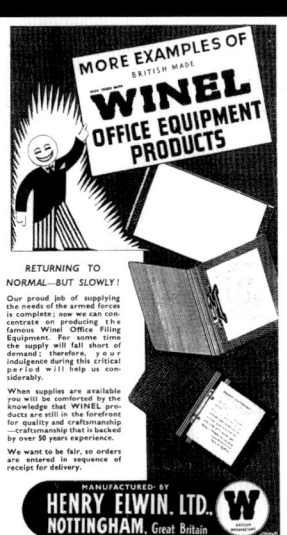

MORE EXAMPLES OF
BRITISH MADE
WINEL
OFFICE EQUIPMENT
PRODUCTS
RETURNING TO NORMAL—BUT SLOWLY!
Our proud job of supplying the needs of the armed forces is complete; now we can concentrate on producing the famous Winel Office Filing Equipment. For some time the supply will fall short of demand; therefore, your indulgence during this critical period will help us considerably.
When supplies are available you will be comforted by the knowledge that WINEL products are still in the forefront for quality and craftsmanship —craftsmanship that is backed by over 50 years experience.
We want to be fair, so orders are entered in sequence of receipt for delivery.
MANUFACTURED BY
HENRY ELWIN, LTD.,
NOTTINGHAM, Great Britain
W

Zoning restrictions now lifted. Obtainable everywhere in moderate quantities
BLUE SKY
GOLDEN SUN
GREEN TREES
PINK BLOSSOM
RED APPLES
WHITE-WAYS
CYDER
ILFRACOMBE
DEVON
WHIMPLE
EXETER
LAUNCESTON
TORQUAY
PLYMOUTH
PENZANCE
1/6
PER SCREW QT. FLAGON
Bottle Extra
WHITEWAYS
DEVON
WHITEWAY'S
FLAGON CYDER
Down in the heart of 'Glorious Devon' — in the path-way of the sun — the Whiteways have been growing apples and making cyder for over 300 years
Medium-Sweet or Dry
WHERE THE RAINBOW ENDS

Advertisements from *The West Country Magazine* capture the flavour of the postwar era

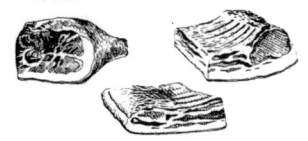

HARRIS BACON
The problem of cutting the bacon ration

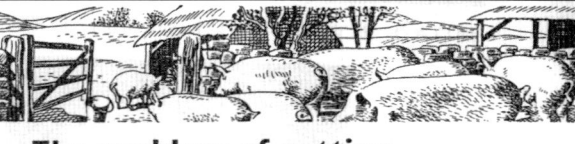

Letter from Henry Williamson to Waveney Girvan written from Ox's Cross

BARNSTAPLE AND NORTH DEVON CLUB.
BARNSTAPLE
TEL. 2075

Ox's Cross
BRAUNTON
N.Devon

28 August
1962 plus 2.

Dear Waveney
I have done nothing since your card, which arrived in the University's term time. I called there some weeks before, and saw the Librarian's secretary. It did seem that my part was done: giving the manuscripts about twenty, including Tarka, Salar, Village Books, Flax of Dream etc etc etc. Originally I wanted it to be a private presentation, then they said if there was a public one it might induce more British authors to give their mss to a 'poor university'. So I agreed, reluctantly. I asked the secretary to Librarian, L J John Lloyd M.A. to contact you and write for dates, or to show dates in May, for she said,'The Vice Chanceller travels a great deal abroad, he may be away in May'. That is all I know, except that I must I suppose find out what covenants to put on the gift, lest various people get hole of the mss, which have various notes on them, not all polite, made at various times. Also they should not be sold, since I have had an offer of several thousand pounds for them, five figures in fact, but wanted them to remain in Devon. RELUCTANCE. Due to conditions of one's life: no cleaner in cottage (4 Capstone Place. Ilfracombe) no cook, secretary, housekeeper or any dam thing at all which means irregular or no meals and consequent pessimism, while one works and works at writing, also looks after 3 acres in this field, contents of large studio, hut, caravan, workshops etc all a liability and one a slave. No doubt this is all

one's own fault, or due to defects of mind, and character, but ... one begins to see why so the new wave let, led by Sam Beckett,....
Now, my dear friend, may I suggest the term president of the West Writers be for three years to give ot er senior vice-presidents a chance to open and bring in new personalities. Such as Lady Vyvyan, A.L.Rouse, John Moore etc. Presidency Lady would ensure presence at the annual meeting, Eden P. was very olde olde man, remember. Also I ha another reason for not wanting to remain President after the annual meeting of 1965, which is private but is due to consideration for the West Writers. Why not L.P. Hartley, a most worthy man in every aspect.

I enclose a letter from Librarian Lloyd sorry I have then back sometime

Every good wish to you & to yours,

Henry

(I need a wife or help-mate very badly!!)

P.S. Lloyd's letter there is Mr Fellowes [?] had a heart attack. He has I know be back in college at Exeter Soon. Will you please write to him?

Henry beside the open fireplace in the writing hut

Top: Snapped with a Jap at Torre Abbey 1971

Right: Henry Williamson and Waveney Girvan on the the River Barle near Dulverton

Below: Postcard to Frank Littlewood

from HENRY WILLIAMSON, OX'S CROSS, BRAUNTON, N. DEVON.

My dear Frank   4 Capstone Place   18 May
                 Ilfracombe   1978

I must write and tell you how much I enjoyed the party at Salisbury this year, and give thanks to you, whose work of organisation and care for everyone's comfort, made it possible. Also your speech — the final one — at the luncheon table was so clear, confident, and right, at the end of the party. I enjoyed too, the presence of our President, & Martin Bourne's description of the work involved with Morality Plays; and of course Anthony Rye, of Sparrow Hedger, Fellow Selborne — the original Stamm Hawk Itself

etc etc love fm NRY

The first Newsletter 1968

Newsletter 1975

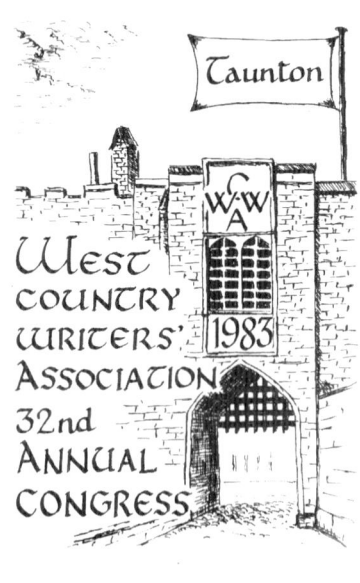
Newsletter 1983

Newsletter 1998

, MAY 27, 1968.

At the Westcountry Writers' Association luncheon on Saturday are (left to right), Lord Goodman (chairman of the Arts Council), the Lord Mayor of Plymouth (Ald. Ivor Lowe), Mr. Christopher Fry, the Lady Mayoress, and Mrs. John Trewin and Mr. Trewin (president of the association).

1968 Congress left to right: Lord Goodman chairman of the Arts Council, Mayor of Plymouth, Christopher Fry, Mayoress, Wendy (Monk) Trewin, John Trewin

Association to admit scriptwriters

Writers' annual congress

NOVELISTS and authors converged on Torquay at the weekend for the annual congress of the Westcountry Writers Guild.

1984 Congress left to right Keith Salter, Rachel Billington, Charles Owen, Deputy Mayor of Torbay, David Keep, Christopher Fry, Nancy Tregenna-Piggott, Deputy Mayoress, Ralph Whitlock

Sketches by Freda Bromhead at annual lunches in the 1970s

Frank was about to take over the running of affairs from Honor, who wished to retire for health reasons - hence the handing over of the small brown cardboard box. Frank's recollection of the delightful tea and the cake stand - and his total blank about the business done - speaks volumes about how things were: the Association was an enjoyable social experience for those who were 'in', but it was not particularly businesslike.

There are no minute books in the archives for the period 1959-1966. That is not to say that Honor Carr was idle - there *are* minutes, but they are all muddled up with correspondence, congress plans and everything else amongst great bundles of papers, haphazardly strung together, bearing these dates. Honor is remembered with gratitude and affection by older members, and at least there was a small brown cardboard box to be handed over this time, an improvement on the previous handover.

Henry Williamson called her the 'Queen Pin' of the Association, and with good cause after she had sorted out the complicated arrangements for the 1965 Congress, which incorporated Henry's presentation of his manuscripts to Exeter University. Instead of a lecture, Henry organized a three-way 'conversation piece' between himself, Ted Hughes and E. W. Martin at the University, where he was supported by some seventy members of the WCWA. In spite of all this, the University failed to acknowledge his generosity with the conferment of an honorary degree. Plans for guests and speakers and receptions fluctuated back and forth until the very last minute, with sheaves of long letters between Honor and Henry trying to sort everything out. 'Honor ran everything' as Frank said, and the Association certainly kept going nicely from day to day, but without much formal business structure - and without looking to the future.

Anyone who has ever had charge of a database will know what a fluid body an address list is. It is *never* up to date: people move, die, resign and disappear without notice at an astonishing rate, and as soon as a list is revised it is certain to need amendments. The turnover of membership in an association like ours is surprisingly high: in ten years from 1990-2000 the membership has changed by fifty per cent. Unless these fifty per cent of members lost are constantly being replaced, the Association can go down very quickly.

In the gracious days of the 1950s, little heed was paid to recruiting. Membership was very firmly 'by invitation of the Committee', and the committee - a well-established group of middle-class friends who preferred to hold their meetings at a prestigious address in London (such as the offices of the Arts Council or the Royal Commonwealth Society) - did not feel the urge to do much inviting. Names of suggested new members were put before a selection committee which met periodically for the sole purpose of vetting nominations, and some of the surviving notes and minutes of these meetings are quite staggering. It was at this time that the qualification for membership crept up from one to three books, published 'at publisher's risk', in hard back - and even nominees who could meet those requirements were frequently considered a little lightweight as yet, and told to apply again in a few years' time when they had a more substantial body of work behind them. One wonders if any of them ever did.

John Trewin's description of that 1961 AGM when '...for some reason neither the then Hon. Secretary or the minutes had appeared'[2] tells us a lot about the state of affairs. As long as Waveney Girvan held the Chair and could perform his conjuring tricks, pulling his '...whole families of rabbits out of a surprising variety of hats',[2] the Association kept going.

Then, in 1964, Waveney Girvan died suddenly and a yawning gap was left. Possibly this is another reason for John Trewin's insistence that the WCWA was Waveney Girvan's alone: not just because he founded it, but because he was able to sustain it by sheer personal charisma. Joan Lowry underlines this in a memory of his days:

> He was also a charming wit, and endlessly entertaining. After he died, the WCWA became rather staid and a bit over-serious.[3]

Without Waveney Girvan to carry things off, impersonating officers, agenda and any other business all rolled into one, the need for an efficient administration became horribly evident, and it has remained a factor that has determined the Association's periods of success and decline ever since.

The chairmanship was not a problem. Who else but John Trewin? - model of all theatre critics, deeply respected writer and poet, the archetypal Cornishman who had held the line at *The West Country Magazine* for so long and who had been instrumental in the foundation of the Association. A recollection from Frank Littlewood gives some measure of his stature: 'On the 20 February 1990, it took *The Times* four three quarter columns and a large photo to pay tribute to the work, scholarship and memory of this man of the theatre, who went each night "...with a feeling of expectation and hope",'[4] - and who went on going each night, without thought of retirement, until the stroke which preceded his death.

John Trewin agreed to take on Waveney Girvan's mantle, and at the same time Lady Mander - 'capable of making any gathering "go",' according to Joan Lowry[5] - resigned her place as vice-chairman in favour of another dominant figure in WCWA history, William Kean Seymour. In 1965 the change in the triumvirate was completed when Henry Williamson, reaching his seventieth birthday, decided to retire as president, ushering in the Christopher Fry era. Henry did not bow out of WCWA completely though, and he continued to be a regular attender at congresses, his infamous bread-roll throwing and other colourful escapades a small price to pay for the loyalty and affection he always showed towards the Association.

What John Trewin brought to the Association was passion. That quality shines through his lengthy *Times* obituary: passion for the theatre in general and for Shakespeare in particular, the sort of passion that meant he could attend the theatre night after night without ever losing his sense of excitement, or that he could enjoy Five and Eighty Hamlets (the title of one of his books) without ever losing freshness. His passion for the West Country, and especially for Cornwall, was equally deep and vibrant - glimpsed in the poem reproduced from *The West Country Magazine* of Autumn 1951:

KINGDOM

Fuchsia-fire and marble shine,
　The green, the frosting spray,
　The embered end of day
In the kingdom that was mine.

Tamarisk and serpentine,
The rose, the crested white,
The sword upon the night,
In the country that was mine.

The gulls in flickering twine,
Wet weed within the cave,
The gold, the toppling wave
In the kingdom that was mine.
                    J. C. Trewin

The new regime found that the kingdom which they had inherited was distinctly rocky. John Trewin in his wisdom could see two basic causes: the lack of an efficient administration and the scant attention paid to recruitment - plus the logical consequence of both, a shortage of funds. The details of members' subscriptions in the small brown box which Honor Carr passed on may have been neat and up to date, but - '...alas, not all the subscriptions were!' Trewin knew just the man for the job of sorting things out, and Frank Littlewood recalls, '...it was John Trewin who came up to me after a Bristol meeting and in his own gentle way persuaded me to take on the job of Honorary Secretary and Treasurer of the Association, not then perhaps in its best state.'[6]

Frank Littlewood was a great administrator. With his sister, Ursula (Sue) Roseveare, he had been a founder member, and Sue recalled in a letter not long before her death that their writing careers had not lived up to the great literary ambitions with which they had set out, but that nonetheless they had thoroughly enjoyed the fellowship and fun of being WCWA members. In Sue's case it was a serious traffic accident which curtailed her career in 1964. Despite her injuries she refused to be relegated to a wheelchair and was always remarkable for her cheerfulness.

Frank's career had taken him away from literature into local government, and he became town clerk of Cheltenham in the early 1940s, an office which he held until 1965 and for which he was made a Freeman of the Borough of Cheltenham and awarded the OBE for services to local government. During this long tenure he was able to help the arts flourish in civic life: he was instrumental in founding the Civic Playhouse, now the

Playhouse Theatre, and he helped to establish the Cheltenham Festivals of Music and Literature. He was 'Mr. Cheltenham', and the mention of his name is met with respect by Cheltenham council officials to this day. It is no accident that Frank took over the administration of the WCWA in 1966 and the first Cheltenham Congress took place in 1967.

It was because of his position in Cheltenham that Frank was able to give way to John Trewin's 'dulcet pleadings', as he had his own secretary, the indefatigable Miss Catherine Irving. She did so much work on the Association's behalf that she should have been made an honorary member. Frank Littlewood acknowledged as much when he admitted, '...but throughout my time I have had the voluntary assistance of Miss Catherine Irving, who had been with me in the Cheltenham office and it was really through her that I was able to do what I did'.[7] As Frank, his wife and his sister were all such kindly and charming people who remained Miss Irving's friends to the end of their lives - they even shared their slice of the WCWA fortieth anniversary cake with her - she probably found this labour of love no displeasing task.

As for Frank himself, Bob Cooper reminds us that '...it would always be Frank who spotted the lonely new members at a congress. He would immediately approach them, introduce them round, and do his utmost to make them feel at home.'[8] One member habitually addressed him as 'Dear Teddy-Bear Littlewood'.

The 1968 Congress at Plymouth was a turning-point. John Trewin and Frank Littlewood had grasped the point about falling numbers and the committee finally came to discuss the qualifications for membership. More new members had to be attracted. The standard requirement that recruits should have been published in hardback had been strictly adhered to; possibly rather more strictly than was envisaged by the founding fathers whose first set of rules had left room for liberal interpretation. Under John Trewin the elitist tendencies were reversed, the insidious demand for not one but three publications was revoked, and the latter part of the stated object - '...as a contribution to the national life' - was changed to read '...as a contribution to the cultural life of the nation', before being quietly dropped in 1970.

But more was needed. It was now over twenty years since the end of the Second World War and the days of rationing: the world was changing - in the 1960s, changing very fast. Publishing was changing too. Paperbacks had become standard, and the media of television and radio had developed out of all recognition. A writer could now be a perfectly respectable professional who had appeared in the dreaded paperback, or whose entire work had 'only' been broadcast - in fact the growth of television meant that TV scriptwriters were probably the most influential and well-paid writers in the business. At the 1968 AGM, held in the Athenaeum at Plymouth (the congress was still in those days scattered around different venues in the town), the decision was unanimously taken to amend the rules and admit both television and radio scriptwriters and people connected with literature who were not writers at all. As a symbolic gesture of the new order, the Plymouth city librarian received the committee's invitation to become the first non-writer member. No longer was the librarian on his knees. John Trewin had begun to stop the rot.

It is significant that Plymouth was the city he turned to for this achievement, because it was the city where both John and his wife Wendy Monk had begun their careers, as journalists on *The Western Independent*. It was the city of his education (at Plymouth College) and it was the subject of the first article he wrote for *The West Country Magazine*, 'Plymouth as it Was', in which he remarks that '...in Devon and Cornwall Plymouth is a word of power. Geographically in Devon, in spirit it belongs to both counties. In the far Cornish village where I was bred it was ambition's height to go "up Plymouth".'[9] He knew his way about here; he had connections and influence - influence sufficient to attract a powerful line-up of speakers for the 1968 Congress. There was Charles Causley reading from his own poetry, Kenneth Macleod of Westward TV (in tune with the move to admit scriptwriters), and as guest of honour no less a personage than Lord Goodman, the Chairman of the Arts Council - quite a coup. Clearly the modernisation of the rules was not to signal any 'dumbing down' of the Association's status as a professional and artistic body.

Frank Littlewood was to write an amusing note on the difficulty of getting publicity even with all John Trewin's pull:

> I was trying to get BBC Plymouth interested in our meetings and Luncheon and was making little progress, but when the name of

Charles Causley came up interest was immediately expressed... theywere much more interested in his poetry, what he was writing and hoped to write, than in the Congress. I couldn't help feeling a bit disappointed![10]

Years later, when our press officer Janet Green was likewise attempting to interest BBC local radio stations in our fortieth anniversary, she met with total apathy - until she mentioned that Charles Causley was a member, whereupon they fell over themselves trying to get an interview. Charles Causley's name has lost none of its potency over the years.

Other reforming measures were on the 1968 agenda. The difficulties of finding a shop willing to host the book exhibition were aired, a poetry competition was suggested, and John Trewin spoke in support of PLR. The WCWA ship was set afloat again at Plymouth, but the officers realized that the new members would need something to keep them on board. It is a long haul from one congress to the next - and what of those members who do not make it to congress? What did they get for their membership fee? In 1967, for the first time, it was acknowledged that something more was needed than an annual letter from the secretary outlining congress plans. Members should know who their fellow-members were. They needed to be kept in touch with changes of office-holders or rules. They needed to know a bit about each other, and about what was going on. So, in 1968, the first ever newsletter was produced.

It was not without opposition. Veterans of the old days remembered the quality of *The West Country Magazine* and feared that a half-baked attempt to revive it on an amateur basis would do nothing for the Association's image and would mar the memory of the original. Others wanted a full-blown revival of *The West Country Magazine*. Anthony Rye of Sparrow's Hanger in Selborne (his major work was a study of Gilbert White of Selborne) was particularly opposed to the concept that Frank Littlewood was forming of a modest *news* letter, just to keep people in touch. As Frank wrote to Charles Irving in 1967,

> I am anxious to circulate to the membership of this Association of rather more than one hundred professional writers, a News Sheet, possibly round about Christmas. It would be a very simple affair,

possibly just one or two pages, and this has not been done before. It holds a most successful annual Congress, but I think that we ought to try and do more than this.[11]

He was, of course, appealing for funding. The Association's finances were still at rock bottom, and a sponsor would be needed before any news sheet could be conceived. A committee member offered some help as long as he could remain anonymous, but getting the funds together and the printing arranged was a lengthy business. In the end the first edition was sponsored by Sir George Dowty, founder of the aeronautical company of Cheltenham, who had previously financed young writers on visits abroad, and who presumably knew Frank through his Cheltenham connections.

Then there was the problem of collecting the material. The letters are all preserved in the archives: Frank's meticulous requests to members to send him some news of their work in progress, and the handwritten - often scribbled - notes back which he carefully transcribed into seven pages of members' news, starting with the president and working its way down to the newest of new members. Henry Williamson at the time was tackling the final novel of *A Chronicle of Ancient Sunlight* and he contributed a message that it was a long, long haul during which, living alone, 'he fails at times to buy food'.

The first WCWA newsletter was at last ready for publication in time for the 1968 Plymouth Congress. It ran to twelve A5 pages and followed a very simple format: messages from the president and chairman, details of committee decisions, congress arrangements, secretary's notes of thanks, and then news of members. At the time the Association was coming to terms with the sudden death of vice-president John Moore, and Christopher Fry paid him warm tribute in the President's Message:

> He was a man made for friendship. His delight in life and people and words and the countryside generated warmth. To be with him, or to read his work, always opened good windows on the world. Days were wider and more free because of him.[12]

The committee's deliberations included a plan to increase membership 'from the present figure of about one hundred (actually one hundred and fifteen) to about one hundred and fifty' by considering honorary or associate members. A poetry or short story competition was also mooted, and there were thoughts of asking members to approach their MPs over royalties and public lending right. With a credit balance of £23. 19s. 0d. it was felt that the finances were fairly healthy, but a small increase in subscriptions to fifteen shillings was proposed for 1968 and members were 'invited to increase their subscriptions accordingly, but there would be no compulsion to do so'.

The newsletter was greeted as a success. Henry Williamson hailed it with congratulations, and asked that the name of Waveney Girvan should be immortalised in every future edition. Even Anthony Rye withdrew his misgivings - 'I was wrong; I retract; I am ready to eat humble pie... it is useful and decorative'[13] - and Frank Littlewood found himself trying to repeat the operation the next year. In 1969 he managed to get sponsorship from the Pergamon Press, so it was a much more splendid publication than in 1968, costing £144 to produce. It had a tasteful green cover carrying an old print of Milsom Street in Bath, and the text was interspersed with engravings of a generally arty kind - muses contemplating their lyres (this one was reproduced for the cover of the fortieth anniversary booklet) or swains serenading their mistresses in a pastoral landscape. It had grown to sixteen pages, and it again carried messages from the president and chairman, congress details, committee activities, reports on the finances and the membership (which had risen to one hundred and twenty-one), and a long section - eight of the sixteen pages - given over to news of members. Laurie Lee contributed the gloriously brief entry:

> Laurie Lee, who has had a bout in hospital, hopes to have a new book out in 1969. He says it is nothing to do with cider or Rosie.

The pattern was established: this was no reincarnation of *The West Country Magazine*. This was simply an in-house newsletter by and for members, with no pretensions to be a literary magazine carrying articles of any length. Significantly the 1969 edition ended with a paragraph headed FORGIVENESS WANTED.

The Hon. Secretary, who seems to have made himself responsible for compiling this affair, wishes to say that if there are any indiscretions he hopes they will be forgiven. He also wishes to place on record his thanks to Catherine Irving for her help in this as in all other aspects of the Association's work.[14]

It was yet another job for the secretary/treasurer, as William Kean Seymour acknowledged when he congratulated Frank on 'your' newsletter.[15]

Consequently Frank found himself trying to do it again in 1970, but this time he could not get a sponsor. Joan Lowry tried to help. She had been looking after a publication called *The Rambler* after the death of its editor and her next-door neighbour, Commander Bertram Faunthorpe, who had been a great WCWA supporter. Apparently he had a particular talent for finding good West Country hotels to be the headquarters for congress - 'Bertram could be relied upon to find one where the beer was up to standard'. She saw to the winding up of the periodical and, as there was some money left over once all the obligations had been met, she felt that nothing would have pleased Bertram Faunthorpe more than to have that surplus ploughed back into the WCWA newsletter, which she saw as a descendant of *The Rambler* - '*Rambler* into *Phoenix*' as she put it. Frank was attracted by the idea of dispensing with an expensive printer and making the newsletter independent of sponsors. He wrote back to Joan on 21 May 1970:

> ...there is much to be said for producing our Newsletter out of our own funds. We shall be just that little bit more masters in our own house, and over the years it could be improved and possibly built up from the simply printed or stencilled sheets with which it may have to start. Also we may indeed think of producing the Newsletter occasionally after Congress so that we can include notes and comments in it about the events.[16]

It was round about the same time that Denys Val Baker managed to get *The Cornishman* going again - he sent apologies for congress that year on the intriguing grounds that his wife was organizing a pottery in Bermuda -

and for 1971 Frank Littlewood was able to put out an edition of the newsletter on yellow paper that was truly an in-house affair. There was no further need for sponsors to meet the costs of printing, but all the workload fell on the ever-willing secretary. Frank had added another hat to his existing ones of secretary and treasurer. Over subsequent years the newsletter was to settle into a regular twice-yearly pattern, its format and contents changing according to the ideas of each succeeding editor, but at the beginning of the 1970s there was no newsletter editor, just Frank, and the strain was beginning to tell. Bob Cooper was to recall:

> For many years, Frank had combined the offices of Secretary, Membership Secretary, Treasurer and Newsletter Editor. Anyone since who has taken on just one of those offices will understand how much work he did for the Association.[17]

By 1970 the twentieth and twenty-first anniversaries of the Association were looming, and it was also a time of great upheaval in local government circles, so Frank was really beginning to flag under the workload. With John Trewin and William Kean Seymour he had kept things going and had started to address the problems, but the work involved in turning things round and refreshing the Association began to seem too much to tackle. John Trewin, too, had alerted people to his imminent retirement from the Chair: he had done all he could, and it was time to hand over to a completely new set of faces. But whose?

William Kean Seymour's idea for the future

There is a whole section of the WCWA archives entitled, somewhat forbiddingly, 'The William Kean Seymour File: 1968 - 1975'. It contains the ongoing correspondence between William Kean Seymour and Frank Littlewood, preserving rather more of his letters to Frank than of Frank's replies to him. He comes over in these letters as quite a character. Living at Old Alresford in Hampshire he was at the edge of the West Country territory, but he was at the centre of literary life in his generation. A Fellow of the Royal Society of Literature he had all the right connections: when he lectured on Blake at the Guildford Literary Festival in 1968, for example, he notes that John and Wendy Trewin were in the front row with Harold Hobson and Arnold de Montmerency (barrister, parliamentary candidate, and then editor of *Contemporary Review*), and one gets a feel of literary elitism - a sense that wherever the top literary people were gathered together, there he would be in the midst of them. He was married to Rosalind Wade, herself a WCWA member, prolific novelist of no mean stature, and an established lecturer on the literary novel. George Eliot was her abiding passion. Their son inherited his parents' literary skills and, dropping the 'Kean' from the family name, became famous first as a journalist and newsreader then as the best-selling novelist, Gerald Seymour.

Rosalind was to take on the editorship of *Contemporary Review*, a highly influential literary magazine which had been going for over a century and which, in the 1970s, was increasing its readership at home and overseas. Together, the Kean Seymours ran literary courses at Moor Park College in Farnham, Surrey (and it is to one of these courses that we owe the recruitment of Bob Cooper), as well as lecturing and holding creative writing workshops worldwide.

One senses, from the letters, that people were a little bit afraid of William Kean Seymour. Bob Cooper, as secretary, felt he was expected to call him 'Sir'. He seems to have had two aspects: one of warmth and generosity that expressed itself in friendships and in the giving of his energy on the Association's behalf, but balanced against it there was also a streak of pettiness. He could split hairs over the finest detail, act with great obstinacy, be rather mean about money, and sometimes speak quite cuttingly. On the other hand he could embrace the new office-holder Bob Cooper with generosity that borders on the patronising - '...Rosalind and I have an instinctive liking for you, and the sort of understanding that seldom misleads us'[18] he wrote to Bob in 1972 - though two months later he could write witheringly, 'Some day - when your typist has your authority to buy a new ribbon - it would be nice to have a copy of the membership roll...'[19] One minute he is pouring praise on Frank Littlewood for all the work he had put into the newsletter: the next he is castigating Frank for omitting his full honours, 'Hon D Litt, FRSL', with a sharp memo that he had just had an honorary doctorate conferred upon him by the Free University of Asia (Pakistan). When this dichotomy was mentioned recently to two elder statesmen of the Association, one agreed that yes, he could be like that, but he was wonderful really. The other rapped out, 'The man was impossible'.

By the time William Kean Seymour took on the vice-chairmanship in 1965 he was not young, and by 1969 he had already suffered a first warning bout of illness. He made light of it in a letter to Frank Littlewood on 1 December 1969, but Rosalind, in a letter of the same date, sounded more concerned. With all the talk of the chairman's coming retirement, the approaching anniversaries, and the reluctance of Frank Littlewood to keep going for ever, he was not at all anxious to be seen as the natural successor to John Trewin. As 1969 marked the one hundred and fiftieth anniversary of George Eliot's birth, Rosalind Wade agreed to lecture on 'George Eliot and the West Country' at the Bath Congress, for which they both stayed in the Francis Hotel, but they wanted no deeper involvement. Throughout that and the next congress, anxieties about the future rumbled on. The changes made in 1968 had helped, yet membership was still falling (and finances with it) and, most discouraging of all, nobody seemed to want to take office.

At this point as never before the importance of the secretary-administrator was thrown into the spotlight. An association cannot keep going without someone willing to do the day-to-day maintenance work, as well as producing the paperwork for committee meetings and organizing the big set pieces for the congress. The secretary holds it all together, including, in Frank's case, running the accounts, the membership list and the newsletter. It must have taken a lot of time even with help such as Frank had from Catherine Irving, and it was a huge amount to ask of anyone who had another job - especially if that job happened to be writing, which carries no regular holidays, weekends or time off. With the twenty-first anniversary looming Frank threw in the towel and presumably wrote a fairly controversial letter to William Kean Seymour (not preserved) because it elicited a handwritten reply of great interest:

...these I've discussed with Rosalind and we both would feel sad if you gave up the Honorary Secretaryship of the WCWA even for the valid reason that your local government work is increasing. In fact, we would think it nothing short of disastrous if you resigned the job which you do so well and is so much appreciated. Hardly a week passes without I feel convinced that I ought to give up something but somehow or other I yield to the entreaties of my colleagues and carry on. Perhaps this will happen in your case when you meet the members of the Committee at Torquay.

I can't help thinking that it would be fatal to the organization if it were decided - as you put it - to 'fold our wings and roost in the branches of the Bath Literary Festival' after celebrating our twenty-first year in that city in 1972: in other words, be put to sleep.

The only thing we can suggest, should you feel unable to carry on, is that Wendy Trewin should accept the position of Secretary-Organizer. It would be asking much of her but it is just possible that she might be persuaded to do it...[20]

The Association, born of the Bath Assembly, came very close to being buried in it.

Needless to say, Wendy Trewin was not over-enamoured of the idea that she should fill the gap when Frank duly gave a year's notice of his resignation to the 1971 AGM. She was willing to give him a hand with membership matters, but not take on the whole administration, and at this stage people were still thinking in terms of one administrator only. This gave the committee a lot to think about at Torquay: should they keep trying to replace John Trewin and Frank Littlewood? Should they give in and let the Association 'roost in the branches of the Bath Literary Festival' (as the Assembly was now called) as Frank suggested? If the old guard had had enough, who was going to replace them? *Could* the old guard face change, and accept 'the younger members'[21] taking over, or would they rather see it all wound up and tidied away rather than altered? - for there were 'younger members' now, four in particular being Bob Cooper, Geraldine Kaye, Meryl Macdonald Bendle and John Brooks who had all made their way on to the committee. But were the old guard capable of relinquishing their hold?

The exchange of letters between William Kean Seymour and Frank Littlewood at this time carries a sense of crisis, of repeated mind-changing and undecidedness. William Kean Seymour himself was torn: on the one hand, he wanted to see the Association survive and he was full of ideas for new developments but on the other hand he could only envisage these developments taking place within the old framework with tried and trusted officers. He could see what had to happen, but found it hard to trust newcomers - especially 'younger' newcomers.

His friendship with Frank Littlewood was cemented when he and Rosalind went to stay with the Littlewoods for the founding of 'The Cheltenham Poets' in October 1971. At the age of 84 this was, surprisingly, William Kean Seymour's first sight of the Cotswolds. The generous hospitality of the Littlewoods elicited a letter of sincere thanks from him, and we see his warm-hearted qualities as he recounts his pleasure at sharing the Littlewoods' home (and admiring Frank's pottery - obviously another dimension to Frank Littlewood the sober administrator) and enjoying the beautiful countryside to which Frank had introduced him. It would be surprising if they had not had some discussion of the WCWA crisis during their time together, and just two days after this visit William Kean Seymour had a Big Idea. On 19 October 1971 he sent Frank a letter which was to turn the whole situation around:

> I've been thinking about the WCWA and wonder whether it might be a good idea for someone to go patiently through the latest edition of 'Authors' & Writers' Who's Who' to extract a list of names and addresses of West Country Writers who might be interested in the Association if particulars were brought properly to their notice. Considered alongside our policy of *inviting* people approved by the Committee this might yield an eventual recruitment of three or four times our present membership and you and John feel it worthwhile carrying on the good work. Each entry in the fat black book contains the author's particulars of publications. If a suitable letter (printed of course) introduced interest and enquiry we might be on the way to a new lease of life.
>
> I can't myself undertake to explore the reference book, but perhaps Miss Irving might be induced to build up a list from it for consideration by the Committee.

Are we having a Committee Meeting in the near future? We might discuss this idea. I feel somehow that an effort might be preferable to handing the organization over to Writers' Clubs.[22]

The idea was on the right lines - the future lay in a concerted recruitment effort - but he could still only see it in terms of keeping the old order together, giving motivation to the same people to keep going, and fighting off those pernicious 'writers' clubs'. Who, incidentally, is 'John' in the context of this letter? There were three Johns on the committee at this time - Trewin, Brooks and Rowland - and two of them (Brooks and Rowland) were potential candidates for chairmanship. If the John in question was Trewin, then the tenor of the sentence about 'carrying on the good work' is that William Kean Seymour still did not want change, and that certainly seems to be the most likely of the three 'John' options. He could see what had to happen, but he still couldn't let go.

Frank very quickly poured cold water on the details, but he could see that a breakthrough in thinking had been made. He developed the vision in his reply the following day: yes, it was a good idea, but the old warhorses just couldn't take it on, and the younger generation must be the people to take it up and run with it:

> I quite agree with the excellent idea about going through the reference books and inviting people to join the Association, and there are a number of other ways in which a knowledge of suitable members can be acquired, but the trouble is we are not short of ideas of how to do this but we are short of people to do it. As I said at the last annual meeting I cannot possibly do this with everything I have on, nor indeed can Miss Irving. We are not handing the Association over to Writers' Clubs, but my suggestion is the running of the Association might be left to the younger members, some of whom are quite active in Writers' Clubs and so forth, and who may be able to find the people necessary to undertake the kind of work you have in mind.[23]

It was at 'the last annual meeting', the 1971 AGM, that various of 'the Bristol members' had made their opinions known as to the way the Association was going. Frank declared himself to be 'stimulated and encouraged'[24] by their ideas, and he defended them against the ingrained elitism of the committee, declaring that although 'a number of them were associated with writers' circles', they were nonetheless 'engaged in professional writing in one aspect or another'.[25] No satisfactory conclusions had been reached at the Torquay AGM, and the committee met at the Arts Council on 16 November 1971 to decide what was to be done. Such was the crucial nature of this meeting that the president himself, Christopher Fry, was invited and attended to give his opinion.

There was a long discussion on Frank's resignation. One party believed that the Association 'should be content with its life of twenty-one years'[26] and close its membership. Arrangements had already begun to inter the minute books and other papers in the Records Office at Bath. The president, however, cautioned against precipitate moves and made two positive suggestions. Why not send out a questionnaire to all the members, canvassing their feelings about the possible directions the Association could take - evolution or extinction - and, in the meantime, why not listen to 'the Bristol members' and see what they had to offer? It was the advice of Christopher Fry that prevailed.

In January 1972 Frank duly wrote his annual round robin to all the members, carrying the details for the next congress - the twenty-first - to be held at Bath. This time, however, the letter was headed, 'The Future of the Association', and it was circulated with an attached questionnaire, as Christopher Fry had suggested. In his letter Frank explained how the twenty-first anniversary celebrations would take place 'in the city where the Association was founded, namely Bath' adding that 'the civic authorities are quite delighted about this, and are doing all in their power to make the occasion a specially happy one'.[27] Apart from the civic reception and the annual luncheon, however, the programme was going to be different in 1972. There were to be no 'formally set functions' so that time could be given to informal meetings at which members could discuss the aspects of the Association's twenty-one year old life and consider its future: 'This would enable any decisions to be made or recommendations adopted formally at the annual general meeting on the Saturday morning'.[28] Before that, there was work to be done as Frank explained:

At the committee meeting, with a view to assisting the discussions about the future of the Association, a suggestion made by the President was adopted unanimously, that a questionnaire which the President, Chairman and myself should draft, should be sent to all members. From the answers a memorandum would be prepared which could be sent to members well in advance of the Bath Congress but which might be a basis of our discussions. With this in mind we shall try and make both the questions and the subsequent memorandum as provocative as possible, and take every advantage of making our twenty-first anniversary a sound foundation for future years.[29]

He ends by emphasising his determination to resign, and his support for a new regime:

...I would like to make it clear, as I did to the annual meeting at Torquay and to the Committee recently, I can no longer continue in the office of Hon. Secretary/Treasurer as I have done for the last five years. I am as enthusiastic as ever in the cause of the Association, but my commitments are such that I must take some firm step towards relinquishing the position I now hold... I would like however to end by saying that I have spoken to a number of members, outside the committee and other meetings, and there is a very real wish particularly among the younger members that the Association should continue in as lively and successful a way as possible.[30]

The questionnaire opened by stating the object of the Association - 'to encourage the love of literature in the West Country' - and explaining that 'at present, membership of the Association is at the invitation of the committee - who have their attention drawn by existing members to potential candidates'. There were then eight questions:

```
1   What do you personally see as the true object of
    the Association?
2   Has it helped you with your work in a social or
    any other way?
3   Would you continue your membership if the
```

emphasis was placed on the Congress being a purely social 'get-together' of writers?
4 Would you wish to see more discussions about the work and practice of a writer?
5 Would you agree to an affiliation to the Association of Writers' Circles in the West Country? [sic]
6 Would you continue to come to the Annual Congress if it was held in turn in three centres, e.g. Bath, Exeter, Plymouth?
7 The present subscription is £1.00 for new members and for those who choose to pay at this rate, but subscriptions at the rate applicable of old members are still acceptable at the same rate as when they joined. Considering postal and telephone increases, would you be prepared to meet a subscription of say £2.00?
8 Can you suggest how the Association's work might be suitably divided? Would you be prepared to undertake any responsibilities? Do you know of any member who you think would like to help in this way?

Before the Bath Congress in May, Frank had collated the responses and sent out the following thoughtful memorandum:

MEMORANDUM FOR CONSIDERATION
by the CONGRESS at BATH, 5 & 6 May, 1972

These notes have been prepared from a study of the answers to the questionnaire sent out on 2 January 1972. They are intended to be the basis for a discussion about the future of the Association at the twenty-first annual Congress at Bath.
  The questionnaire was sent to all Vice Presidents and members (including the Committee), a total of one hundred and twenty-five. By 18 January, forty-eight replies had been received.

Most, it not all, of those who replied had taken a great deal of trouble to do so; and the President, Chairman, and Hon. Secretary are most grateful to them. Obviously some questions were easier than others. Sometimes it has been hard to decide on which side of the line an answer has fallen, though here the general tone of other answers has been a final guide. Such figures as are given here are as precise as possible in the circumstances; the intention is to find some kind of concensus of opinion rather than a form of arithmetical nicety.

Three or four members felt it would be right for them to resign (some thought they had already done so). Clearly these decisions had been made with sadness and continued affection. Besides the formal replies, the Hon. Secretary has received a number of letters; a few he has already answered and the others he will answer as and when possible.

It was thought logical to deal with the replies in the same order as the questions, and to end with some general observations and deductions.

   1. First, members were asked what they considered to be the true object of the Association. A relatively small number (eight) accepted as satisfactory the phrase used in the Constitution: 'To encourage the love of literature in the West Country'. Many members, while accepting the idea, found other ways of stating it. The largest group (twenty-two) - that is, nearly half the replies - stressed the social side. Several spoke of the loneliness of a writer's life; the annual Congress was a change to which they looked forward with pleasure.

   2. Next, members were asked whether the Association had helped them with their work in a social (or any other) way. Eleven said 'yes' in a general way; only two acknowledged that it had helped with their *work;* fourteen said pretty firmly that it had not helped their work at all;

and another dozen emphasised the social side.

3. Would membership be continued if the Congress were arranged as a purely social gathering of writers? Whether from loyalty or not, the replies were overwhelmingly affirmative (thirty-four). Some eight or so deprecated a purely social occasion, but there was only one resounding 'No'.

4. Should there be more discussions about the work and practice of a writer? Many answers were qualified with the comment, 'It all depends on the kind of discussion, doesn't it?' Obviously, talks were unwelcome unless given by someone eminent. Yet, as a helpful pointer, nearly half (twenty-three) of the replies came under the heading 'Yes' with a fairly firm 'No' from a dozen. Quite a few sat on the fence.

5. Writers' Circles. Possibly the question was not phrased in the best way; and, to make it more difficult, a 'clerical error' crept in. Still, generally, the point was taken well. The answers were a good example of what seems to be called polarisation. Seventeen members agreed without reserve to affiliation with Writers' Circles; fourteen said 'No' just as plainly (some with a suggestion of hostility). Four could be put down as 'Don't knows', and six answers, hedged about with conditions, might be described as a courteous 'yes, on a carefully selected basis'. Four others would vote 'Yes' if the Circles were professional; otherwise they would vote 'No'.

6. Thirty-four members said they would continue to come to the Congress if it were held in turn in three centres: Bath, Exeter, Plymouth. Six at least pleaded for more variation, a view probably shared by quite a few more. Half-a-dozen (with a couple of definite 'Noes') said that travel was becoming increasingly difficult for them, if not impossible. These answers would have been sad if the members had not said what a delight it had

been to attend past Congresses.
7. Raising of the subscription to £2.00. About thirty members gave an unqualified 'Yes'; half-a-dozen were clearly against the idea; and a small handful said sensibly, 'It all depends on what we get for our money'. It might be helpful to add - supported by some other answers - that writers do not have much money to spare and have to watch expenses carefully.
8. Organization. Except for a very few carefully thought out suggestions, the first part of this treble question drew almost a blank. Moreover the suggestions depended on other answers (Would any member be prepared to undertake actual work? Or did any member know of anybody who would do so?) In the circumstances they must remain in mid-air.

Looking ahead to the next Congress after what he said last year, and has written since, the Hon. Secretary/Treasurer feels disappointed that there is no one to whom he can really hand over his responsibilities (or any part of them) in any substantial way. He proposes to lay them down at the Annual General Meeting on 6 May.

F.D. LITTLEWOOD

This is a fairly gloomy conclusion. However positive or negative the responses had been, the bottom line was that both Frank Littlewood and John Trewin were determined to lay down their responsibilities in Bath, but pleas for suggested replacements 'drew almost a blank' and no one person seemed to have emerged as a likely successor to either. The chairman appended his valedictory message to Frank's memorandum:

> At the Torquay AGM I said that, most regretfully, I would have to retire from the Chairmanship. Now we approach the Association's twenty-first conference, one at which we shall be thinking, as always, of Waveney Girvan, the moving spirit in the formation of the WCWA at Bath in 1951.
>
> We have long missed Waveney's irresistible Chairmanship; but

since his death (and the Exeter conference of 1965) I have been proud to carry on; to work with Christopher Fry and Frank Littlewood - there could have been no better or kinder President and Hon. Secretary/Treasurer - and with the Committee and all the members who have become my own, and Wendy's friends across the years. And may I express affectionate gratitude here to Mrs. Honor Carr, who was Frank's predecessor and to whose tireless endeavour we owed much.

I do want to say Thank You, warmly, to you all; to wish the Association and its officers every imaginable success in any fresh venture; and to say that, of course, I shall always be ready to help in any other way I can.

Other work has been pressing in recent years; and though the difficult business of the Association has been conducted expertly by Frank Littlewood - has anyone ever seen Frank lose command of any situation? - I feel it would be unfair of me not to be able to give more substantial help to a new Hon. Secretary.

The Association has done splendid service across the years. Especially I think, in getting professional writers - who can be lonely souls - to meet on such occasions as ours, and to talk informally. That has been important; so many friendships have grown from it. And we have been so happy to have Christopher Fry with us at every conference; you know what an inspiration that has been.

From Wendy and myself, thank you all again for friendliness we have valued deeply and hope to keep. And may the future be bright, for everyone.

John Trewin

It cannot have seemed very bright, at that juncture. The archives contain a most confused succession of notes and letters exchanged during these last months before the congress. In March it was suggested that Berta Lawrence of Bridgwater should be secretary. A month later Frank Littlewood wrote to William Kean Seymour that the committee had made their decisions: Rev. John Rowland was to become chairman, and Bob Cooper - 'first interested in the Association after attending one of your courses at Moor Park'[31] - would be secretary. John Trewin and William Kean Seymour were to be made vice-presidents, and the rest of the committee would be honorary members. Kean Seymour replied, somewhat tartly, 'We congratulate you on achieving so much in the way of planning for the secure continuation of the Association to which we are all so deeply attached. You must be on the General Council.'[32]

About the same time, William Kean Seymour suddenly announced that he and Rosalind would not even be attending the congress. This seems very odd, as the congress was not only a crucial decision time for the Association, but was also its twenty-first anniversary, but apparently William and Rosalind had to conduct a weekend writers' craft course at Moor Park which had completely slipped their minds. A week later, William Kean Seymour resigned from the committee as well:

> I think I have served long enough - seven years on the Committee and would like to withdraw in favour of a writer resident in the West Country. If in order I wish to nominate for membership of the Committee Mrs. Berta Lawrence, Novelist, Biographer and Anthologist, of Bridgwater, Somerset, and I have elicited that she would be willing to serve.[33]

To complete the confusion, the next letter in the archives is from Bob Cooper, the new secretary, writing after the congress to William Kean Seymour - to congratulate him on his election as chairman!

The Gang of Four

During the 1972 WCWA Congress at Bath my wife and I found ourselves, owing to a clash of dates, conducting one of our 'Writers' Craft' weekend courses at Moor Park.

On our opening evening there I was telephoned by John Trewin from Bath and persuaded to accept nomination for the Chairmanship on his retirement from that office the next morning at the Annual General Meeting. I pleaded my age and multiple engagements, but he made it seem only fair that he should be relieved after seven years of devoted service - and that is why I am facing this year's Congress at Exeter.[34]

This is how William Kean Seymour, writing in the 1973 newsletter, explained his unlooked-for election to the Chair. Quite what led to John Trewin's eleventh hour phone call from Bath is not clear, bearing in mind that the committee had approached the congress with quite different plans, but what is quite clear is that John Trewin's silver-tongued powers of persuasion were as irresistible as ever. As a result, the WCWA was not after all laid to rest at Bath. On the contrary, a revolution had taken place and 'the Gang of Four' were in power - but under the watchful eye of Chairman Kean Seymour. He concluded his first chairman's message with a brief self-portrait:

> I am a founder member of the Association, in my mid-eighties, and have had a passion for books and authorship, particularly poetry, since my earliest schooldays.
> Lectures, articles and book reviews now take up most of my time and I am associated with various literary societies. All have taken their toll of time and energy, but have been worthwhile in their yield of interest, friendship and esteem.
> No man is an island in the world of literature, and in this gathering at Exeter we can count ourselves happy not only in our heritage of books but in the company of those who make them.[35]

In the same issue, the new secretary, Bob Cooper, takes up the story:

> After the Bath Congress the new Committee of The West Country Writers' Association decided to try and give the Association a new look. The position had been that, prior to the Bath Congress, as nobody had offered himself as Secretary to fill the post that Frank Littlewood had so ably held, it had been decided to wind up the affairs of the Association and put all the relevant matter in the Bath archives.
> It seemed too good an Association to finish in this way, so four of us split the duties that Frank had been carrying alone and it was decided to carry on. It is a measure of how much work Frank did that it has taken four of us to replace him.
> We have been enthusiastically supported by both Committee and Membership, and the response has been such that the affairs of the Association are very healthy. This has nothing to do with

the fact that you have a Doctor of Medicine as your Secretary. It seems, to date, that the Exeter Congress is going to be the largest yet, and already all the accommodation available at the Rougemont has been taken up. Our Guest of Honour will be Lady Lee, who was Minister of Arts in the last Government.

I would like to take this opportunity of thanking the Members, Committee, and particularly Frank Littlewood, for all the help and support they have so far given.[36]

Political events in China at the time led to the inevitable christening of Frank Littlewood's four replacements as 'the Gang of Four'. They divided up the administrative work as follows:

> Bob Cooper - secretary, assisted, like Frank Littlewood, by his own secretary
> Geraldine Kaye - the first dedicated membership secretary
> John Brooks - treasurer
> Meryl Macdonald Bendle - newsletter editor and public relations officer

This new arrangement was commended by Frank Littlewood, who added a warning that never again must the work fall too much on one person, 'as it has done now for many years'.

Bob Cooper had attended the Moor Park courses in writers' craft because he has always been a doctor with a difference: as well as being a full-time GP he has a parallel life as a medical columnist and author. The life of a doctor is never without incident, and Bob's sense of humour and his eye for the ridiculous have enabled him to write a series of highly successful humorous books about the ups and downs of his daily life - all under a pseudonym, of course. As Robert Clifford he began with *Just Here, Doctor* which was swiftly followed by *Not There, Doctor* then *What Next, Doctor* and *Oh Dear, Doctor!* and on until a dozen titles had been published, in large print and in audio books as well as standard editions, with translations into several languages making him a productive best selling author. And all this with his left hand, while continuing his medical career - *You're Still a Doctor, Doctor!* is an apt title - so that he has often felt himself developing a split personality:

> ...it is fun to have appeared in print enough to be able to enjoy the company of writers. It is also a great help in becoming completely schizophrenic as you soon find that, in the company of doctors, they think of you as a writer, and in the company of writers, they think of you as a doctor.[37]

A raconteur who can delight his audience, Bob has also become a prized after-dinner speaker, radio performer, and judge of literary competitions, all a bit to his own surprise as he still modestly denies having done anything but scribble.

Both as a doctor and as an observant writer, however, Bob's great gift is his ability to relate to people - he has to perfection what a modern CV would describe as 'interpersonal skills'. This ability to put people at their ease, to listen to them and win them over - 'I think we were all a little in love with Doctor Bob', suggested his supportive practice secretary, Honor Butler - has made him WCWA's 'Mr. Fixit'. Whenever there is a problem, wherever there is friction, fraught committee members generally turn to Bob for advice. This skill with people has also enabled him to make hundreds of contacts in his life, and that has rescued the Association from more than one crisis. Simon Rocksborough Smith remembers a March committee meeting at which the chairman had unexpectedly gone to America and no programme had been arranged for the approaching congress:

> 'While we all sat in the Committee Room, I remember Bob Cooper spent most of the time in a telephone booth along the corridor, ringing his numerous contacts to try to rustle up some speakers for congress'.[38]

With Bob to front the arrangements and his assistant Honor Butler to keep the paperwork in efficient order, the organizational side of things was in good hands. Frank Littlewood, in congratulating Bob on his appointment as secretary, had mentioned in passing, '...it is only fair to warn you that the Association funds don't in the ordinary way run to payment of travelling or other expenses, but no doubt the Committee will have to assess the situation when they look at the future Constitution and subscription rates...'[39] In fact the committee had, in 1968, made the innovatory decision to reimburse the secretary £5 for 'general expenses'. No wonder they had found it difficult to fill the vacancy! Bob took a very practical approach to his new role and wrote to his new chairman on 9 May 1972:

> 'I heard that unless a Secretary were found, things would grind to a halt. I am in the fortunate position of having good secretarial help and the use of duplicating and Photostatting facilities, and it is with the mechanics of secretaryship that I shall probably be most useful'.[40]

William Kean Seymour replied in a tone almost gushing with good will:

> John Trewin's dulcet pleadings prevailed, and when I reflected that you had accepted the secretaryship I yielded, for I can think of no one I could work with more congenial and efficient than yourself.
> Rosalind and I have an instinctive liking for you, and the sort of understanding that seldom misleads us. We can, I think, work together to recover the WCWA from the decline in which it has been slipping; and you will be able to confer with me with the knowledge of the reconstruction that is taking place.
> So let me know more, and we will get together and see what can be done. But remember, I am old, and you must be patient with me.[41]

Bob was, to a degree that few could have matched. He formed a good working relationship with William Kean Seymour based on his respect for the great man's achievements, and displayed admirable diplomacy in coping with his increasing demands - even to the point of giving medical advice as Kean Seymour became more frail.

'The Four of us', said Bob, 'set out with certain objectives'. The first of these was staring them in the face: 'The membership had to be increased.'[42] This is where Geraldine Kaye became so vital, having herself been the victim of the old, elitist arrangements.

I joined the WCWA in 1968. It was quite a difficult process. Having discovered there was such an organization I managed to track down a member. At the time I was chairman of the Bristol Writers' Circle and when I told him this, he became very doubtful about my eligibility for WCWA though I had been a professional writer for many years. However, several letters and phonecalls duly established my credentials. I attended my first Congress at Plymouth entirely ignored in lounge and dining room while a flurry of old friends greeted and embraced each other. Eventually I was rescued by the ever friendly Frank Littlewood, then Secretary and general factotum. But it did occur to me at the time that a society so indifferent to recruitment and so unconcerned with new members would find it difficult to survive, and so it proved.

Increased membership was a first essential. I wrote to a number of central libraries all over the West asking for names of writers in their area, combed newspapers and periodicals for further names, asked the Society of Authors for a list of members who lived in the West, and abstracted all such names from the PEN membership lists myself. This was only possible because of Bob's generous help and that of his secretary. I sent names and addresses to her and she despatched letters of invitation. Quite a task, it was before the days of word processing! We wrote to far more writers than we gathered in of course, but by 1977 the membership had reached 260 and there was no longer any anxiety about the WCWA's viability.[43]

It is a remarkable tribute to Geraldine's determination that she ever bothered to persist in becoming a member - especially in the light of Kean Seymour's rude remarks about writers' circles - let alone spend so much time and effort in pulling the Association round. She was, after all, a full-time writer with a growing list of children's titles to her credit, and the amount of time it must have taken to research all those lists, even with secretarial help for the letter-writing, is something that would make a more selfish person turn and walk away. Geraldine, however, was so motivated by her dislike of in-crowds, of snobbery and unfriendliness of any kind, that she was prepared to invest her energy not only (and this is significant) in *recruiting* new members, but in 'trying to ensure that new members were recognized and welcomed when they arrived at Congress'.

This mature and humanitarian approach reflects the tenor of Geraldine's writings which have become classics for children, especially those facing the awkward years of adolescence and learning to cope with adult problems such as racial disharmony, lack of friends, broken families, or teenage pregnancy. That sounds a fairly depressing catalogue of social ills, but the books are quite the reverse of depressing as Geraldine always explores problems with a positive and non-judgmental attitude that looks for practical solutions and has no time for wallowing in self-pity. Prejudice and the setting-up of barriers are the worst enemies of her young protagonists, and she was able to bring the same attitude to the business of opening up the WCWA and blowing away all the fusty air that had accumulated there. Why shouldn't new, younger members be encouraged? Why should all the committee meetings be held at a prestigious London venue? Why shouldn't people *enjoy* themselves at meetings? So, in the newsletter for 1973, Geraldine was able to report that '...so far we have fifty-three new members and we are hoping to improve on this'. It did mean change.

> Of course such an influx has greatly altered and updated the character of the Association, a change not always appreciated by 'the old guard'. All our new recruits had to have published a book or, if they worked in other media, to have accomplished 'a considerable body of work' but the atmosphere is distinctly less literary, less elitist and there is less talk of being distinguished. However, some of our members certainly justify this label and many more are competent professionals. Committee meetings are less formal, and I may say more enjoyable, and the custom of having at least one a year in London has been suspended.[44]

The fifty-three new recruits included many who have gone on to be stalwarts of the Association: Freda Bromhead, Honor Butler, Evelyn Hilary-Szydlowska, Jean Paton, Raymond Tong, Angela Tuckett. There were two future chairmen in Jacynth Hope-Simpson and Simon

Rocksborough Smith. There were also some star names, notably Rachel Billington and Daphne du Maurier who, at this stage in her life, would not attend congresses. She always maintained that she was not, as people often said, a recluse: she simply did not like social occasions or giving interviews. She did, however, show her support of the Association with messages of greeting and by accepting the vice-presidency. Of course there were also some notable refusals, including Lord Snow, Lord Longford, Tom Stoppard and V. S. Pritchett.

Once recruited, the new members needed to be nurtured. The second objective listed by Bob Cooper involved the newsletter -

> 'It was felt that the Newsletter should be prestigious both in content and presentation, and under Meryl's guidance a first class quality Newsletter was produced. It is the only thing members who can't get to Congress receive, and it is the only outward sign of what the WCWA is all about.'[45]

Meryl Macdonald Bendle, the third of the Four, was the ideal person to take on the Association's 'shop window'. Her writing career had led her to journalism ('I fancied myself as a photo-journalist in those days and sported a heavy twin-lens reflex', she recalls of the 1971 Congress[46]) and thence to television, where she was a presenter with the old Harlech TV channel for many years. As luck would have it, the person whom she was asked to interview as a demonstration of her skills when she applied for the job was none other than Bob Cooper. Bob tells a very good story about how he had just completed one of his regular medical advice programmes when the producer asked if he would mind being interviewed again by a potential new girl. Just one look at this smart and personable young lady made him determined that the interview should go well for her. He had a feeling that she looked vaguely familiar... but it was only after Meryl had landed the job and he went to congratulate her that she reminded him that they had met before, in fact just a few weeks before, at a WCWA Congress.

Meryl's practised eye brought consistency and professionalism to the newsletter so that it became a regular production. It listed all the practical details for congress, introduced new members, gave a comprehensive listing of members' news and work in progress, and carried an extremely useful series of 'Biographies in Brief' which allowed the general membership to know more about their officers and fellow members. As Christopher Fry put it in his message for the first of the 'new look' newsletters:

> 'This new year brings us the first issue of our "periodical", which should help to keep us all in touch with what each other is working on; and also an encouraging increase in membership to welcome the Association's twenty-second year'.[47]

The administration was in order, new members were being recruited and looked after, and behind the scenes the finances were being sorted out. John Brooks, the fourth member of 'the Gang', became the new treasurer and tackled the problem of the unpaid and inadequate subscriptions. John, a novelist and one of 'the Bristol members', has never been a person to court publicity and not many people realize how much he has done for the good of the Association.

He did not altogether expect to be a novelist. In his early years he seemed to be destined for a career in music or science: a musician's son, he was a gifted chorister at St. Mary Redcliffe Church in Bristol, but it was his brilliance at chemistry that took him to Cambridge where 'he had barely got his knees under the amateur theatricals' keyboard when war was declared'.[48] Once war service was over he embarked on a new passion - still not writing, but flying. Experience in the University Air Squadron led to a career as a flying instructor and then finally, via a magazine called *The Aeroplane*, to writing. His poetry won awards, and he tells a lovely story about winning the Guinness Poetry Prize at Cheltenham Literary Festival and being asked to read his collected poems at the Poetry Society in London. That meant he had to sit down and write a collection, pdq. His shorter prose works have appeared in such distinguished periodicals as *Blackwell's Magazine*, but when it comes to novels John has always been a believer in size. His first novel, *Hat*, was huge, and further hefty tomes were to follow.

The WCWA is indebted to John Brooks for two big things: in his period as treasurer he sorted out the finances, and later, as chairman, he was to propose and shape 'Congress Aid', a fund to subsidise members who had difficulty with the spiralling cost of attending congresses.

As the new treasurer in 1972 he inherited a balance of some £50. He made the tough decision to double the subscriptions to £2.00 (they had been raised to £1.00 only two years previously) and worked hard to encourage payment by bankers' order, a recurring theme for all treasurers. As a result he was able to report in the 1973 newsletter:

> That your Association is in an unusually strong financial position is attributable to an increase in its membership and an aligning of its subscription rates with contemporary values. There is every reason to suppose that the position will become even stronger, at least until membership steadies at the new figure.
>
> I look for a departure from an annual cycle in which expenses were met leaving a negligible balance to carry into the following year. I believe that the establishment of a sound financial base must be a first priority, stimulating the confidence to take a fresh look at our activities; confirming our established ones while taking a glance in new directions from a position of strength. It is the means of the Association's representation and encouragement of what is best in West Country letters.[49]

His success in building up a reserve meant that when he left office in 1976 he was able to say:

> After four years, this is my valedictory message as your Honorary Treasurer. It is pleasant that it should be one of prosperity.
>
> During this time my policy has been to try to build a financial foundation on which future plans may be constructed. To the extent that I have succeeded, I am greatly indebted to other officers for their help.
>
> It is my belief that revenue should be returned, in one way or another, to those who provide it - our members. There are many ways in which this might be accomplished. A literary prize, awarded periodically, has been spoken of. As has been the possible growth of our Newsletter into something more like a magazine. I would like, as Vice Chairman, to invite your suggestions.

I hope that my successor (yet to be appointed, perhaps someone will kindly step forward) will extend a favourable situation and I shall hope to co-operate in any way that I can.[50]

As we reach our fiftieth anniversary that financial stability has enabled us to expand our activities, and although John is not one for attending congresses these days we owe him a great debt of thanks.

But, straight after the Bath Congress of 1972, all these successes still lay in the future. The 'new look' committee had a lot of work to do, not least on amending the Constitution and Rules to provide for a committee of ten, 'the Chairman, the Honorary Treasurer and the Honorary Secretary being for this purpose counted as members of the committee' - although, this being the eccentric organization that it is, the 1973 newsletter promptly listed a committee of ten members as well as six officers. It is interesting to see that in those days the election of officers and committee was by postal ballot of the whole membership.

Over the summer of 1972 business in general was smartened up. John Brooks, seeing the need to gather in subscriptions by bankers' order, needed a new form for the purpose. Bob Cooper perceived the need for smart new headed notepaper to promote the Association's image to the world. Geraldine Kaye needed recruiting letters and membership application forms for her three-stranded recruitment drive, and Meryl Macdonald Bendle needed a means of getting enough material from members to make an interesting newsletter. Reworking the rules, designing the new headed notepaper and bankers' order forms, and deciding on the wording for the letters were to exercise the minds of the new committee greatly. First, however, the new committee had to meet, and that proved not to be without problems. William Kean Seymour started as he meant to go on as chairman, questioning everything in detail.

The members of the 'new look' committee were trying to make a point by meeting outside London, and as quite a number of them lived in or near Bristol (including three of the Gang of Four) that seemed the logical choice of venue. William Kean Seymour did not like the idea. In a prickly exchange of letters with Bob Cooper he argued over the travelling distance for non-Bristol members, the possible need to stay overnight at a hotel, and the cost of petrol. He did not like the time chosen, or the idea of meeting on a weekday. A compromise proposal to hire some rooms in Salisbury on a Sunday afternoon made him even more cross as it had been put forward without consulting him first. Bob poured some soothing oil on these troubled waters, reminding Kean Seymour that the Association would have folded if it had not been for 'the Bristol members' - '...we must be so careful not to alienate the few people who are prepared to give their time and energy to resuscitating the Association...'[51] - and the point was finally conceded. In the event, the Kean Seymours' car broke down at Romsey en route to the first meeting, and the ever-capable Bob drove them home and worked his magic. Warmth and harmony were restored when William Kean Seymour wrote again, thanking Bob for coming to the rescue - and bemoaning the fact that repairs to his clutch had cost him £44.61.

During these teething troubles, the Gang of Four ploughed steadily on with their tasks, sometimes meeting as a sub-committee to thrash out the wording of the bankers' order forms, headed paper, invitations to prospective new members, and revised aims and objectives. William Kean Seymour wanted to see proofs before he would sanction anything to go ahead.

The headed paper began to seem more trouble than it was worth, with arguments over whose names should be on it and whose not. It is illuminating to look at the changing styles of the headed paper over the half century. Like everything else about the Association, they have reflected their respective times. In the first days, Westaway Books could see to the printing, and a smart, professionally produced heading flaunted the new Association's big names to the world. All the vice-presidents and all committee members were listed, vertically, so that the heading used up nearly half of the page. By Frank Littlewood's day, some space was saved by listing the names across the page. The printed paper was used only for official letters, while circulars to the membership came on cyclostyled sheets with a typed heading - but it still listed every last committee member. It could be changed more readily when the committee membership changed, but sometimes it looked rather amateur. The 1972 committee wanted to go in for a professional look, but committee members change and vice-presidents are mortal, so the commitment to a print-run would always run the risk of being very quickly out of date. The green-headed paper with the WCWA logo introduced in the 1980s had this problem. A long print-run brought vast discounts, so committee members' names were omitted to make it more long-lasting. Unfortunately Daphne du Maurier died while it was still with the printer, but her name seemed too good to lose so the problem was solved by surrounding it with a box. The Association went on using up this enormous quantity of paper until the mid-nineties, by which time more than half the vice-presidents listed had been consigned to boxes too. Fortunately the arrival of word processors and desktop publishing freed succeeding committees to design their own headed paper to suit the changing times, using different colours and fonts, never committed to a long print run, and changing names as vice-presidents disappear or are elected. It is now possible, at minimal cost, to personalize paper so that it carries the appropriate address of the president, chairman, secretary, treasurer or membership secretary.

In 1972, though, the problem was still to avoid wasting half the paper's surface on long lists of names that could soon be out of date. William Kean Seymour would not have anyone - or any of the letters after their names - omitted. He rejected various sets of proofs. Bob resubmitted them, suitably adapted to make him happy - though remarking wryly that, '...we must be one of the few organizations that has more than a quarter of its membership's names on their writing paper...'[52] The master stroke was to fit all the committee members' names, in minuscule font, at the *foot* of the paper. Alas, when the amended set of proofs arrived, Bob had to apologize to William Kean Seymour for one 'gross error... the omission of yourself and John Trewin as Vice Presidents.'[53]

With that sorted out, the chairman's attention was turned to the bankers' order forms. Existing forms still carried the old subscription rate of 10s. 6d. and a variety of subscription dates. John Brooks wished to standardize the date at 1 October each year, and raise the subscription to £2.00: simple enough, one might suppose. William Kean Seymour took the wording apart and quibbled over every detail. Should the form be returned to the member's bank direct, or to the treasurer to be returned to the bank? - and why had his FRSL been missed out *again*?? The drafts went backwards and forwards between the chairman, the treasurer and the secretary until at last things seemed to be perfect and they were sent to Honor Butler for typing and duplicating. One can only imagine the scenario that lies behind Bob's apologetic note to Kean Seymour - 'It is unfortunate that the duplicating paper turned out to be pink. But Mrs. Butler's stencil was just a *little* bit crooked...'[54]

In August 1972 the membership finally received their multiple mailing. It contained a letter from the secretary listing the decisions of the new committee, with a form for confirming their correct address; a letter from the membership secretary outlining her recruitment drive, with a nomination form for the proposal of new members; a letter from the newsletter editor asking each member to submit a 500-1000 word 'potted biography' and to send regular news of their publications; and a letter from the treasurer explaining the need for raised subscriptions, with a copy of the new bankers' order form.

William Kean Seymour was not the only one who disliked the new bankers' order form, and not just because of the colour. The whole issue of bankers' orders can rouse quite strong feelings of antagonism in any membership group, especially when combined with a large rise in the subscriptions, and various members resigned (or, as Bob wrote of one lady, 'Edna Manning is *trying* to resign'[55] - my italics). Crispin Gill, editor of *The Countryman*, was one of them, and expressed his views on the new arrangements in forthright manner. 'I think he is obviously a literary snob', wrote Bob, 'and this is possibly typical of why the Association has become run down'.[56] William Kean Seymour wrote to Crispin Gill and was able to talk him round, remarking to Bob that, '...in the course of the present transition from the moderately exclusive to the free for all there may be others taking his line'.[57] That crisp exchange sums up the pull between old and new that was taking place.

All the same, Geraldine Kaye sent out her first two waves of letters - William Kean Seymour insisted on drafting one of his own in December 1972 - and the process of evolution moved on. By March 1973 the campaign was bearing fruit: membership had risen to 186 with every prospect of reaching 200 by the next congress. There were, however, still limits to the 'free for all', as a terse note from William Kean Seymour reveals:

> 'Associate Membership. Mellersh is right. No more campaigning of this kind until we have expanded the actual membership'.[58]

With the spadework done on rules, recruitment, newsletter and finances, the Gang of Four could turn to its final objective. In Bob's words:

> Prior to 1973 the format of a Congress was that members booked their own hotel accommodation, individually, in different hotels. There was a lecture on the Friday afternoon, a civic reception on the Friday evening, the AGM was on the Saturday morning followed by the Annual Lunch, then everyone went home. Thus it was possible to be the only member of the WCWA staying in your hotel and, sadly, there was a chance that nobody spoke to you.
> We decided to double the length of the Congress, make a package deal at one hotel, and all of us go out of our way to make people feel welcome. Our Chairman William Kean Seymour felt that to attract members to a Congress we must have a very prominent Guest of Honour and first class speakers, and if possible all go to the theatre together on the Saturday night.[59]

Planning for the 1973 Exeter Congress was meticulous. Bob's businesslike files preserved in the archives show his attention to every detail. He admitted it was 'a formidable undertaking' and to this day it remains a major task to organize all the bookings in one hotel, make arrangements for eminent guests and speakers, sort out a book exhibition and possibly a theatre trip or outing, and cope with the last minute crises, but at least we now have a tried and tested routine for going about it. To take this on for the first time must have been not only a huge logistic nightmare but an enormous risk.

The risk paid off. The new arrangement was such a success that by the time the 1973 newsletter came out, all the accommodation available at the Rougemont Hotel (no small hotel, as members who attended the 1999 Congress at what is now called The Exeter Thistle Hotel will agree) had been taken, and latecomers were advised to find their own accommodation elsewhere. This rather spoiled the point of getting everyone under the same roof, but the principle of inclusiveness and contact had been established.

The speakers were as prestigious as even the chairman could have wished.

Mirroring John Trewin's achievement in landing Lord Goodman, William Kean Seymour managed to get the Rt. Hon. Jennie Lee PC, recent Minister of Arts, as guest of honour. 'Thomas' Stoppard unfortunately declined, but Professor Moelwyn Merchant filled the bill on Friday. An overall theme of 'The Theatre' was reflected in panel discussions, lectures - no less an authority than Professor Wilson Knight was the main speaker - and a visit to the Northcott Theatre to see *The Tempest*, after which the director came back to the hotel for a discussion on the production.

Despite the success there was a lot to be learnt from this first venture at the 'package' congress, and some fine tuning was required. Exeter 1973 had left the finances 'parlous', so the idea of a congress fee (then £1.00) to help cover the speakers' expenses and the other incidental costs incurred over the weekend was introduced.

The transition from 'the old guard' was soon to be complete. Although William Kean Seymour made it to the 1973 Congress and chaired the annual lunch, the signs of his illness had increased in March 1973 when he had to go into hospital for a serious operation. His energetic flow of correspondence with the secretary at this stage gives way to a series of gentle handwritten notes and postcards from his wife, Rosalind Wade, confirming the date of the operation and describing progress afterwards. Through the autumn of 1973 he was spending most of the day in bed, with breathing difficulties, though a spurt of improved health in November had him up and about and demanding reimbursal for some WCWA letters he had written, complaining that the stamps had cost him 37p. It was to be a last flurry: later in the year he suffered a cerebral spasm, on Boxing Day 1973. He lost the use of his right hand, and suffered speech and swallowing difficulties. He made sufficient progress to get through the 1974 Congress where he retired from the chairmanship, with the thanks and praise of committee members. Revd. John Rowland moved up from the vice-chairmanship, and before the next winter was out, William Kean Seymour was dead.

His achievement was, however guardedly, to preside over the 'new look' and to see the new style congresses in place. Exeter 1973 and the following congresses run by Bob Cooper at Bristol in 1974 and 1975 were ambitious, well-planned, efficient operations which had seen the WCWA reborn with a new style, a revitalised membership, and a new sense of purpose. It had achieved this by responding to change in society at large and refusing to lie down with the dodo. It was different - 'less literary, less elitist, less talk of being distinguished' in Geraldine's words - but the influx of new members far outnumbered those who left, disgruntled.

It had taken nearly ten years since the death of Waveney Girvan in 1964 to remodel his creation and equip it for modern times, and it had taken two stages for this to be fully accomplished, with John Trewin's expansion of the membership in 1968 followed by the comprehensive re-invention of 1973. It is difficult to overstate the role of the Gang of Four. If John Trewin insisted that the WCWA was the creation of one man, Waveney Girvan, it was also the re-creation of four people: Bob Cooper, Geraldine Kaye, John Brooks and Meryl Macdonald Bendle.

The Secretary's Tale

Time does not stand still. Once the Association had been roused from its stasis and started to change, change began to happen at an ever-increasing pace. Never again were chairmen and vice-chairmen to hold office for years on end as Waveney Girvan and Lady Mander had done: the new rules stated that a chairman should be elected for one year at a time and not more than three consecutive years. By the time of the twenty-fifth anniversary in 1976 it had been decided that two years should be the regular tenure. There was a reshuffle in the cabinet: John Rowland - who combined his work as a Unitarian minister with a second career writing crime thrillers - relinquished his chairmanship to John Brooks, who in turn bequeathed the treasurer's role to the 'specially meticulous'[60] care of Meryl Macdonald Bendle. Her old job of editing the newsletter and looking after public relations went to John Rowland, and Bryan Little became the vice-chairman. Only Geraldine Kaye remained in her original role as membership secretary.

Once again, though, the big problem was finding a secretary. Bob Cooper had done wonders, and his three congresses in 1973, 1974 and 1975 had set completely new standards. Following the theme of 'The Theatre' in 1973, the two Bristol congresses in 1974 and 1975 (the Royal Hotel was offering a very good deal) had the themes 'Literature and the Media' and 'Biographers and Biography'. Themes gave a satisfying cohesion to the weekend - but they did make life difficult when guests dropped out late in the day, as A. L. Rowse did in 1975. Not only did a replacement have to be found at short notice, but a replacement who would fit the overall theme. And members now expected their speakers to be well known. They also expected all their hotel arrangements to be made for them, and their theatre bookings, and everything else. When Frank Littlewood's job had been divided into four it had made life easier for the office holders, but the big new package congress had multiplied the secretary's tasks to the point where he was back where he had started. Bob, who was also very busy as a committee member of English PEN, decided that the time had come for him to give up WCWA office, and around 1974-5 the committee began casting about to find a replacement.

No-one volunteered. It is hardly surprising. The work load had again become enormous and it demanded a lot of a busy person - and not just their time. Things had not changed much since Frank had warned Bob about the lack of expenses, so the secretary still had to find a lot of the resources himself, including access to reprographic resources. Bob had, like Frank, been fortunate in having his own secretarial backup to help with office work, but 'the mechanics of secretaryship'[61] were becoming more problematical all the time as the quality of typewriting and reproduction improved. People expected higher standards at a time when even quality electronic typewriters with golfballs and daisywheels were beginning to give way to the first word processors.

Not that the WCWA was looking for a secretary with a word processor. Just someone with a typewriter and the time to use it was the extent of its demands, but no-one was forthcoming and the process of persuading a member to take it on every few years was becoming both time-consuming and frustrating. The committee came to the inevitable conclusion that the only long-term solution was to advertise outside the Association for professional secretarial help. This of course meant that, for the first time, the WCWA must pay its secretary both expenses and a remuneration.

Bob duly placed an advertisement in the *Western Daily Press* as follows:

> The West Country Writers' Association require an Honorary Secretary (male or female) to take on the responsibility of the running of the Association. Secretarial expenses and an honorarium of £50 per annum will be paid.
>
> Applicants need not necessarily be writers, but should be interested in, and able to give some time to, the Association and to further its aims 'to foster the love of literature in the West Country as a contribution to the cultural heritage of the nation'.

It produced four applicants. Bob duly sent them all a letter:

> Thank you for your enquiry. The duties of the Secretary of the West Country Writers' Association involve running the Annual Congress (which is held in a West Country city), room bookings, etc. All correspondence and circulars come from the Secretary, and this probably accounts for most of the work load. There are usually three Committee Meetings a year in a West Country town (Bristol, Bath or Salisbury). These are evening meetings. A Council Meeting is held in London in the early part of December. We have also begun to have Regional Meetings, and there was one in Plymouth this year which I managed to get to.
>
> We are an expanding organization at present, and to date have about 250 members. It is difficult to say exactly how much time it requires, but one would think in the order of an hour a day over the year.
>
> It is mainly a labour of love. This is the first year that we have been able to offer the Secretary all his expenses, and what we are offering is an honorarium of £50 plus expenses (this includes stationery, telephone, typing etc.) of up to £200 a year.
>
> The main enjoyment of the job is that one meets and mingles

The West Country Writers' Association

with some very interesting and distinguished writers and one does facilitate the getting together of writers who are, by and large, rather lonely, singular people.

If you are still interested, please let me know, and I will be happy to put your name before my Committee in due course.

This remains a very accurate summary of the secretary's role. To put the figures into perspective, the £50 per annum plus up to £200 in expenses has, over twenty-five years, risen to £400 per annum but expenses (which now include travelling to meetings) still run at something between £200 - £300 per annum. Meanwhile subscriptions have risen from £2 to £10 per annum.

That the Association could afford to offer remuneration at all was due to the financial forward planning of John Brooks, who had broken the chain of year-to-year subsistence. All the same, an application for funding from the Arts Council was prepared. It set out the brief history of the Association and its objectives, describing its activities with particular reference to the congress, book exhibition and newsletter. Then it reaches the nub of the matter:

> It is now clear to the Committee that if the Association is to continue, and the existing and potential membership could well increase, it must have some financial help. There is an acute need for assistance on the secretarial side to obviate the very considerable call on the time of members on the administrative aspect of the Association's work.
>
> There are a number of important reasons why the Association should continue. In these days of mass media and technological processes there are many tendencies to produce uniformity in all walks of life, and the preservation of West Country thought and expression is more vital than ever, particularly as the part the West Country is now called upon to take as a play or leisure area for the nation is increasing. This had developed in so many ways that it leads to a destruction of the traditions and customs of the area in pursuit of contemporary pleasures, sometimes out of keeping with the West Country environment. Additionally there is a need to encourage reading and writing amongst the young,

and this the Committee feel is more than important in present circumstances.

With financial assistance the Association, through their writer membership and otherwise, might be able to consider support of local periodicals, and though it is perhaps too ambitious to consider at the present time, the revival of 'The West Country Magazine' for so many years most successful and whose closure it is thought was due to a misunderstanding more than anything else[sic].[62]

The arguments fell on deaf ears: *The West Country Magazine* accordingly never was revived, but there was enough money in the kitty to seek the required secretarial help from among the four applicants.

In the end the successful candidate was a professional secretary and WCWA member, Ann Manning, and another candidate, Doris Hodges, was asked if she would consider relieving Meryl of the treasurership instead. More of them both anon, but before taking up the story of Ann Manning there is one other person who deserves a mention: one of the four external applicants, a lady called Miss Diana Stephenson. She did not get the job and she is of no further importance to WCWA history, but her application is worthy of a digression because it is such a good story.

Diana Stephenson must have been quite a character. Not many people would bother to apply for a secretarial position which involved travelling when they had no car, no telephone - and no typewriter.

> ...My secretarial experience covers the political and medical fields and prior to my retirement last year I worked in an administrative capacity for VSO in Sierra Leone after ten years with the Grenfell Medical Mission in Labrador and Newfoundland.
>
> On the debit side, I have no telephone and have not yet managed to find a typewriter - but I continue to haunt auction sales 'with a view'!
>
> I have a particular interest in books and writing and am a member of the Association of Commonwealth Literature and Language Studies.[63]

Obviously a lady who was not easily daunted - and Bob's tactful reply was not enough to put her off. She wrote straight back, enclosing an impressive curriculum vitae which revealed that her father had founded Letchworth School while she, before her time as a medical secretary in 'the frozen north', had joined the Transport Unit of the Women's Auxiliary Territorial Service and driven everything from minicars to ten-ton lorries in Ceylon, Singapore, and Hong Kong, returning home after demobilization via Malaya, Siam, Sumatra and Japan. Then came her medical work which included '...helping with Annual Chest X-ray surveys, radio air ambulance control and various odd and unexpected things which seem to occur in outpost hospitals! ...Became particularly interested in tubercular and mental patients...' Later she sorted out a friend's airline agency in the Virgin Islands, before starting her own travel agency. I do wish that someone had recruited her. She sounds like one of those redoubtable daughters of Britannia who had rolled up their sleeves, donned a pith helmet, and sorted out the Empire, and it would have been child's play to her, running the WCWA without an office.

> Your letter of 31st December has fired me with enthusiasm and I would very much like to be considered for appointment as Honorary Secretary to the West Country Writers' Association... Lack of a telephone, car and typewriter are obvious handicaps which may be overcome as follows:
> 1. <u>Telephone</u> A phone box is near and arrangements could be made with a neighbour for incoming calls, if necessary.
> 2. <u>Car</u> Public transport available to Bath, Bristol, Salisbury, Plymouth and other West Country towns (at time of writing!). Would be prepared to stay overnight at my own expense, of course.
> 3. <u>Typewriter</u> No problem as I am intending to buy one at the first opportunity. Just waiting for a suitable, solid machine to appear at an auction sale.[64]

It is understandable that the committee should feel that a typewriter in the hand was worth several in the potential auction sale, and by now some more candidates had applied - interestingly they were members, who had presumably not been attracted by the job until it carried a remuneration. Miss Stephenson heard in March 1975 that:

...in the end we had six candidates for this position, three were already members of the Association, and we have invited one of our members - Ann Manning, who has considerable secretarial experience - to be the next holder of this post.[65]

Miss Diana Stephenson duly disappeared from WCWA history, but perhaps the committee could have done worse than appoint her, for they soon found that their new super-secretary was not quite what they had bargained for.

It is the practice nowadays for each secretary, upon appointment, to keep the minute books of her immediate predecessor on hand for quick reference, and deposit any earlier ones in our archives at Bath. Upon taking over from Dorothy Stiffe I accordingly prepared to consign the old minute book to Bath, but first I thought I ought to read through it to get the feel of the Association. Dorothy, as one of the first secretaries to use a word processor and printer, had begun a new loose-leaf file for minutes, but the old minute book stretched back through several secretaries between 1975 and 1984, and its first entries were meticulously recorded by Ann Manning. These were the first words I read:

> The Treasurer then asked the Secretary for her estimation of administration costs for the period to Congress, giving the reason that he needed to know what he could spend on the Newsletter. The Secretary indicated that it was difficult to make a quick assessment off the cuff at this stage. Abruptly, F. Littlewood told the Secretary to answer the Treasurer's question. A member of the Committee then expressed the view that the Treasurer might have requested the Secretary to prepare an estimate prior to the meeting. The Secretary attempted to close the matter satisfactorily by pointing out that it was very difficult to foretell costs, as it would depend so much upon the cost of circulars to members, the increasing costs of duplicating and printing, postage and stationery. F. Littlewood persisted with his acrimonious attack upon the Secretary, which provoked some surprise from the meeting. A Committee member pointed out that the work of the Secretary involved a great deal of time, especially for a writer. The Secretary then indicated that as it would be very difficult for her

The West Country Writers' Association

to carry on, in view of the hostile attitude of the Treasurer and Hon. Solicitor, it would seem that the only course for her in these regrettable circumstances, was to relinquish the secretaryship. F. Littlewood then left the meeting.[66]

I did wonder what I had taken on, and made a mental note to watch my expenses if I did not want to be so summarily dismissed, with the full weight of Frank Littlewood in his capacity as 'Honorary Solicitor'. This is certainly not the impression of Frank Littlewood that appears anywhere else. Bearing in mind that it was Ann Manning herself who wrote this minute, one can only imagine what a painful and unpleasant meeting it must have been. I did speak to Bryan Little about the circumstances behind this incident, and he had a hazy memory that it was to do with excessive taxi fares pushing up the travelling expenses. The resourceful Diana Stephenson must have begun to look very attractive in retrospect, with her modest demands and her offer to pay her own overnight expenses. This scene occurred at the annual Council Meeting in December 1975, and Ann Manning sent her apologies to the next committee meeting as she was 'unwell'. From the Chair, John Rowland stated that there was to be '...no discussion about the discord at the Council Meeting; it would be left in the past. Ann Manning was carrying on until the AGM, but her work commitments would prevent her from continuing after that time'.[67] It was proposed that Honor Butler should succeed her. She had done all the duplicating for some years, and now that she had retired from work she would have more time to devote to the Association. Honor was accordingly elected secretary at the 1976 AGM, which voted that a letter of thanks should be sent to Ann Manning. So the first venture into advertising and paying for a secretary did not have the desired effect, and once again the Association was back to looking for an administrator from within its own ranks.

Honor Butler remained in office for two years until a move to a smaller flat meant that she just did not have the space to cope with the paperwork any more. Soon afterwards, she moved to New Zealand to look after an ageing relative, and there she remarried and became Honor Allingham. It is good to know that in the late 1990s, as a widow, Honor returned to Bournemouth where she had the great good luck to find her

-143-

old flat available so that she was able to move into it again. She rejoined the WCWA and enjoyed three more congresses in her Indian Summer, before her death in the year 2000. She left us a delightful little poem dedicated to WCWA members, in which her own modest nature is conveyed as well as the atmosphere of a congress afternoon:

WRITTEN IN ADMIRATION OF ALL THE MEMBERS OF THE WCWA

As they stand at the bar
with their whisky or beer,
Are ideas going round in their heads?
And while they are eager
to start a new work,
Do they hear every word that is said?
While they sit most attentive
to hear the guests speak,
Is their subconscious making a plot?
Though they nibble their scampi
or munch a ham sandwich,
Their minds must be working a lot.
In amazement I watch them
these verbal constructors;
Their brains must be all of a churn.
But I - a beginner
Just sit at their feet,
While I ponder, and listen and learn.
Honor Butler

After Honor, the reliable Doris Hodges - once passed over in favour of Ann Manning - took over as secretary in 1978. She went on to do the job splendidly for three years, running congresses and knocking off correspondence with one hand, while with the other she continued to produce a steady stream of novels.

One wonders how she had the time. She was also a member of the Crime Writers' Association, as she wrote thrillers with an occult and mystery flavour under the name Charlotte Hunt, including the five 'Dr. Holton' mysteries for Ace Books of America. Under her own name she wrote books about healing, and a textbook *Writing for Profit* - a subject on which she also lectured at adult education classes, until her sudden death of a stroke in 1997. Doris was a stalwart who picked up the pieces for WCWA and just got on with the job, until 1982 when Elizabeth Churcher and Nancy Tregenna-Piggott took it over for a year apiece before moving on to other offices. In 1984 Dorothy Stiffe took on the role for six years, becoming one of the best-loved secretaries ever to hold the position because of her unassuming, thoughtful attitude and her genuine interest in the people around her. One of her duties was to organize a short story competition designed to bring in some new blood, and that was where I came in: I won the competition, and the prize turned out to be a ten-year stint as secretary, with one year's break in 1999 when Caroline Stickland took it on.

In the whole fifty-year history of the Association, that completes the list of secretaries: just thirteen people -

 John Nance/John Keast 1951 - 1959

 Honor Carr 1960 - 1965

 Frank Littlewood 1966 - 1971

 Bob Cooper 1972 - 1975

 Ann Manning 1975

 Honor Butler 1976 - 1978

 Doris Hodges 1978 - 1981

 Elizabeth Churcher 1982

 Nancy Tregenna-Piggott 1983

 Dorothy Stiffe 1984 - 1989

 Anne Double 1990 - 1997 and 1999 -

 Caroline Stickland 1998

It remains a lot of hard work, but as David Keep enticingly said, 'You'll make a lot of good friends, and acquire a formidable collection of autographs' - both true, even if the autographs do tend to be at the foot of letters from famous authors declining our invitation to speak at the next congress...

Henry

It would be absurd to leave the 1970s without some mention of the tall, gaunt figure whose stature dominated the congresses of that era: Henry Williamson. Although he had resigned the presidency in 1965, he continued to be a loyal attender at congress and he seems to have had a genuine affection for the WCWA. He is, for example, well known for his aversion to signing copies of his books - 'I don't know why Henry Williamson disliked autographing his work', recalls Joan Lowry, 'I was once told that it was because certain people sold their copies with his name in it at a profit'.[68] With the WCWA however it was quite a different case, and he not only signed books for Bob Cooper but pressed signed copies on him unsolicited, as a token of thanks for Bob's work as secretary in organizing congress bookings - and Henry's booking requirements were never simple, involving female guests with complicated travel arrangements, dogs to be accommodated at the hotel, and tortuous negotiations on route maps or railway timetables. One year he invited twenty-four personal guests to the annual luncheon. Bob, who kept Henry's hand-written correspondence in a neat file, was unfailingly equal to the challenge of getting Henry plus assorted guests (human and otherwise) eventually to the right place at the right time, and Henry obviously responded to Bob's good-humoured helpfulness. Funnily enough, Bob recently went to look at one of his signed volumes from *A Chronicle of Ancient Sunlight*, only to find that the signed page had been carefully cut out and removed, presumably by one of the many guests who have passed through his house over the years - so Joan Lowry must have been right about the market value of a Williamson autograph. Joan goes on to say:

I didn't even know Henry. I think few people did - perhaps not even Henry himself. I was never more than a casual acquaintance, meeting him at WCWA Congresses or occasionally in North Devon, but the force of his personality was such that each encounter left a lasting impression. He could be maddening, charming, teasing, perverse or angry. But I could be wrong about everything to do with Henry. The King of the Hill went where the winds took him, when he wasn't marching stubbornly to a different drum.[69]

This is one of the commonest remarks that members of those days make about Henry Williamson - that nobody really knew him, that he could be maddening or brilliant in equal proportions. Tales abound of the things he got up to at congresses over the years. Joan Lowry remembers one occasion when he had omitted to book, found there was no room at the inn, and made his point by insisting on sleeping in his car outside all weekend. On another occasion, when the principal lunch guests were lining up for a press photograph outside the hotel, Henry summoned a passing street sweeper to join them. William Kean Seymour once tartly remarked that Henry always looked as if he'd just left his plough in the cloakroom, and yet the pictures of him taken by Meryl Macdonald Bendle at Torre Abbey in 1971 show a figure respectable to the point of restrainedness. There is a trapped, uneasy look about Henry in his formal wear - maybe because he is hemmed in against a wall, or maybe because he did not approve of the camera. Meryl tells us that when she produced a state-of-the-art Japanese model, Henry spotted it and gave her a long lecture on the superiority of German manufacture. It was only with a certain reluctance that he consented to be 'snapped with a Jap'.[70] The air of restraint did not, however, extend to his behaviour at the lunch where he was as exuberant as ever, yet even silly schoolboy pranks like trying to lock ladies in the lavatory were met with indulgence by his fellow members because of the greatness of the man.

Christopher Fry, writing just after Henry's death, recalled 'Congresses of a few years ago when there was always the inimitable pleasure of conversations with Henry Williamson to look forward to'. He calls him 'a fine writer' and 'an invigorating companion'.[71]

The 1973 Congress at Exeter was one of particular significance to Henry Williamson. In WCWA mythology it was not just the first 'new look' residential congress, but it is also known as 'the Kenneth Allsop Congress'. It is a poignant moment in WCWA history because, very shortly after attending the 1973 Congress, Kenneth Allsop committed suicide (or at least was found dead at home in bed with all the appearance of having taken his own life). It is something that has long troubled the members who were there, and yet it has its positive side because that WCWA congress played a part in reconciling Allsop to Henry Williamson before his death.

Kenneth Allsop and Henry Williamson had been close friends for years - since Kenneth Allsop has been in his teens, in fact, when he admired a book of Henry's so much that he went out of his way to meet the author. The friendship lasted and deepened with Allsop and his wife spending many holidays in North Devon, and there is a lovely photograph of them all together with their children on the beach at Woolacombe Bay. In the 1970s, however, two things happened which caused a lot of hurt between them. First Kenneth Allsop, by then a successful broadcaster, conducted an interview with Henry for a BBC TV programme. As an old man in his seventies, and as an old friend, Henry thought it was going to be a fairly complimentary affair; he would talk about his work and get a plug for his latest book. But as many an unwary interviewee has found to his cost, friendship does not count for much when a professional journalist scents a good story. Kenneth Allsop wrong-footed Henry with some very personal questions about his marriage and family, and the interview was a most unpleasant experience, though by all accounts, Henry fielded the questions with great dignity. All the same, in 1969 Henry dedicated his last novel, *The Gale of the World*, to his old friend, Kenneth Allsop. This was not just any book; it was the culmination of his whole life's work, the fifteenth and final episode of his mammoth series, *A Chronicle of Ancient Sunlight*. Henry really expected to get, at last, the acclaim he felt he deserved, and he thought that Allsop would be heedful of the honour he was being paid. Not only, however, was his book badly received by the critics and public at large, but Kenneth Allsop found it quite abhorrent, and their relationship broke down completely.

Then they found themselves thrown together at the 1973 WCWA Congress and the rift was healed, and soon after that Kenneth Allsop was dead. It has never been easy for fellow-members to think that he went home and ended his life so soon after spending a weekend in their company, but at least they have the privilege of knowing that the occasion was a source of peace-making.

Whole volumes have been written about the enigma of Henry Williamson, most notably the book *A Shadowed Man* by WCWA member Lois Lamplugh who knew him personally from the days of her childhood, and *Henry Williamson: Tarka and the Last Romantic,* the definitive biography so lovingly prepared by his daughter-in-law, Anne Williamson, who had access to all the family papers and archives. There has always been a warm friendship between the WCWA and the Henry Williamson Society, and thanks to the genuine relationship which Bob Cooper formed with him during his years as secretary we are fortunate to have quite a set of Henry Williamson's handwritten letters and papers in our archives. One of these, the last, is of quite exceptional importance, describing as it does his mixture of emotions upon reaching the end of the last volume of his enormously long novel sequence, *A Chronicle of Ancient Sunlight* - and in effect reaching the end of his life's work. Written on Tuesday 28 May 1974 to thank Bob for his 'splendid services to our West Country Writers', it ends:

> Do please forgive the sloppy way this letter is put together. But since one has run out of Inspiration - or ambition - or will (one has lived entirely alone since 1962, when the Blizzard swirled over the South and East, and held for many weeks - and my wife ran into the storm, and things were difficult. E.S.T. at Exeter Hospital - 15 or more at the same time -
>
> But I had A Chronicle to finish: and steadily one wrote, until the final and 15th volume - the Great Storm over Exmoor - 3 RAF colonels practicing [sic] gliding (object - the rescue of Hess in Spandau prison) and all things under the flail, and the hammer - Wagner's Gotterdammerung on a smaller scale: but able to stand up to that great work of a lifetime? In its own way, I think so - and, writing the last words of The Gale of the World, I wept and wept, that it was all over, in my little hut (open fireplace!) at Ox's

Cross - my final sentence -
'The flame of the taper falters. We have come to wax end, our chronicle with it'.⁷²

An era had truly come to an end, not just for Henry Williamson but also for the WCWA. William Kean Seymour's sudden death came in 1975, and Bob Cooper ended his spell as secretary soon afterwards. In 1976 a new regime took up the challenge, with John Brooks as chairman, Bryan Little as vice-chairman, and Honor Butler picking up the pieces as secretary after the Ann Manning saga.

By August 1977, Henry Williamson too was dead. There could be no greater tribute than the obituary which John Trewin recorded in the WCWA Newsletter for 1978:

> Inevitably, Waveney Girvan (who had been his bibliographer) first introduced me to Henry Williamson - some time around 1949 to 1950. A formal introduction, as many of us know, was needless because HW had a way of plunging in at once and asking the name of the other person about half an hour later.
>
> He was a charmingly loyal man. As soon as he made a friend, it was a personal relationship, and he regarded the West Country Writers, collectively, as a friend to welcome every year: an annual release from the work to which he gave himself single-mindedly.
>
> Some people found it hard to get on terms with him. I think this was because, in the couple of days when he released his concentration and came to Bath or Exeter or Bristol to 'play' (as he would put it) he let the boyishness in his nature take charge. It was never far beneath the surface. He delighted in the simple joke; putting seriousness behind him, he behaved cheerfully like a boy on half-term holiday.
>
> He was a striking figure anywhere. Reginald Pound once wrote of the 'small lantern-skull, the burning woodland eyes, the drawn-back smile'. Moreover, he moved with almost balletic lightness. Always he seemed to be far younger than his age. Generally he did not much like public speaking, shying away from it whenever he could, though once he did accept an invitation to propose J. B. Priestley's health at Bath. That afternoon, in one of his discursive moods, he spoke at large rather than about his subject. This

inspired Priestley - who had listened, twinkling - to begin his own speech with the words: 'I might have come off better if I had been an otter'.

We shall greatly miss Henry Williamson. He was a founder member; he succeeded Eden Phillpotts as President; later he served for many years as a Vice President. At conferences he would rarely talk of his own books except to murmur now and again about the strain of writing them; he was a compulsive writer who would not leave the desk for long. At heart, I think he knew that the WCWA was proud of the Author of Tarka, one of the enduring books of its century, and of so much else besides.

Shy, boyish, loyal, deeply compassionate, moody sometimes haunted still by the shadows of the first world war, he was always ineffably himself, never seeking to offer any false 'image'. Henry Williamson is bound to remain in our memories; at every conference a loved and loving ghost.[73]

The West Country Writers' Association

Letter reporting Waveney Girvan's death

WEST COUNTRY
WRITERS' ASSOCIATION

PRESIDENT: HENRY WILLIAMSON

Hon.Sec. Honor Carr

Address: 99, Kenilworth Court,
Putney Bridge,
London, S.W.15.
Telephone: PUTNEY 9022.

Vice-Presidents:
A.J. Coles (Jan Stewer)
St.John Ervine Christopher Fry
L.P.Hartley John Moore
A.L.Rowse Marguerite Steen
Brian Vesey Fitzgerald
Lady Vyvyan

Committee:
Kenneth Hopkins Bryan Little
Lady Mander Gilbert Phelps
J.C. Trewin Rosalind Wade

November, 1964.

Dear Members of the West Country Writers' Association,

  It falls upon me to tell you the grievous news that our Chairman, IAN WAVENEY GIRVAN, is dead. This letter would have been written to you earlier – for Waveney, as he liked to be called – died on 22nd October, but I was away from my home for some weeks at that time, and no letters were forwarded from either the Savage Club or my Devon address. It therefore was a great shock when, on going to London, I found our Honorary Secretary's letter awaiting me there, just before Remembrance Day.

  Ian and I were together when he decided to buy the WEST COUNTRY MAGAZINE, towards the end of the Hitlerian war. It was the day of the 'little magazines'. Denys Val Baker was one of the pioneers. No new periodicals were allowed at that time of dearth owing to paper and other shortages – Europe prostrate, the cousin nations bled white – but magazines which had been published previously were permitted revival. Ian and I met at the house above the woods of Lee Bay in North Devon, where Malcolm Elwin was then living, and talked about the revival. Elwin accepted the editorship.

  It was evident that the magazine would soon need advertisements if it was to continue. Elwin had made it a literary magazine, and published a fine first number, with Powys and other good writers. Ian suggested the magazine should be of general interest, thus to get advertising from hotels in Devon and Cornwall, etc. Elwin felt that he could not continue as editor, and Ian did the job himself. From this beginning came the West Country Writers' Association.

  Here is no place to mention Ian's proposal to the Duke of Bedford that tax might be saved by going into publishing, but this idea materialized in the WESTAWAY PRESS. New publishers were springing up, there was a shortage of books. It was the time of 'the sellers' market'. A current phrase was 'one can sell old rope', such was the scarcity of all commodities. Rationing was severely general. Publishers were still short of paper; they were rationed during the war, printers were not. So several printers started publishing on their own. (The only firm I know of which remains, was sponsored by a printing company started by an ex-service man after the war of 1914-18, on a £50 gratuity. By proper use of talent and hard work, and always in a spirit of generosity and rectitude, the original company ultimately expanded to a group with a capital of several millions, inspired and controlled by that ex-infantry sergeant.

  In due course The Westaway Press ceased to publish books, and Ian later joined Odhams Press, becoming Joint Editorial Manager, and was working with the International Printing Corporation (which took over Odhams Press) when he felt he needed a rest, went into hospital for observation, was operated on five days later, found to be fatally ill, and died in the early hours of Thursday, 22nd October, 1964.

The West Country Writers' Association

Waveney was the mainspring of our West Country Writers' Association. He worked for us without rest, for his other job was most exacting. We all know the stresses and strains of this age of anguish. Also, he had an outstanding interest in 'Flying Saucers', being editor of "The Flying Saucer Review". Every pioneer and artist is a dedicated man. The physical world is based on ideas, or an Idea: what Keats called the Imagination. The evolution of species reveals manifold use of the Imagination.

I met Waveney Girvan in the valley of the Bray in the early thirties. He had proposed a visit to us at Shallowford, a thatched house beside that river, to ask me if he might publish a bibliography of my writings. I have a photograph of him sitting beside me on a timber-waggon in the shallows of another river, the Barle, by Dulverton. We had gone there to buy fish from the trout farm, to put into my beat on the Bray. We are hatless, and sitting with my eldest son, then a small boy. The water ripples in the May sunshine, around the great wheels of the timber waggon. We are holding up pint pots of beer, toasting the photographer. It was a happy occasion. I must look out the old photograph and, if I can find it, get it blown up and copied, as a memorial to our founder and friend.

That is all I can think of at the moment. Perhaps there will be a better memorial. It is to be hoped that the West Country Writers' Association will go on, that we will all rally to the annual meetings.

I have written to Mrs. Girvan, for myself and on behalf of us all, to tell her and her family how we are thinking of her at this time, and of the dear man who lives with us in that source of all terrestrial life, the Imagination, by which mankind is sustained in spirit by the Creator.

I have the honour to be,

Your obedient Servant,

(Sgd.) HENRY WILLIAMSON.

President of the
West Country Writers' Association.

The West Country Writers' Association

Programme for the 1973 Congress - the first residential one

THE 22ND ANNUAL CONGRESS
OF THE WEST COUNTRY WRITERS' ASSOCIATION
Founded by Waveney Girvan, 1951

EXETER - 1973. (11th, 12th & 13th May)

Friday, 11th May

2.45 p.m.	Welcome to Members and Guests by President, Christopher Fry, F.R.S.L.
3.00 p.m.	* Professor The Rev. W. Moelwyn Merchant, M.A.,D.Litt., will speak on Robert Herrick, in many ways one of the most notable writers of the district. Chairman - Christopher Fry.
4.00 p.m.	Tea.
4.30 p.m.	* A Panel consisting of Professor Moelwyn Merchant (Chairman, Christopher Fry, John Trewin, Miss Jane Howell and Peter Redgrove will answer questions on the Contemporary Theatre Objectives and the Repertory Theatre.
7.00 p.m.	Buffet Supper, Rougemont Hotel.
8.30 p.m.	Reception by His Worship the Mayor of Exeter in the Guildhall. Henry Williamson will reply to the Mayor's welcome to the Association.

Saturday, 12th May

10.00 a.m.	Opening of the Book Exhibition in the Chatsworth Room, Rougemont Hotel, by J.C. Trewin, F.R.S.L. (Vice Chairman).
10.30 a.m.	Annual General Meeting, Chatsworth Room, Rougemont Hotel.
1.00 p.m.	Annual Luncheon. Chairman - Christopher Fry.
	Toasts - City of Exeter. Dr. William Kean Seymour, Hon.D.Litt.,F.R.S.L., Chairman West Country Writers' Association.
	Response by His Worship the Mayor of Exeter.
	Guest of Honour - The Rt. Hon. Jennie Lee, P.C., Baroness Lee of Asheridge - will propose the Toast, The West Country Writers' Association.
	Response by Rosalind Wade.
3.30 p.m.	* Devonshire Room, Rougemont Hotel. Professor Wilson Knight, C.B.E.,M.A.,F.R.S.L., will speak on Shakespeare's Dramatic Challenge. Chairman - Dr. Frances Stevens.
4.30 p.m.	Tea.
6.30 p.m.	Buffet Supper, Rougemont Hotel.
	Tickets will be available for Members and their Guests for the evening performance of The Tempest at the Northcott Theatre.

Sunday, 13th May

10.30 a.m.	Coffee - Rougemont Hotel.
	An address by a Representative of the Arvon Foundation.

* Open to members of the general public

The West Country Writers' Association

Henry Williamson's last letter to Bob Cooper
The little hut with the open fireplace is shown in the photographs

4 Capstone Place, Ilfracombe, N. Devon
28 May; Tuesday: 1974

My dear Dr Cooper!

Pray forgive a letter, much delayed by travel and other events (one such being the arrival from Seattle, Mass. U.S.A. of a young woman hoping to receive her doctorate (:) by writing at length about the longest novel in the world – to wit, <u>A Chronicle of Ancient Sunlight</u>) and as for the Sunday 19th May – my guest, Melloney Berry, was looking after her father, a don (Eng. Lit.) at a University in Surrey – She had driven him, before appearing at Bristol, to Cambridge – arranged help (he had, comparatively young, several 'strokes' – and before midday of Sunday 19th, left for Cambridge, in order to motor him home to Englefield Green, his home.

Then, a day or so later – after leaving Melloney – I had to meet my visitant from U.S.A. and that evening, to whisk her to the Royal Society of Lit. for a poetry reading : then descent from No 1, Hyde Park Gardens, to the Chelsea Arts Club, for supper.

So this letter of thanks for your excellent services to the West Writers has been too tardy, and comes with my apologies.

(I don't know if the young U.S.A. lady will find any College or University to finance her. She arrived recently: and after two days at the Nat. Liberal Club I had to return here – in N. Devon. (I did write to Exeter University (where Miss Berry acquired her BSc (sic?) – & asked particularly if they could help Miss Bonney Blackleigh, from Seattle: I have given three of my MSs in my handwriting – <u>Tarka the Otter</u>, <u>Salar the Salmon</u>, <u>and The Peregrine's Saga</u> (said MSs being valued at £70,000 – £80,000. Thus I wrote to Exeter Univ. but received no reply: the letter, perhaps, is under discussion . , ..

Do please forgive the sloppy way this letter is put together. But since one has run out of Inspiration — or ~~ambition~~ Pity — ambition — or will, (one has lived entirely alone since 1962, when the Blizzard swirled over the South and East, and held for many weeks — and my wife ran into the storm, & things were difficult. E.S.T. at Exeter Hospital — 15 or more at the same time —

But, I had a Chronicle to finish: & steadily one wrote, until the final and 15th volume — the Great Storm over Exmoor — 3 RAF Colonels practicing gliding (object — the rescue of Hess in Spandau (prison) and all things under the flail, and the hammer — Wagner's Götterdämmerung on a smaller scale: but able to stand up to that great work of a lifetime? In its own way, I think so — and, writing the last words of The Gale of the World, I wept and wept, that it was all over, in my little hut (open fireplace!) at Ox's Cross — my final sentence —
'The flame of the taper fallen. We have come to wax end, our chronicle with it.'

If you have no copy of No 15, may I send you one, please; as a small tribute to your splendid services to our West Country writers.

Yours sincerely Henry Williamson.

The West Country Writers' Association

Honor Carr's Letterhead 1960s

```
                THE                      President:    HENRY WILLIAMSON
      WEST COUNTRY                       Vice-Presidents:  A. J. COLES ('JAN STEWER'), ST. JOHN ERVINE,
                                                           CHRISTOPHER FRY,         L. P. HARTLEY,
      WRITERS' ASSOCIATION                                 JOHN MOORE, A.L. ROWSE, MARGUERITE STEEN,
                                         Chairman:        BRIAN VESEY-FITZGERALD,  LADY VYVYAN.
                                                          WAVENEY GIRVAN.
                                         Committee:      KENNETH HOPKINS,   BRYAN LITTLE,
      99, KENILWORTH COURT, PUTNEY BRIDGE,                LADY MANDER,      GILBERT PHELPS,
      LONDON, S.W.15.        Tel.: PUTNEY 9022            J. C. TREWIN,     ROSALIND WADE.
                                         Hon. Secretary: HONOR CARR.
```

1st May '68

Bob Cooper's Letterhead 1974

```
Past Presidents: EDEN PHILLPOTTS 1951-1960   HENRY WILLIAMSON 1960-1965    President:   CHRISTOPHER FRY, F.R.S.L.
                                                                           Vice Presidents: CHARLES CAUSLEY, F.R.S.L.    LAURIE LEE, M.B.E., F.R.S.L.
                                                                                            L. P. HARTLEY, C.B.E., F.R.S.L.    WILLIAM KEAN SEYMOUR
                                                                                            MARGUERITE STEEN, F.R.S.L.         BRIAN VESEY-FITZGERALD
                                                                                            LADY VYVYAN                        HENRY WILLIAMSON, F.R.S.L.
                    THE                                                                     J. C. TREWIN, F.R.S.L.   A. L. ROWSE, M.A., D.LITT., F.B.A., F.R.S.L.
          WEST COUNTRY                                                     Chairman:        WILLIAM KEAN SEYMOUR, Hon. D. LITT., F.R.S.L.
          WRITERS' ASSOCIATION                                             Vice Chairman:   Rev. JOHN ROWLAND
                                                                           Hon. Treas.      JOHN BROOKS
                                                                           Hon. M'ship Sec. GERALDINE KAYE
                                                                           Hon. P.R.O.
                                                                           and Newsletter   MERYL BENDLE
                                                                           Hon. Solicitor:  F. D. LITTLEWOOD, O.B.E.
     Hon. Sec. Dr. R. A. COOPER, M.B., B.S., L.M.S.S.A.
         THE DENE - THE STREET - ALDERMASTON - BERKS
         Telephone WOOLHAMPTON 2188
```

Anne Manning's paper subsequently used by other officers

```
Past Presidents: EDEN PHILLPOTTS 1951-1960   HENRY WILLIAMSON 1960-1965
                                             President:       CHRISTOPHER FRY, F.R.S.L.
                                             Vice Presidents: CHARLES CAUSLEY, F.R.S.L.         ROSALIND WADE
                                                                                                BRYAN LITTLE          LAURIE LEE, M.B.E., F.R.S.L.
                                                                                                LADY VYVYAN           BRIAN VESEY-FITZGERALD
                    THE                                                                         J. C. TREWIN, F.R.S.L.   HENRY WILLIAMSON, F.R.S.L.
          WEST COUNTRY                                                                          A. L. ROWSE, M.A., D.LITT., F.B.A., F.R.S.L.
                                             Chairman:        REV. JOHN ROWLAND, B.Sc.
          WRITERS' ASSOCIATION               Vice Chairman:   JOHN BROOKS
                                             Hon. Treas.      JOHN BROOKS
                                             Hon. M'ship Sec. GERALDINE KAYE
                                             Hon. P.R.O.
                                             and Newsletter   MERYL BENDLE
                                             Hon. Solicitor:  F. D. LITTLEWOOD, O.B.E.
     Hon. Secretary: ANN MANNING
         THE COTTAGE, Nr. STOKE GIFFORD, BRISTOL BS12 6PT
         Telephone WINTERBOURNE 772315
```

The West Country Writers' Association

A Typical Frank Littlewood Letter requesting items for the first newsletter. This one was sent to Henry Williamson - and returned with interesting annotations.

Past Presidents: EDEN PHILLPOTTS 1951-1960.   HENRY WILLIAMSON 1960-1965

THE WEST COUNTRY WRITERS' ASSOCIATION

'LITTLE ASHLEY', 5 RYEWORTH ROAD,
CHARLTON KINGS, CHELTENHAM, GLOS.
Tel. CHELT. 24143

President: CHRISTOPHER FRY
Vice-Presidents: ST. JOHN ERVINE, L. P. HARTLEY, JOHN MOORE, A. L. ROWSE, MARGUERITE STEEN, BRIAN VESEY FITZGERALD, LADY VYVYAN, HENRY WILLIAMSON
Chairman: J. C. TREWIN
Committee: JOHN BAYLISS, LINDA BOSCAWEN, HONOR CARR, KENNETH HOPKINS, BRYAN LITTLE, LADY MANDER, ANTHONY RYE, WILLIAM KEAN SEYMOUR
Hon. Secretary: F. D LITTLEWOOD

28th November, 1967.

Dear Williamson,

As one of those who helped to instigate the idea, could I have a line of your present activities for our News Sheet. I would like to put in something like this -

"Our one time President and now Vice President is still working hard and is tackling another novel This time, and possibly for the first time, on a fully planned basis."

Henry Williamson Esq.,
Ox's Cross,
Georgeham,
Braunton,
Nr. Barnstaple,
N. Devon.

The West Country Writers' Association

Honor Butler's headed paper, late 1970s

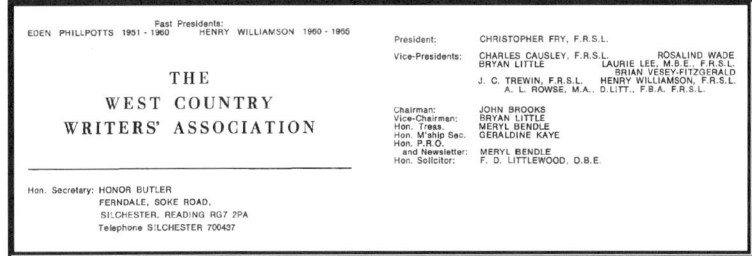

The green Letterhead incorporating the logo. Designed in 1982, supplies lasted until 1995.

PHOTO: JANET GREEN

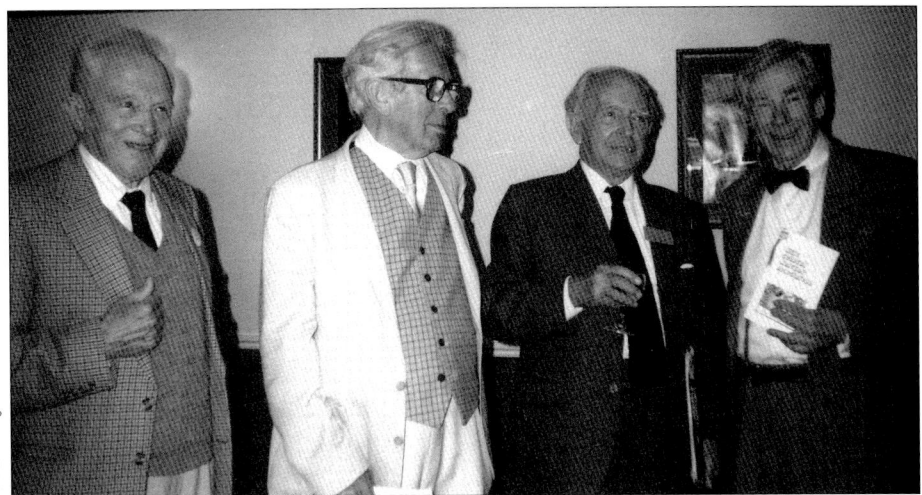

The 40th Anniversary Congress at Salisbury, 1991. Left to right Ralph Whitock, Laurie Lee, Christopher Fry and actor Michael Gough who was Guest of Honour that year (he is holding a copy of the 40th Anniversary Booklet)

PHOTO: JOHN HARCUP

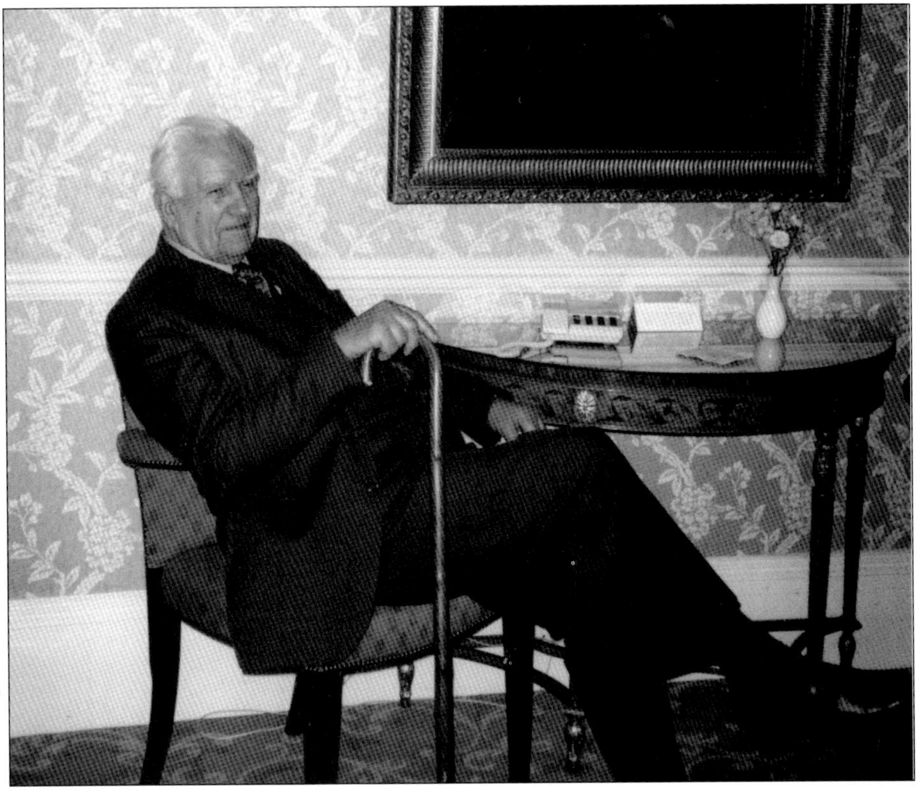

Victor Bonham-Carter, founder member, at Bristol in 1966

Left: Christopher in the mid 1960s when he became President of the WCWA
Below: Christopher with Bob Cooper in 1999
Bottom: Christopher at work on his faithful typewriter

OUR LAURIE Top left: Laurie with Jean Steward, Cheltenham 1994
Above: Mollie Hince with Laurie at Torquay, 1995
Above right: Laurie always refused to make a scheduled talk "I'm simply no good at making speeches" he says in his postcard, but he would generally give an impromptu performance at the annual lunch
Bottom right: Laurie's gallant response to the poem written in his honour by Christopher Fry, Bristol 1996

The committee – Torquay 1995 left to right John Wroughton, Bob Cooper, John Harcup, Geraldine Kaye, Meryl Macdonald Bendle, David Keep, Anne Double, John Paxton, Rosemary Jeffery, Simon Rocksborough Smith, Jo Andrew, Janet Green, Helen Rowett, Gillian Lindsay and John Rowe

Three out of four Bristol 1996: Chairman Bob Cooper makes a presentation to Meryl Macdonald Bendle and Geraldine Kaye, marking their 25th year of service on the committee

Civic reception John Harcup tries out the Mayoral Mace at Weymouth in 1998. Looking on is Margaret Bacon.

Annual Luncheon A group of members enjoying lunch at Cheltenham in 1994 Peggy Lossemore-Jones is seated furthest from the camera on the right.

THE 1990s – TWO SECRETARIES
Dorothy Stiffe and Honor Butler/Allingham meet again at Plymouth in 1997

Below **LORD ST. LEVAN** Patron of the WCWA at home at St. Michael's Mount 1992

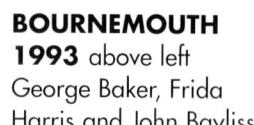

BOURNEMOUTH 1993 above left
George Baker, Frida Harris and John Bayliss

FORTIETH ANNIVERSARY left
Geraldine Kaye cuts the cake, watched by Chairman David Keep and his wife Carolyn

BOURNEMOUTH 1993 far left John Paxton proposes a toast in entertaining style

SOME MOTHERS DO 'AVE 'EM left Raymond Allen at his first Congress in Bournemouth 1993

PREPARING FOR HOME Leslie Grinsell sets off to walk to the station with his rucksack

Bryan Little gives his last speech to the WCWA at the 1990 luncheon

1995: Chairman John Paxton leads the applause for Bob Cooper after his reading of Victor Bonham–Carter's address

Above: At the Plymouth Congress 1997 Bob Cooper congratulates Adele Ziolkowska on reaching 90 years
Left: Charles Causley read from his poetry in Exeter 1990 – here with Laurie Lee

OUTSIDE ACTIVITIES
left: **VISIT TO HARVEY'S WINE CELLARS** in Bristol, 1996: Paul Hyland and Raymond Allen among the soleros

Above: **THE ASCENT OF ST, MICHAEL'S MOUNT** some of those who made it to the top: back row left to right Vivien Foster, Ron Jeffery, Rosemary Ellerbeck, Fay Sampson, Olwen Reed front row left to right Ken Randall, Dorothy Stiffe, Rosie Gerrish, Frida Harris, Angela Tuckett and Rosemary Jeffery

REGIONAL LUNCH *left to right* John Harcup, Geoff and Penelope Ruddock, Astrid Klemz, Jean Steward and friends were among the many guests who celebrated the new Millennium at Pat Daly's home in Bath

PART IV

THE INFORMATION AGE: 1978 - 2000

> *The first thing a new Chairman realizes is what a wonderful job his predecessor did.*
> Antony Hippisley Coxe

Into the Eighties

For a whole year, from November 1978 - November 1979, *The Times* did not appear because of a protracted and bitter dispute over what was then called 'the New Technology'. It was perhaps the most public and symbolic manifestation of a revolution that was sweeping through the whole printing and publishing world, and as Fleet Street gradually began the process of decamping to new quarters at Wapping the revolution was met with a modern form of Luddism. A trade which still carried some of the mysteries of a medieval guild, which still called its union leaders 'the Mother/Father of the Chapel' and wrapped itself in arcane working practices, just could not come to terms with a change that was so sudden and so total. A whole way of life was overturned with a speed that was frightening.

Looking back, we already view the giant computers and early word processors of those days with a touch of mockery because things have moved on so much further. Desktop publishing, modern PCs, Internet access for all: we constantly demand better, quicker, easier. The last twenty years of the second millennium saw change happen at a pace that could be brutal, and the gentle sunlit days of Henry Williamson's reverie beside a Devon stream, or Lady Mander taking the spa waters at Bath, seem centuries away from the Year 2000.

In its own modest way, the West Country Writers' Association of the 1980s was changing at a swifter pace as well. The 'new look' brought in during the seventies had changed more than just the structure of congress. The new constitution, with chairmen holding office for only two years at a time, meant an inevitably swift turnover of officers so that never again did one person's viewpoint dominate and never again could one speak of 'the Waveney Girvan days' or 'the William Kean Seymour years', which is not to say that there were not outstanding personalities whose contribution was invaluable. The Association continued to be served by a succession of great characters, it was just that the succession happened at an ever-increasing pace, and the history becomes more fragmented than in the solid days of the fifties.

Janet Green, our current public relations officer, made a wise observation when she was reviewing the Association's development at the time of the fortieth anniversary. Lots of writers' associations, she pointed out, had sprung up in the immediate post-war years, but had fallen by the wayside or been choked by thorns as the decades passed. It struck her that the WCWA had made it through forty years because it had learnt to cope with change, and by regularly re-inventing itself it had weathered the shock of the new.

The developments which were to bear fruit in the eighties all had their roots in the overhaul of the seventies. The concept of associate membership, flatly dismissed by William Kean Seymour in 1972, was brought up again in 1976. In the same year John Brooks began his chairmanship with an enigmatic item on the AGM agenda: 'C. A.' Much speculation was aroused about what the letters might stand for. The answer turned out to be 'Congress Aid' and it was John Brooks' first endeavour to return revenue, as he had wished, 'to those who provide it - our members'.[1] Certainly, by 1978, several mutterings were to be heard about the cost of congress, and some members had even made a plea for a return to the old days when everyone made their own accommodation arrangements. For the concept of 'under one roof' to be defended, something had to be done about costs. Discussion went on throughout 1977, when it was suggested that the fund should be called 'the Henry Williamson Travel Award' in recognition of the great vice-president who had died that year. Inevitable arguments then arose about whether grants should cover the cost of travel, or just the hotel accommodation. It was in any case always going to be a delicate subject. The eventual arrangements agreed for Congress Aid were described in the 1978 newsletter by Frank Littlewood, who had found himself unexpectedly acting as editor again when John Rowland's health had collapsed:

> Among the matters on which the Council deliberated at their London meeting were several aspects of the scheme touched on several times before but much more seriously considered at the Congress at Plymouth last year, to help members of the Association who would like to come to the Congress but who cannot afford - and there is not a great deal of money in writing these days - to come both to the Congress with its interest and also in some cases to meet considerable travelling expenses. For obvious reasons this is a delicate and difficult matter. The Council finally decided to dispense with complicated rules and formalities, and to leave the matter largely in the hands of the Chairman who will consult in confidence and with the discretion one would expect, representative members or officers of the Association. Though it is understood the Council would not wish to restrict him, the present Chairman's views tend to helping more in the direction of covering expenditure at the Congress rather than those concerned with travelling. As the acting Editor understands it, suggestions to the Chairman as to the name or names of members who would be suitable to benefit, can come from someone other than the member personally involved. In fact some members might find the help of a friend less embarrassing; others of course might find this just the opposite. The guiding principles will be confidentiality and simplicity. It should be said clearly the amount of money available is very strictly limited.[2]

Whether because of delicacy or the limitation of funds, no applications for

Congress Aid were received in 1978 or 1979. Any awards of course would have been confidential, but speaking in general terms to past treasurers I have uncovered no evidence that Congress Aid was ever taken up in the 1980s either. The offer remained on the books though, and a big push in the newsletter led to some use of the fund in the 1990s, specifically to enable people to attend congress for the first time. Since then its use has increased, and it will always be there if it is needed, a lasting testimonial to the vision of John Brooks and the other pioneers of the seventies.

The Gang of Four themselves had gradually been trying to pass on the baton as the seventies went by, but with varying degrees of success. Bob Cooper had finally sorted out a successor as secretary by initiating the payment of an honorarium and expenses, but when John Brooks gave up being treasurer to become chairman for 1976 and 1977, Meryl Macdonald Bendle - who was trying to retire from the newsletter - found herself looking after the finances as well. In 1977 it was all change again when Doris Hodges took over from Honor Butler as secretary, and John Rowland briefly relieved Meryl of editorial responsibilities only to be forced into resignation by health problems, so that Frank Littlewood was pressed back into temporary service.

At this point the rotation of roles between officers begins to resemble an eight-handed reel. By 1978 Geraldine Kaye was able to lay down the burden of recruiting and nurturing when Olwen Reed agreed to become membership secretary, but Meryl was still treasurer, and the newsletter post remained vacant until Jacynth Hope-Simpson offered to keep a holding brief. Bryan Little had acceded to the Chair in 1978 but his tenure was overshadowed by the illness of his wife in 1979. They had married late in life, and when she died her loss was a great blow to him. The shortness of the chairman's term of office was producing a new problem: the need for a constant supply of members willing to be the chairman. After four or five years of recycling the same officers into different roles a halt was called, and the committee was refreshed with some new blood to meet the new decade.

The 1980 AGM saw a great step forward for the WCWA. Thirty years into its history it elected its first woman chairman, Jacynth Hope-Simpson. That a woman should take the leadership at this particular date is significant, and not just because, in Bryan Little's words, 'If the country could have a woman prime minister, then the WCWA could have a woman chairman!'[3] Women had held office before, but Jacynth was no Lady Mander, quietly occupying the role of back-up for thirteen years and graciously acting as 'hostess' on grand occasions; she was a working mother with that 'classic women's problem of reconciling a profession with domestic responsibilities'.[4] Once again we see the times reflected in the development of the Association, as more and more women began to tackle the problem of reconciling those two roles - and coming out as leaders.

The other elections in 1980 saw Elizabeth Churcher succeed Doris Hodges as secretary, Olwen Reed continuing with membership, the energetic Jean Harding setting about the rebranding of the newsletter as *Stepping Westward*, and - lest it be seen as a complete feminist takeover - a new treasurer in the person of David Keep, who was to become another in the long line of faithful servants to the Association: 'Meryl... at long, long last has managed to bow out of what is not the most enviable of jobs; that of treasurer. The gentleman who has so gallantly taken over from her is Dr. David Keep'[5] - more accurately Revd. Dr. David Keep, as David is a Methodist minister whose writings encompass many religious subjects as well as his great interest, that champion of women's rights, Mark Rutherford of Bedford.

Jacynth, the 'first lady' of the WCWA, was at the time of her election just moving from children's books to adult fiction, which she wrote under the pen name of Helen Dudley. A First World War novel, set against the background of the birth of Yugoslavia was to follow her first success, *The Hooded Falcon*. Under her chairmanship, Jean Harding did great things with the newly named *Stepping Westward*. It began to develop into a magazine rather than a newsletter, still concentrating on members' achievements and activities, but incorporating editorial comment and inviting contributions on literary subjects - for example, there was an ongoing correspondence on writers' work patterns. The periodical began to look a much smarter publication and it carried more photographs than ever before, although these early attempts at printing photocopies were never very satisfactory.

One of Jean's first ideas was to run a history of the Association and in 1980 she declared her intention to begin with a feature on 'Waveney Girvan as the man he was'. Sadly, it was not to be. Jean's husband became seriously ill and she had to give up her role as editor - and eventually her writing career, though she later discovered her talents as an artist - in order to look after him. John Trewin contributed his piece on the early years of the Association which served as the standard 'history' ever since, but no further work was done on the history for another twenty years.

Following the 'first lady' into the Chair was someone who had become a member in Geraldine's great recruitment drive of the seventies, Antony Hippisley Coxe. Principally a journalist, he was a man of many parts - and of great energy, despite his seventy years. He had started out by training in architecture and then designing film and stage sets, before becoming associate arts editor of *Harper's Bazaar*. War service in naval intelligence interrupted his career, but afterwards he became features editor of the *News Chronicle* and then press and/or publicity officer for bodies as various as the NFU, Granada TV, Shell International Petroleum and the British Plastics Federation. He contributed to everything from *The Encyclopaedia Britannica* to *The Horseman's Year*. His was just the sort of new blood that John Trewin had hoped to infuse into the Association when he changed the rules to include journalists and other writers as well as the authors of books.

Antony Hippisley Coxe did write books too, the most successful being *Haunted Britain* - a sort of 'Who's Who' of the ghostly world - and he collaborated with his wife, the cookery writer Araminta Hippisley Coxe, on a highly idiosyncratic concept - *The Book of the Sausage*. This compendious work covered five hundred different kinds of sausage from thirty-two different countries, listing their history, how to make them, how to cook them, and even what to drink with them. He loved good food and drink, but more than anything else he loved the circus. His book *A Seat at the Circus* remains the classic work on the circus arts because it was written from the heart. He had been collecting circus memorabilia since he was a boy, and the collection grew to such size and importance that it was purchased by the Theatre Museum in Covent Garden. When the Festival of Britain was planned in 1951, he organized a tightrope crossing of the

Thames - he even had his own circus act of trained domestic cats who performed acrobatic tricks. He was an exceptional character, and by all accounts a charming person, who could turn his hand to anything, from thatching his own cottage and laying its parquet floor to curing his own hams.

Antony Hippisley Coxe brought to the committee the sort of mind that gets on with things. He quickly picked up on the good ideas that had been mooted in the pioneering seventies but had not yet been developed. With his early background in visual arts he could see the need for a corporate symbol and he brought up the idea of a logo at the 1982 Congress. As he put it in the newsletter:

> The Treasurer has made a number of remarkable savings, particularly in print production, for which we must all be most grateful. Now, I feel, we must build on this to establish our own individual house style, so that our letter heads, publications and so on instantly proclaim who we are - and show that we are proud of it.[6]

The idea was received with enthusiasm and art work was drawn up, producing the familiar intertwined WCWA logo which we use to this day. Attempts to develop this into a tie, scarf or badge for members were not so successful, and although David Keep put a lot of work into obtaining designs and quotations in 1984, not enough orders were forthcoming to make the project viable. West Country writers remain resistant to being badged or labelled, and a similar suggestion for ties and badges by Frida Harris and John Harcup met with equal apathy ten years later. The letterheads, however, were produced, and the new house style was proclaimed by the bold new official paper which carried the logo prominently on a green background. The only drawback to this was the old problem of mortality which meant that 'the green paper' carried Daphne du Maurier's name in a green, rather than a black, border for the greater part of its existence.

With his journalistic background Antony Hippisley Coxe was also rather more keen on campaigns than had previously been the case with the WCWA. In July 1982 he was up in arms about the threat to the

-167-

Theatre Museum, of which he was a lifelong supporter:

> Although some of the links which tie the Theatre and our Association are obvious - the work of our President, Christopher Fry, Past President Eden Phillpotts, Vice President J. C. Trewin, to name but three - some members may not know that Frank Littlewood also has strong theatrical connections. His father was Dramatic Critic of *The Morning Post* and Editor of *The Stage*. He recently gave a collection of important books on the subject to the Theatre Museum, on whose Advisory Council I happen to sit.
> So when the future of the Museum appeared to be in jeopardy it seemed proper that we should come to its aid, not only because of past ties, but because I know that the plans for its development stress the importance of facilities for research, which will be invaluable to historians, biographers, playwrights and all authors interested in any aspect of the performing arts.
> Unfortunately the Rayner Scrutiny, which contained the threat of abandonment, was not issued until the holiday season had started and action had to be taken before the summer recess, there was therefore no time to circularize all members with much hope that individual action could be taken by the majority. We did, however, make our voice heard - loud and clear. The President wrote to the Prime Minister; a number of Vice Presidents wrote personally to their MP, as indeed did a number of ordinary members, one of whom at least followed the President's lead and wrote to Mrs. Thatcher. I, as Chairman, wrote to all MPs in Cornwall, Devon, Somerset and Dorset urging them to add their name in support of the Early Day Motion on the House of Commons Order Paper supporting the Theatre Museum Project. I understand that some hundred MPs from all Political Parties had indicated their support by the end of July. What the final result will be is not known at the time of writing. Members, however, should know that the Association took action.[7]

A year or so later he 'took action' again in another cause, as Dorothy Stiffe, the secretary in those days, had reason to recall:

> I was up to my eyes preparing for Christmas and Antony

> Hippisley Coxe phoned to say he had composed a letter protesting against the tax the government was thinking of putting on books. 'Could you send copies to all West Country Members of Parliament', he said, 'And if you could type them individually it would be better. Photostats wouldn't have the same impact'. I went to the library and came back with the names of over fifty MPs.
>
> Icing my Christmas cake after that stint, my arms were decidedly wobbly! Antony didn't take it for granted, he really appreciated the effort made.[8]

In the days before PCs, that must have been a marathon task.

Life with Antony Hippisley Coxe was always going to be lively. He had introduced himself as chairman in that vein:

> The first thing a new Chairman realizes is what a wonderful job his predecessor did, and the second is that one cannot hope to please all the members all the time. And I don't think one should try. It is not a bad thing for a few people to get hot under the collar about something of which the rest approve, as long as the dissident voices are not always the same. It helps to keep our Congresses lively.[9]

He also acknowledged that, 'The main problems that face a new chairman, I find, are concerned with next year's congress, particularly where? and who? But one must also try to learn from the past'.[10] He encouraged the revival of another seventies idea, the themed congress:

> At the moment your Committee is considering holding a Congress with a theme. Any theme is bound to appeal to some more than others. So it is up to us to find speakers who will attract more than the theme might detract... We will see how we get on.[11]

But far and away the most important issue that Antony Hippisley Coxe tackled was the question of associate membership. John Trewin had breathed new life into the Association by expanding eligibility to script and media writers in 1968, and ever since that date committees had toyed with the possibilities of further expansion. Librarians were in, but what about budding writers; people who were not *yet* writers but were trying hard; people who had not only not published three hardback books, but had not yet published at all in any medium? William Kean Seymour had sat upon the idea firmly in 1972 - 'No more campaigning of this kind'.[12] For him, even the idea of the active recruiting campaign was a 'free for all' after the days of vetting, sifting, blackballing, and occasionally admitting the *right* sort of person 'at the invitation of the Committee'. It was an idea that refused to lie down though, and the committee had deliberated long and hard on the subject under John Brooks in 1976 and 1977 and in subsequent years, without ever accepting the idea. Once Antony Hippisley Coxe took command, things started to move. At one of the first committee meetings he chaired, in October 1982, he set up a sub-committee under the chairmanship of Charles Owen to look into the rules about membership.

Even one of the old school like Bryan Little was prepared to admit that paperbacks could now be of very high quality - though he ruthlessly excluded vanity publishing. Two categories of potential 'Associate Members' were to be considered: those in the associated professions (e.g. librarians, agents, publishers, booksellers) and those who were described as 'cadet writers'. All sorts of objections were raised, based mostly on the premise that 'opening the floodgates' would lead to a huge inflow of new applicants who would outnumber and drown the established membership. It would create too much work for the secretary and treasurer, some said. It would mean congress being hijacked by ruthless agents touting for custom, said others. Things would never be the same again. The professional Association would become no more than a writers' circle. Against this point of view were those who complained of 'elitism' and 'snobbishness', or who counselled the necessity to find younger members if the Association was not to die of sheer old age. The arguments will sound very familiar to any present-day committee member who has ever sat through discussion of an application by a self-published author.

Antony Hippisley Coxe, believing it to be no bad thing for people to get hot under the collar, carried the idea of a sub-committee through the 1982 AGM, and the fruits of their researches came in a recommendation for an amendment to the rules to be placed on the agenda for the 1983 AGM at Taunton. It was formally proposed that Rule 3, on membership, which had always stated simply that

> 'Admission to membership of the Association shall be by invitation of the Committee', should in future read:
>
> '3. Admission to membership of the Association shall be by invitation of the Committee. A full member may be either any adult who was born or is living, working or studying or for a reasonable period has lived, worked or studied in the West Country and is the author of at least one full length published book or has had a substantial body of work published or produced in one or more of the other media; or any adult living, working or studying in or doing work about the West Country who for at least five years has been engaged in an occupation involved directly with writers and their profession such as those of publisher, editor, producer, literary agent, illustrator, indexer, bookseller, librarian, literary or TV critic or author's researcher. An associate member may be an adult living, working or studying in the West Country who can show evidence that he/she is an aspiring and practising writer who expects to be able, within a reasonable period, to qualify for full membership and so far has been published or produced to only a limited extent.'

This was much more in keeping with the spirit of the guidelines on eligibility drawn up by the provisional committee in 1950 than with the official rules as laid down in 1968.

The report on this significant Taunton AGM is carried in the subsequent newsletter, which was produced by Jacynth Hope-Simpson. Caretaker editor Doris Hodges had finally given up, and Jacynth agreed to hold the fort for just one edition. She recorded:

> A very full discussion took place. The advantages of attracting more members, producing more revenue and bringing in younger people were weighed against the question of altering the traditional character of the WCWA. The possibility of setting a quota was suggested, and fears of a take-over by the 'avant garde'

were expressed. The questions of voting rights and of differential subscriptions were raised by several members.

A vote was finally taken to see if the meeting accepted the principle of admitting associate members. A 2:1 majority was in favour of doing so.

It was decided, however, that the membership rules should not be changed in isolation. David Keep, the Treasurer, and Simon Rocksborough Smith, who is a barrister, are examining the rules of the WCWA and will report to the Committee.

The final draft, including proposals on membership, will be put to the next AGM. It is hoped that as many members as possible will be there to record their votes.[13]

A significant name makes its appearance here: Simon Rocksborough Smith. Bob Cooper had greeted his recruitment in 1972 by pointing out to William Kean Seymour that this was just the sort of person that the Association needed to attract, and that there was nothing to be feared in the idea of giving the same welcome 'to somebody just launching himself as to somebody who is already established'.[14] Simon at that time was a young barrister whose passion for public transport had led him into writing about steam trains - particularly GWR - for David & Charles ('David' - i.e. David St. John Thomas - was an early member of the WCWA). He was swiftly head-hunted on to the committee, and by the time of his retirement in 1998 he had served for twenty-three years as a committee member and was looking forward to what would be only his third congress as an 'ordinary' member. His appointment as a circuit judge did nothing to allay his fascination with the idea of getting to any given venue without a car, and it has become part of the congress to see the Rocksborough Smiths waiting, timetable in hand and surrounded by luggage, at the nearest bus stop as soon as proceedings have ended. During his long stint on the committee Simon has taken his turn as vice-chairman and chairman for a few years, but throughout the duration - and still today - he has been the wise man to whom the Association has turned for advice on any problem that could be said to be of legal significance. As he himself put it:

When we revised the Constitution to bring in Associate Members, I was assumed to be good at draftsmanship, since I was a barrister. I was always expected to give an opinion on whether a proposal was within the Rules, and I had to make sure I brought a copy with me to every meeting.[15]

The sub-committee met several times at Charles Owen's home in Topsham, first to consider the existing rules as amended in 1968, then to consider a discussion paper, make suggestions for drafting by Simon, and then scrutinize the results. The proposed new set of rules was studied and approved by the president, and it was then printed in the newsletter for 1984 so that members could consider the changes in good time to vote on them at the AGM that year. The 1984 Rules are reproduced after Part IV, as they appeared in the 1984 newsletter. Bill Pickard was the new editor in those days, and he gave them the flamboyant heading inspired by the fashion at the time for proclaiming '***rules OK!' The concluding paragraph is crucial:

> During the years 1982, 1983 and 1984 a great deal of thought and hard work on these Rules has been done by Charles Owen, David Keep, Simon Rocksborough Smith and others, and we are grateful that a clear and workable revision has now emerged. Even our President made a gracious concession on membership, and we should now try to implement the new possibilities to the full extent that they can be implemented in Rule Three[16]

Rule Three was the big one. It meant that, for the first time, associate membership could be held by any 'aspiring and practising writer', even if he or she had not yet published anything.

Twenty years on we can evaluate what a good piece of work this was. The Association has not been submerged - the membership has remained fairly constant at just below three hundred - and it has not greatly changed its nature. There has been the sort of lightening up that Geraldine Kaye observed in her recollections, but that probably owes as much to changes in society and mores generally as to any change in membership qualifications. Life, customs, dress, social occasions are all more relaxed and informal than they were in the 1950s. But what the WCWA has gained from introducing associate membership far outweighs anything it might have lost. Quite apart from keeping the numbers up to a viable level and hence protecting the finances, congresses have been enriched by the presence and personality of many an associate member who has attended regularly and supported loyally, though without perhaps ever attaining the status of successful author. We have been the better for their company and friendship, benefiting from the increased 'exchange of ideas' without ever departing from 'the love of literature in the West Country'. The 1984 Rules have served us well ever since, with only one small amendment in 1995 to tidy up a detail of committee membership.

So 1984 was a year of significance *within* the Association, but as always it is impossible to divorce Association affairs from what was going on in the world outside. 1984 always was a date to be conjured with, and the 1984 Congress at Torquay faced head-on the big issue for writers of the day: Information Technology. The theme was 'Looking Forward'. This was the programme:

Friday 11 May

2.30 pm   Book Exhibition at W.H. Smith, to be opened by Ralph Whitlock
3.15 pm   Terry Tapp: 'Communication; Close Encounters'
6.00 pm   Civic Reception at Torre Abbey, followed by tour of the Mansion House and Tithe Barn
8.00 pm   Dinner
9.00 pm   Mark and Kim Millon: 'Authors and some aspects of Food & Wine'

Saturday 12 May

10.00 am AGM

12.30 for 1pm   Annual Luncheon
                Guest of Honour: Rachel Billington
3.15 pm   Keith Salter: 'George Orwell'
5.00 pm   Demonstration of Word Processors by Devon
          Computers
7.30 pm   Dinner
9.00 pm   Jean Stubbs: 'The Writers' Chip - her Word
          Processor Merlin'

Sunday 13 May

10.00 am Coffee & Conversation before we all depart North,
          South and West.
          Don't go East, it's wet and salty.

(Remember that the venue was Torquay if you are baffled by the last remark!)

Inevitably there had to be a talk on George Orwell in 1984, and even the talks that appear unrelated had their place in the overall theme. Terry Tapp's 'Communications' lecture outlined the need for a 'New Concept about Education, Creativity and Work' from his viewpoint as Tutor/Organizer of the Workers' Educational Association. It was certainly controversial and had people talking until long after dinner. The food and wine talk by Marc and Kim Millon might have sounded conservative enough, but they were great exponents of the new technology who made good use of visual aids and demonstrated how they thought that the word processor would put the author in total control. They could now, they said, plan, package and prepare the text and pictures of their cookery books so precisely that 'no editor in the world could remove one full stop'.[17] If only.

When it came to the demonstration of computers - well, word processors in those days - the membership had been helpfully briefed in advance through a newsletter article by Michael Hartland. He tried patiently to explain to the most reactionary and suspicious member that word processors were nothing to be afraid of and could in fact be an enormously helpful servant to the writer:

What is a Word Processor? There are four pieces of equipment -

KEYBOARD - a normal QWERTY typewriter-style keyboard with some extra control keys.

A VIDEO DISPLAY UNIT (VDU) - like a small TV screen on which the text appears as it is typed.

A SMALL DESKTOP COMPUTER - which stores what is typed on small portable discs, and subsequently enables it to be revised very quickly and simply.

A PRINTER.

How does it work?
Despite this battery of electronic paraphernalia, it is all quite simple to use. You type your text on the keyboard and it appears, not on paper, but on the VDU - mine displays about half a page at a time, black on white. As you type you can pick up and correct errors and edit the text, if you want, while the material is still in the computer. Once you are satisfied with what has been typed, you press a control key and it is stored on a disc in the computer. You can then print it out automatically on the Printer, from which it emerges looking like typing done on a high quality electric machine - while you have a cup of coffee or do something else.

Or you can just store it on the disc, to be edited or printed out later.

A whole book can be stored on six or seven discs, the box for which takes up about two inches of shelf space.

What are the advantages?
A Word Processor has one enormous advantage over conventional typing, particularly for an author. Revision and editing of a manuscript is unbelievably fast and easy. All you do is retrieve the chapter or section stored on the disc, then 'scroll' through to the part you want to change, press a key and type out the change.

The rest of the text automatically adjusts and stays put. Gone are the miseries of scissors and paste, tippex, white tapes, let alone all the dreary and time-wasting checking of passages not changed but re-typed as a result of other alterations.

You can change the text as much as you like, fast, and without any need to check the rest which you haven't touched. The output is always well-typed and always presents a good appearance.

What are the drawbacks?

The biggest drawback is cost. My computer is a Digital (DEC) Rainbow 100 which has a large capacity - it can be used for all sorts of other things also e.g. Accounts and Stored Research Data. The PRINTER is a FACIT daisywheel 4560 which produces an attractive result. I have six daisywheels, giving a choice of typefaces.

One can get cheaper versions of both, but I found them unsatisfactory when trying equipment out before I bought. The equipment in my set-up cost getting on for £4,000, which is not cheap.

Even if you go for the LEAST expensive gear available, it will cost thousands rather than hundreds of pounds. Prices may well fall in a few years, as the technology develops, but there is no sign of it yet.

The only other general drawbacks are:

You, or your secretary, have to learn to use it. Once you've mastered the computer programmes and its controls it becomes easy, but it takes time and practice.

You will still have to be able to type. A Word Processor won't turn you into a touch typist if you aren't one already, although it makes it simple to correct your mistakes.

The whole set-up takes up considerably more space than a typewriter. Mine has taken over a whole room.[18]

I have quoted this article at length because it illustrates vividly the sheer *pace* of change in our age. Remember this was less than twenty years ago - word processors at £4,000 plus, six or seven disks needed for a book, and the whole concept needing such careful explanation. The report on the 1984 word processing demonstration sounds equally quaint, describing early keyboards and VDUs that had to use an electronic typewriter as a printer, and a top-of-the-range model that 'will do anything except sing an operatic aria' which came in at £3,500 plus, with disks at £40 for a box of ten, and an estimated annual maintenance cost of £450. Nowadays we would definitely expect our computers to be able to deliver a whole opera on CD - and print in full colour, as well as connecting us to the Internet and carrying our e-mail - for a quarter of the price.

In 1984 Jean Stubbs gave a humorous and enthusiastic talk on the sheer usefulness of the new machines to the writer, describing her developing love affair with her own 'Merlin', which could hold a million words of research notes for her historical novels. But for all that, many of the members remained sceptical and the divide widened between those who embraced the new technology and those who resisted change with a strong affection for the ways they were used to. Most writers now accept without question the advantages offered by IT - in fact two committee members were recently heard admitting that they had lost the knack of writing creatively with pen and paper - but there will always be some who know they perform best in the old way. Laurie Lee claimed he could only write with a soft pencil on the back of recycled BBC scripts. Christopher Fry will never abandon the small portable manual that has served him so well, and John Paxton was only half joking when he referred to retirement as 'hanging up his quill...' On the whole, though, a change of massive proportions had come over the business of writing, and come over it with astonishing speed.

The chairman at the futuristic 1984 Congress had been Nancy Tregenna-Piggott, but family pressures prevented her from carrying out her full term and a third lady ascended to the Chair for 1985 and 1986. This was Rosemary Jeffery, who combined local journalism around Plymouth with sterling work for the Soroptimists. Not many people conversing with this gentle, erudite lady of letters realize that she also just happens to be a nuclear physicist. After Rosemary, Simon Rocksborough Smith and David Keep each held the Chair for their allotted two years, and it was during this era that another idea which had been simmering for ages finally reached the boil.

The notion of holding a competition, primarily to attract new members, had been mooted since the days of William Kean Seymour, but nobody had ever got down to the business of organization. When the decision was taken to go ahead in 1986, the committee members discovered just how much work is involved in such an apparently simple exercise. They had expected a time-consuming job in reading the entries, but perhaps had not grasped what a business it would be to set the rules and then to obtain those entries by spreading the publicity. The number of entries received was not as great as had been hoped and the committee even thought of abandoning the whole project, but in the end there were enough entries to give the judges a busy time. As the object was specifically to attract younger members, its success was debatable: only in WCWA circles could a winner approaching her fortieth birthday still be regarded as young blood! It did, however, solve one perennial problem for some time to come. Having won the competition, I discovered that the prize seemed to be a very long stint as the secretary. The idea of running another competition, possibly for poetry, is raised again from time to time, but so far no-one on the committee has been able to commit the time required to run such an exercise well.

President Fry

As the 1980s came to their conclusion it occurred to various committee members that a significant anniversary was approaching. Christopher Fry had become president of the WCWA when Henry Williamson had retired in 1965: 1990 would therefore be his twenty-fifth year in office.

It is difficult to know where to begin to describe all that Christopher Fry has done and been for the WCWA. He has been no passive figurehead, looking on from an exalted distance or dipping in and out of annual lunches from time to time: he has always been a real presence, taking the interest of a friend in all the doings of the Association and its members. It was Christopher who was there at the emergency meeting in 1972, when the Association could so easily have folded, advising against dissolution and suggesting positive change. It is Christopher who can summon up guests of honour and distinguished speakers at the shortest notice - 'If Christopher calls', one very famous actor responded, 'I am yours to command.' His name on our headed paper was enough to make a hotel halve its prices in order to get our business - it turned out that the manager's wife was named Jennet after the heroine of *The Lady's not for Burning*. He has been a member since the very first days and he was a founder vice-president, and in his ninety-fourth year he has seen us into a new millennium.

In the first place, Christopher is undoubtedly a very great writer whose work as a dramatist has made him one of the classics and whose reputation is worldwide. In January 1988 his eightieth birthday was marked by a tribute from the great theatre critic himself, John Trewin:

> No dramatist of his day has written himself so surely into the theatrical record of the period. His most recent work, *One Thing More;* or, *Caedmon Construed*, written, performed and published in 1986, showed that time had not dulled the man who wrote, during an extraordinary passage nearly four decades ago, such plays as *The Lady's not for Burning, Venus Observed, A Sleep of Prisoners* and *The Dark is Light Enough.*
>
> To know Christopher Fry is to recognise his blend of extreme modesty and artistic integrity, his entirely original slant on any speech or scene, and the personal sense of humour unmatched among dramatists of our century: certainly by none who have written in verse. We have to agree with his publishers who say that one of his achievements has been 'the long-needed re-instatement of the comic spirit in English poetic drama'.
>
> Far more than this. I suggest that those of you who have not done so give yourselves the pleasure of reading *The Firstborn,* an Old Testament drama that does not trail away on a cirrus cloud of pseudo-Biblical idiom. Or, say, *Curtmantle,* or *One Thing More.* Fry's publishers talk also of the 'metaphysical content' of his plays; we should remember his depth of seriousness, a quality that has been glossed over too often.
>
> It is a blessed relief to hear, or read, Fry in a world where the music of English speech has been endangered far too long. Only the other night I was caught up again, at an amateur performance of *A Sleep of Prisoners,* by these wholly unadorned lines that I recalled quoting after I had first heard them thirty-six years ago:
>
> > Good has no fear;

Good is itself, whatever comes.
It grows, and makes and bravely
Persuades beyond all tilt of wrong:
Stronger than anger, wiser than strategy,
Enough to subdue cities and men
If we believe in it with the courage of truth.

Ever since I heard Fry in the theatre for the first time I have felt like Edgar in *King Lear* when he says, 'Mark the high noises'. Fry has restored sound and meaning that may delight even those (bless them) who would define poetry as 'the expression in a generalised and abstract way of the dynamic relation of the ego to the elements of outer reality symbolised by words'.

Really, it is best to take the plays as they come and glory in them without bothering about 'the dynamic relation of the ego'. By this time, I daresay, many of you will have heard a radio revival of *Venus Observed* (1950), the autumn comedy of the four 'seasonal' plays, with a depth and haunting sense that no mere recital of the narrative can indicate. It begins and ends marvellously, and midway is the now famous speech for the girl Perpetua in which she asks why a sentence, once begun, need ever end: 'Phrase in linking phrase, with commas falling / As airily as lime-flowers'.

As I look back now, I remember Evans, Gielgud, Olivier, Clunes and Scofield in some of his plays; nights of rapture; poetry on many levels, never shouting that it is blank verse; phrase in linking phrase; occasions that must long outlive the transient, defiant ugliness of much hastily lauded work of the same period. Let us, then, be grateful always for Christopher Fry, and (no need for me to say this) let the West Country Writers' Association be ever grateful for his presence and his sustained friendliness across the years.[19]

Christopher's plays have been ground-breaking, and, as John Trewin emphasised, their humour and the love of life expressed in them has been matched by a philosophical seriousness. Over the years of his presidency we have been blessed by the opportunity to hear many of his thoughts on life and literature expressed in the lectures and papers he has given us.

Looking for a Language is perhaps the one most directly concentrated on the struggles of the artist to find true expression - and it contains Bob Cooper's favourite quotation, '...the sensation of overtaking what had always been waiting for us'.[20] How characteristic of Christopher's philosophy that the struggle should be seen in such a positive light.

Christopher's talk on the Brontes, *Genius, Talent and Failure,* leads us not only into his sympathetic understanding of the lesser Brontes, but into an exploration of the question of creativity itself. Why did so much literary ability manifest itself in the different members of one family? And as it was one family, sharing a common nurture and environment, how could it manifest itself so differently in each child? In fact, what *is* creativity, and why should it occur at all?

Christopher's own creative history is outlined in a talk which he gave exclusively to the WCWA at Torquay in 1995, entitled *The Early Days*. The sobering truth that this revealed is that Christopher felt he has had to be pushed, coaxed and driven into writing by the encouragement (and occasional bullying) of friends: left to himself, he would never have considered his writing good enough. Laurence Olivier was one of those who kept him at it by commissioning *Venus Observed* and then nagging him, in terms of increasing desperation, to finish it. He told us this amusing story in another paper in 1996. How very thrilling it is for us to rub shoulders with someone who was on 'Larry and Vivien' terms with two of the most star-spangled film stars of their generation.

Christopher's vein of humour and his sheer delight in life shine through two readings he has given us from his favourite books, *Turning the Pages* and *Things Come Across.* There is no substitute for hearing these selections read in Christopher's own rich, characterful voice. More than once, questioners from the audience have queried whether he was ever on the professional stage himself (he gives the answer in a very funny story about the shipwreck scene from *The Tempest,* his first and last foray on to the boards) because words seem to gain so much through his reading of them. In *Turning the Pages* he showed us how he could find poetry and food for thought even in the dark days of the war. As a Quaker and a pacifist, Christopher's war work involved digging mud out of the bombed-out sewers of Islington to be transported onto Thames barges for disposal.

Christopher, in a wartime letter to Phyl, his wife, turns the wet, yellow sewage mud into a golden transformation scene, shot through with the humorous remarks of passers-by. 'It's a shame', said one man carefully negotiating the slippery planks across the diggings, 'You ought to be earning £3 a week!' Later a poem came from this experience when Christopher pronounced himself grateful, in the face of so much death and destruction all around, '...to be the hand that digs the muck - and not the muck I dig'.

A great dramatist, a thoughtful lecturer whose talks have been part of the Association's history, a president who has been most diligent and conscientious in his oversight of affairs: Christopher Fry has been all these - and yet there is one thing more. Above all these, Christopher has been a real friend to the Association and to its members as individuals. This friendship has been a great privilege, and its warmth and sincerity are the reasons why, within the WCWA, Christopher is regarded not just with respect for his work and gratitude for his presidency, but with genuine personal affection. So it was that in 1990, his twenty-fifth anniversary at the helm was marked in Exeter by a delightful evening of excerpts from his plays, read or acted out by various members of the Association and by local talent from the Devon area, and interspersed by musical items from Clyst Valley Choral Society. Janet Green's reading of Pharoah's Sister was a highlight of the evening. David Keep, chairman at the time, arranged this lovely offering for Christopher, who had brought along his old friend George Baker to share what was in effect a mini-festival of Fry (and George, being a scriptwriter and cookery writer as well as an actor, was promptly recruited). Many warm words were spoken, not least Harry Guest's poem of tribute:

THE DRAMA'S THE OBJECT
for Christopher Fry - 5 May 1990

Words fail the tribute-bringer
for here on the shelf are stored
such images that keep their fire
igniting chancel, studio or stage.

A lad dazzled by prophecy
hauled his mother over the green
domes of the downs. Alien,
uneasy farmers witnessed
the advent of the thunder-cloud
cancelled by seraphs.
They moved on a land in flux
where leaf becoming rock
turns into flame - where man
breaks from his brittle
case of ordinariness
to surprise us with the brilliance of his wings.

One performer
eyeing the love-star in an ageing sky
savours the paradox of time
where the heart finds humour in its end-stopped
    cage
and voyagers walk the plank of their desires
blindfold, smiling.

For laughter saved
the lithe witch from the pyre
as wryness rescued
a countess from her loneliness.

Four captives shared a dream
and the dream became words
ringing among us.

Images evade the tribute-bringer.
The bones
of gratitude alone
remain.
                  Harry Guest

'Laughter saved the lithe witch', and Christopher's ability to find humour in the world, and truth in humour, are encapsulated in a note he wrote for the WCWA newsletter in 1978:

A friend tells me that there is a librarian's notice in a West Country Library which reads: BOOKS MUST BE STAMPED OUT. Before or after burning, I wonder?[21]

When Christopher reached the age of 90 he was again celebrated by his WCWA friends, at the annual lunch in Plymouth 1997. All four aspects of his writing were included. The theatre was represented when George Baker returned with his wife, Louie Ramsay, and Shakespearean actress Barbara Leigh-Hunt, to give readings from the plays - at last a chance for Barbara to do one of her favourite speeches by Jennet whom she felt she was, alas, too old ever to play on stage. Bob Cooper read that favourite passage of his from *Looking for a Language* to represent Christopher's prose writings, and John Bayliss read one of his occasional poems - with the remark that he had often urged Christopher to collect and publish these lesser-known treasures of his non-dramatic poetry.

Translation is the fourth branch of Christopher's work: his version of Anouilh's *Ring Round the Moon* is justly famous, and an RSC director is said to have called his *Peer Gynt* 'much better than Ibsen'. His translation of Rostand's *Cyrano de Bergerac* provided the typically life-affirming tone:

> This is what life's about!
> Not lifting the frail glass to a cautious lip
> But slaking our heartfelt thirst by drinking deep![22]

Another long-standing member, Adele Ziolkowska, was also celebrating her ninetieth birthday at that lunch, and celebration became its appropriate theme. 'A life-long, life-imbibing celebrant', Christopher's phrase from his poem in praise of Laurie Lee, very nicely sums up his own philosophy, for his writings ring with the love of life. Nothing escapes him, from the tiniest details of the natural world to the huge issues of war and peace, and it sounds very much as if Christopher himself is speaking through the lines of his last hero, Caedmon:

> I've been shown such a universe! These not-
> so many years, what vastness has filled them, though
> I made so little of it. Before I am lost and found

in God's love I should like to make one thing more,
a song or half-song or no-song, but
one thing more in thanksgiving for having
seen and known and lived and died.[23]

The End of a Century

When, in 1991, the WCWA reached its fortieth anniversary, Christopher Fry and Laurie Lee sat side by side at the annual lunch as they had done so often over the preceding years. Another milestone had been reached: WCWA had risen phoenix-like from decline in the seventies and had broadened its member base in the eighties and all seemed well established and set fair. Cake was eaten, champagne consumed, and kind speeches made. But, after all the energy of the eighties, the nineties yellowed into a more elegiac phase. So many of the old familiar faces were being lost, one after another. Antony Hippisley Coxe had died in 1988, and Rosalind Wade a year later. Joan Purgold had just taken over the reins as treasurer when she died very suddenly in 1990: her loss was grievously felt by her friends. In November 1990 John Keast, secretary and treasurer of the early days, also died, and the same year saw the loss of another founder father, John Trewin. In fact 1990 was a crossroads for the Association because the congress at Exeter that year was, as it turned out, the last to be attended by Frank Littlewood and his sister Sue Roseveare who died within a year of each other soon afterwards.

Few people attending the 1990 annual lunch would have dreamt that it would also be the last congress for Bryan Little. His death came very suddenly in the winter of 1992, but he had been prevented from attending Salisbury 1991 or Penzance 1992, so the toast which he proposed to Exeter in 1990 was his final public word on our behalf. He had diligently continued to attend committee meetings almost up to the time of his death, and our last sighting of him was in October 1992, at Sea Mills Station after a committee meeting at the Bristol home of Meryl Macdonald Bendle, almost missing his train in his usual enthusiasm to impart knowledge - about the engineering feats involved in the construction of that particular length of railway line, as I recall. This was typical Bryan: a fund of information about *anything* to do with Bristol, Bath or Exeter, not just the pretty buildings and soaring spires. At his Requiem Mass in Clifton Cathedral the preacher paid tribute to his role in the foundation of the building in which we stood. Bryan had patiently used his position in local affairs to smooth the path of planning permission, design and construction even though this modern structure was not at all to his personal taste. The man steeped in Wren and Pugin could yet see that a church, like a society, could not live by only looking backwards. In Clifton Cathedral Bryan left his very real mark on a city whose fabric had meant so much to him, and with his death we lost the last link with the three people whose 'triangular correspondence' at the end of the 1940s had built the foundations of the WCWA.

But life - and deaths - went on. Ex-secretary Elizabeth Churcher died in the same year as Bryan, and in 1995 another name synonymous with rural life in the West Country was lost upon the death of Ralph Whitlock. One of the founder members, he had delighted generations of radio audiences as 'Farmer Whitlock' in the 'Cowleaze Farm' broadcasts on Children's Hour. Janet Green remembered fondly the special quality they held:

> You have to be my contemporary in age to appreciate the nostalgia that his name conjures. I can still see myself, in the early 1950s, aged about 12, plaiting my long pigtails whilst listening to the wireless before setting out for the Grammar School. 'Thought for the Day', the News, and Ralph Whitlock talking about the countryside.
>
> I have always been a townie. Seaside towns preferably. Blackpool was the town of my childhood. There was something, however, in Ralph Whitlock's country brogue which mesmerised me; something so comfortable, comforting and timeless. I brushed my hair and felt that all was well with the world.[24]

Ralph was thrilled to have been elected a vice-president of the Association he had loved for so long, and he was able to see his name on the headed paper shortly before he died.

The list of vice-presidents on the headed paper was dwindling fast -

only four names from the 'green paper' still remained, whereas the committee had stipulated in 1969 that there should be eight vice-presidents at any one time. Of course, this being the WCWA, there were usually either more or less but rarely the prescribed number. The intention was, however, that election to vice-presidency should be seen as 'a signal honour' awarded for 'special service to the literary profession or the Association',[25] with a new vice-president created only to fill the vacancy left by the death of a previous incumbent. Bryan Little had accordingly been made vice-president in 1973 on the death of L. P. Hartley. Laurie Lee and Charles Causley had already been vice-presidents for a long time, and Frank Littlewood and Bob Cooper had been similarly honoured for their services to the Association as vacancies arose. With vice-presidential numbers floundering, the 1990s saw a spate of new creations. Victor Bonham-Carter and E. V. Thompson were both elected in 1993 as a mark of their services to literature and to the West Country.

Victor, another founder member, had one foot planted firmly in either camp as he tells us in his autobiography *What Countryman, Sir?* On the one hand he has had the experience of coaxing a living from the uncompromising Exmoor soil when, returning from war service, he took up farming at Brushford, near Dulverton, at the age of thirty-four. These days it is impossible to think about Exmoor and the Exmoor Society without the name of Victor Bonham-Carter coming to mind. On the other hand he has performed distinguished service to literature with two books in particular: one the official history of the Dartington Hall Estate in Devon which has contributed so much to the artistic and literary life of the West Country, and the other a comprehensive history of the writing business, *Authors by Profession*, a tour de force commissioned by the Society of Authors in 1963. This was a book which was to grow and grow until there were moments when Victor wished he had never started it, but the final result was a landmark of which Michael Holroyd said:

> It needed all Victor's military and farming skills, as well as his more academic expertise, and perhaps the muscle of a coal miner, to grapple with and finally quell the monstrosity of paper work. The archivist was lowered into the basement and was not seen again for several years.[26]

Victor is one of the stalwarts of the writing profession to whom all professional authors owe a great debt of gratitude. He had worked hard for the Society of Authors, the Royal Literary Fund, and the campaign for PLR. And like all true West Country writers he has his idiosyncrasy - you will never see Victor far from his cats.

Ernest Thompson is so well known by his initials, E. V., that he once found a bookshop assistant who was convinced he was a she, called 'Evie'. His colourful career has taken him all over the world in a variety of exciting professions - serving on gunboats in Hong Kong, chief of security for the Civil Aviation Authority in the former Rhodesia - but he gave it all up to return to Cornwall and do what he really wanted, full time writing (augmented by sweeping floors at the local clay works). It was these years of struggling that led to his eventual runaway success, because it was while doing the menial jobs at the clay works that he really came to know the Cornish characters who were to inspire his books. Living on Bodmin Moor in two derelict cottages surrounded only by wild moorland and deserted mine workings, he found the material for *Chase the Wind*, the novel that was to establish him as a writer. Cornwall has always been his material, because Cornwall, in Ernest's eyes, breeds characters.

Cornwall also bred a Patron for the WCWA in the early nineties when the congress was held at Penzance. For the first time the committee had decided that the Sunday mornings of congress weekend were being under-used, and that we ought to organize an outing to some local place of interest. Staying at a hotel on the waterfront overlooking Mount Bay, where else could we go but St. Michael's Mount? Lord St. Levan most graciously invited us to visit him at his castle, for drinks after morning service in the church which tops the Mount. He even sent his boats for us - because one problem about visiting the island is negotiating the tides: at high tide the causeway disappears and St. Michael's Mount is completely cut off.

That will always be a memorable day in Association folklore, not just because St. Michael's Mount is so lovely and so fascinating, but also because of the people who were there in all their characteristic West Country eccentricity. Getting the WCWA afloat proved no mean task. Not all were in the first flush of youth and there was one lady in particular who was so disabled that she could scarcely walk, despite the aid of two sticks, let alone climb into the boat. But she was not to be defeated. 'Lord St. Levan will be expecting to meet me', she declared, 'I must not let him down', and we ended up with two passing members of the public lifting her bodily and carrying her into the boat.

The problems didn't end there. On disembarkation there was a long walk down the quay which nearly finished her off, and *then* the climb began - up and up, on stony footpaths of ever-increasing steepness, to the pinnacle of the isle where the castle towers above. It was quite a challenging climb for several of us, but for this lady it was a physical impossibility. Employees of the estate, working at the gift shop on the quay, pleaded with her not even to make the attempt. They came out and tried to reason with her. We were beginning to gather a crowd. It was only when a large man in an official uniform came along and actually forbade her to go any further that she was talked round, and the kind ladies from the shop thought she looked so upset that they took her into the Visitor Centre and sat her down with a nice cup of tea for a free viewing of the tourist video, while those who had been trying to remonstrate with her went puffing uphill to catch up with the rest of the party.

It was all worth it when we reached the top. The view back to the mainland, the unique gardens moulded out of the rocky hillside, the castle itself with its haunted history were all equalled by the kindly generosity of Lord St. Levan's reception. We promptly recruited him. Moved by this extraordinary day, chairman Dorothy Stiffe and public relations officer Janet Green began to hatch the idea of creating a Patron for the Association. Lord St. Levan accepted the invitation and has been our first and only Patron ever since.

Another face from that day lives in the memory. It was Peggy Loosemore Jones who bore the brunt of looking after that difficult disabled member on her wayward course to St. Michael's Mount. Always thoughtful and kind, Peggy saw her through the day and safely home, consequently missing a lot of the excitement herself. Peggy was both an excellent poet and a great encourager of others, helping many people find their voice at her local writers' circle. Peggy was as well known in the literary circles of Teesside, where she lived for many years, as she was in

Barnstaple, but her roots were in North Devon and her sense of family continuity echoes through this elegaic poem:

THE LAST ON THE BEACH

We'll be last on the beach
I see, as always.
Always a sandcastle
Cannot be left
Till the incoming tide
Has filled up its moat
And swirled it away.
Other folk leave
With deckchairs and surfboards,
Carrying pushchairs
Or dragging their children.
And as they depart
The sky becomes suddenly
Flashy with seagulls.
Clattering, swooping
They skim to the sand
And scavenge the leavings.
Lundy hangs low
On a silver horizon,
Part of my childhood
And part of my children's.
Now it's my grandchildren
Digging and channelling,
Last on the beach.
The seagulls scream
And the hooded crows gather.
One lone pigeon
Potters and pecks.
Taking possession
As everyone leaves,
They'll be last on the beach,
As always.
Peggy Loosemore Jones

Peggy's death in the nineties was another loss to the Association, as was the death of Freda Bromhead, also a long-standing member and superb poet whose work has strangely failed to meet the recognition it deserves. She was over ninety when she gave a reading to the Cheltenham Congress in 1994, enthralling her audience and seeming to gather new strength when she stood up to read.

Freda had lived an amazing life. As a young girl she worked in the pioneering days of cinema, from the silent movies to the establishment of the Gaumont chain, before going off to Hollywood as secretary to the novelist G. B. Stern. She wrote a novel herself and had several short stories broadcast and published, but it is first and foremost as a poet that we knew her, after she settled in Bristol in 1970. All her poems combine observation of the real things around her with a sense of their deeper significance, and this poem - very definitely rooted in Bristol but speaking of infinite possibilities - is no exception.

BALLOON FIESTA
Bristol - 18.08.84

Making us all look up
These quiet presences,
With their lack of menace,
Inexplicably there -
Unexpectedly gone -
Returning, are as petals
From variegated flowers,
Unplayed musical notes
Grouped on the treble stave.
Their gentle use of air
Their under-emphasis
Float them across the sky,
As enigmatic thoughts
Float into consciousness,
Reaching our street-bound minds,
Making us all look up.
Freda Bromhead

The West Country Writers' Association

Forty years on from the Association's initiation it is not surprising that the loss of old members overshadowed the 1990s, but at the same time the Association was actually going through a very healthy period of growth. After the fortieth anniversary in Salisbury, the congress travelled to all four corners of its territory: Penzance in the south, Bournemouth in the east, Cheltenham in the north, and then back west to Torquay.

David Keep had been followed as chairman by Dorothy Stiffe, a prize-winning member of the Society of Women Writers and Journalists, whose previous years as secretary had made her one of the most loved incumbents of the office. Always a good listener, Dorothy's sensitivity to the needs of other people ensured that her congresses were friendly, enjoyable experiences for all comers. No-one was ignored or passed by in her term of office.

She in turn was followed by John Paxton, recently retired as editor of the prestigious Statesman's Year-Book, experienced committee member of PEN, and author of an impressively long list of reference books. During his leadership the Association consolidated and regrouped after the loss of the old faces; loose ends were tidied up and old problems solved - not least the problem of the book exhibition.

This had been an integral feature of every congress from the very first: professional writers needed and appreciated a shop window for their work. Increasingly, however, it was becoming difficult to find a bookshop willing to volunteer a window, or even a couple of shelves, as changes in the world of publishing were resulting in a new generation of bookshops.

The small, old-fashioned independent bookseller running the sort of business that Christopher Milne describes in *The Path through the Trees* was becoming rare. The big names proliferated and ate up many small bookshops through their huge buying power, while the conglomerate publishing houses became less and less keen to provide small numbers of members' titles on a sale-or-return basis. Cost-conscious managers of the new stores took a dim view of the amount of work involved in setting up an exhibition and the expense of returning unsold copies. Sometimes the WCWA exhibition found itself allotted a dark corner on the back stairs, and on one occasion received just a few hours' notice that the bookshop had no intention of returning unsold books to the publishers, and would dispose of any that were not immediately collected by their authors.

Instead of moaning that things weren't what they used to be, John Paxton solved the problem by starting the in-house book exhibition at the congress hotel. With the help of his wife Joan, the first do-it-yourself book exhibition was mounted at Cheltenham in 1994 and it has gone from strength to strength since. The Paxtons had plenty of experience to fall back on, having in 1950 established 'The Cotswold Book Room' in Wotton-under-Edge - one independent bookseller which has not been swallowed up and is still going strong today. The in-house book exhibition has been a very popular innovation, allowing more space and leisure for looking at the books without even the need to walk into town to do so. Once again the Association adapted to overcome the changing conditions of the time.

During the first half of the nineties, congress attendances had been gradually increasing year on year until the Association began to be the victim of its own success, outgrowing many of the characterful country hotels which had hosted weekends in the past. For 1996, with Bob Cooper in the Chair (he had been secretary and vice-president, but never chairman before) it was decided to think big and hold the congress in Bristol.

It was the first time for twenty years that the WCWA had been there, the high cost of hotels in this prosperous city having proved a deterrent since the days when the old Royal Hotel had offered such a bargain for three years running. This time, the biggest and most expensive hotel in the whole city, the newly refurbished Swallow Royal, offered to slash its prices for us because of Christopher Fry's name on the headed paper.

Bob was soon back in the swing of things and using his skill to talk famous names into coming as guests, so the programme that year featured a distinguished line-up. Talks by Christopher Fry, Melvyn Bragg and Debbie Moggach preceded an unforgettable annual luncheon where John Mortimer was guest of honour at a top table shining with literary talent. An international hotel in a big city with good communications proved a popular venue, and the attendance was a record. Over one hundred and twenty members and guests sat down to that lunch in Bristol and enjoyed the wit of the scheduled speakers as well as some unscheduled extra treats - Christopher Fry reading his poem 'Of Laurie Lee' in honour of Laurie's eightieth birthday, and Laurie's gallant response when he rose from his seat, took Christopher's hand, and raised it to his lips. It was one of those rare moments.

We had grown used to Laurie's presence at annual lunches: like Christopher, he just always seemed to be there. He had become a member long before the appearance of *Cider with Rosie* in 1959. Laurie famously wrote his own blurb for the book's jacket - 'sure to become a classic' - and the founding fathers clearly shared his faith in his ability, enrolling him many years before his rise to fame. By 1971 he had been made a vice-president for his services to literature, and though he was not the sort of person to sit on committees or attend meetings, he was very rarely absent from the annual luncheon, always accompanied by his wife, Kathy. In 1987, when Laurie was not able to get to Weymouth, I well remember Adele Ziolkowska settling herself in an armchair in the lounge after lunch and proclaiming, 'Oh, isn't there something *missing* when Laurie isn't here!'

From time to time an eager committee would try to pin him down to giving a formal talk but that was not Laurie's way. All invitations were politely declined in his chunky handwriting, usually with the unlikely excuse that he was no good at public speaking. Everybody knew, though, that while he insisted that he was not going to make a speech, he would always rise to his feet at the end of proceedings and delight everyone with an impromptu, sparkling cameo.

Even on a rare occasion when he missed the annual lunch he still managed to raise a laugh when he sent a telephone message to the assembly. He meant to send greetings to the immortal Christopher Fry, but the girl who took the message was not the world's best speller, and rendered his telephone message as 'Greetings to the *immoral* Christopher'.

Laurie always kept the committee on its toes, resisting their attempts to round him up into the formal sherry reception for honoured guests before luncheon, and preferring to find his own way to the bar for a more convivial beer. Many's the time he had to be cajoled into coming to meet the mayor. Once he was there, though, he never failed to charm the most bland of civic dignitaries, and however brief the encounter he always had a way of making people feel better about themselves after talking to him. He was so very famous, almost mythical, and yet he would remember your name.

Like Henry Williamson, even at his most famous Laurie retained a particular affection for the WCWA and displayed remarkable loyalty in his attendance. It was always a great boost for members to be treated as his friend and fellow-writer; well known for his depressed moods in the dark days of winter he always joked that the springtime lunch of the WCWA marked his 'annual rejuvenation', the warmth of his fellow-members' welcome encouraging him to put away all thoughts of obituaries for another year.

'The well-loved stranger' would never be pushed into taking the limelight, even if he enjoyed it when he took it for himself. When he reached his approximately eightieth birthday - he liked to be as enigmatic about the date of his birth as about the rest of his private life - he stubbornly refused to be guest of honour at the annual luncheon or to let the Association make any official fuss of him.

In the end his birthday tribute was something far more precious, the poem written for him by Christopher Fry which, because a touch of flu forced Christopher to go home before the annual lunch at Torquay in 1995, was not actually read to him by the author until that magical day at Bristol in 1996.

Laurie, Valerie Grove tells us, was 'dumbfounded', and wrote a thank you letter to Christopher of a warmth that is very moving to those who were at that lunch in 1996 - 'Dear friend, you have been kinder to me than I can find thanks for, or the merit to deserve it'[27] - especially with the hindsight that it was to be his last WCWA appearance.

Next year, at Plymouth in 1997 where the ninetieth birthday of Christopher Fry was being celebrated, a card was signed by everyone to be sent to Laurie, absent because of illness.

He never did see the card, because he died in May within days of that congress, and the poem which Christopher had written for his eightieth birthday became the centrepiece of the memorial service at St. James's, Piccadilly, where the great and the good of literary life gathered to celebrate his memory.

OF LAURIE LEE

'Born I was to meet with Age,
And to walk life's pilgrimage' -
   (That's Robert Herrick.)
'But I'll spend my coming hours,
Drinking wine, and crowned with flowers' -
   (Sang that Devon cleric.)

'Far-fetched with tales of other worlds and ways,
My skin well-oiled with wines of the Levant' -
   (That's Laurie Lee.)
But how the hell is one to celebrate
A life-long, life-imbibing celebrant?
   (That's simply Me.)

Treading the grapes of time and people
He made that earth-engaging tipple
   His vintage Slad.
Then with his music charmed the sun
Of Mexico, Tuscany and Spain
   And Trinidad.

But still I find my eager feet
Return to Slad to attend the Whitsun Treat,
   Standing to gowp at
The headlong charge of children and our Laurie
In triumph past the bullying Walt Kerry
   Sprawled in a cow-pat.

I like to imagine at that Whitsun Fair
The gift of tongues was hovering in the air
   Waiting to stoop
Headlong with equal triumph, Leeward bound,
To snatch him up into a field of sound
   Laurelled and cock-a-hoop.

> And when the pilgrimage is made,
> The shadow meeting with the shade,
> The graver music will be purling still
> By Painswick stream and Birdlip Hill.
> *Christopher Fry*

Not long after Laurie's passing, another larger-than-life figure of the West Country, A. L. Rowse, died at the fine old age of 94. Unlike Laurie Lee he never attended WCWA congresses or lunches, but he had been a member from the very beginning and a vice-president for as long as anyone could remember (and he had *once* been lured to a regional lunch at the home of his Cornish neighbour, John Rowe) and the loss of two such eminent figures in swift succession had left the list of vice-presidents looking depleted again.

How do you replace such giants? The criteria for vice-presidency, 'special service to the literary profession or the association', were reflected in the four new vice-presidents created in 1998: Joanna Trollope, whose name was regularly topping the best sellers' list, and Rachel Billington, who had recently become president of English PEN, for their services to the literary profession; John Rowe and Geraldine Kaye for their outstanding contribution to the Association.

Bristol, Plymouth, Weymouth, and back to Exeter - and so the Association moved steadily towards the millennium and the goal of the fiftieth anniversary. The big Bristol Congress of 1996 was a hard act to follow, but the habit of attracting distinguished speakers went on, with Francis King, Margaret Drabble, Michael Holroyd, and Ann and Anthony Thwaite all joining the list of those who succumbed to the persuasive powers of Bob and his successors in the Chair.

Gloria Cottesloe, a good friend and loyal supporter of the Association, had hoped to relieve Bob of his duties in 1997 but was frustratingly prevented from doing so by the need to convalesce, so Frances Brown, who had first entranced her audience at the Bournemouth Congress in 1993 with the story of how she came to write about her colourful ancestry of fairground folk, was the next person to hold the office. She in turn is followed by John Harcup, chairman for the millennium and the fiftieth anniversary.

For some ten years past, apart from one short break in 1998, I have acted as secretary of the WCWA and, being so closely involved, it is a decade which I find hard to discuss with objective detachment. I feel I cannot end without listing some of those members who have always been there at congresses - and I regret that it can be no more than a list, space precluding the fuller acknowledgement that they all merit - and who make the WCWA what it is because of what they are. Firstly, they are friends, and secondly, they are people in whom the West Country spirit lives on like 'brandy burning on the Christmas pudding'.

Friday afternoon is the best bit of the congress for the secretary, with an air of cheerful chaos as everyone starts arriving at once and the reception area becomes a happy blur of smiling faces, greetings and kisses - like the family reunion of a large and decidedly singular family. From every corner of the expanded West Country they come.

The Isle of Wight contingent are usually among the first - Mollie Hince, prolific novelist and long-serving committee member, with husband Derek and guest Cecily Gould and fellow-member Raymond Allen. The Rowes are never far behind - John, historian and Cornish Bard, and his wife Constance who is famous for her pasties (especially the ones that are savoury at one end and sweet at the other). The Jefferys, Rosemary and Ron, also arrive from across the Tamar.

The arrivals tend to come in pairs because 'members' spouses' are always welcome to the congress: as Bob Cooper says, in his wide experience of writers' organizations, he has never known another at which husbands, wives, friends and family are made so much part of the proceedings. And more than once the secretary has been baled out in a crisis by the invaluable helpfulness of a member's husband or wife!

The familiar faces continue to appear: there are the Paxtons, and the Harcups, and of course the Coopers. Mayfair agent Gerald Pollinger arrives, usually by the same train as the poet John Bayliss and the Rocksborough Smiths. Then there's Frances and Henry Brown, David and Carolyn Keep, Janet Green, Ken Randall (who comes all the way from Carnforth), Pat Daly from Bath, ditto John Wroughton - historian of the Civil War in the West - and Dorothy Stiffe from Wales. Botanist Jean Paton knows everything there is to know about her specialism, the liverwort family. There is a whole contingent from Bristol, including Geraldine Kaye, Meryl Macdonald Bendle, Peter Macdonald, and the poet Pamela Gillilan. There are the ladies from Cheltenham - Florence Jackson, Jenery Howard, Joyce Richell, Eva Bailey, Audrey Andrews and assorted friends. From round about Plymouth come Helen Rowett, Angela Tuckett, Roy York and Barbara Fenton.

At some stage of the afternoon Christopher Fry arrives, with his driver Julie who has become part of the family. From a Dorset direction come novelists Caroline Stickland and Rosemary Ellerbeck aka Nicola Thorne, and from more easterly parts we have Margaret Bacon - our wonderful membership secretary who follows Olwen Reed, Jean Steward and Gillian Lindsay in the tradition of making new members feel at home - and Marina Oliver, our treasurer. Then there's Fay Sampson, Bill Pickard, Pam Sykes, Anne Ashurst, Evelyn Hilary Szydlowska, Brian le Messurier (when he isn't walking the four corners of the globe)... I could go on and on. The full list of our fiftieth anniversary membership is printed in Appendix III.

There are always some new members to be greeted, but there are always some faces missing, most recently Honor Allingham who, as Honor Butler, helped the Association through a tricky time in the 1970s. We miss the characters - Adele Ziolkowska, a stalwart attender up to the age of ninety, or Leslie Grinsell, who generally arrived in shorts having walked the distance from the station with a rucksack on his back. Now there *was* a character. A bank clerk and then a museum curator by day, he had a weekend life as an archaeologist, and his lifetime's achievement was to record, classify and map every single Bronze Age burial mound in southern England. He did it alone, and he was self-taught. He admitted that he struggled for ages to rewind his measuring tape until a chance meeting with someone who showed him that it would retract automatically. Leslie attended congress every year - though one always felt that he found fiction writers just a *little* lacking in gravitas - and he was always a striking figure. Even in death he caught the imagination, leaving provision in his will for a highly unusual wake in his beloved Mendips. After his cremation, his friends from the Bristol and Avon Archaeological Society enjoyed a meal at the *Castle of Comfort Inn* and then took his ashes in a burial urn 1,000 feet up on to one of Priddy Nine Barrows, where they were scattered to the winds of the West Country, and the urn smashed according to Bronze Age tradition. Leslie was one who kept the brandy burning on the Christmas pudding right to the very end.

Over fifty years the faces have changed, though some things never seem to alter. The arguments about recruitment and membership qualifications go on with a certain endearing familiarity now as they did in the fifties - perhaps even more so, with the rise of respectable self-publishing making it even more difficult than ever to dictate what constitutes a 'published' author. The congress still dominates the secretary's life, as it always has, with the annual struggle to find hotels, speakers and guests of honour, and get them all into the right place at the right time in spite of last-minute cancellations. There is still an ongoing difficulty in finding people willing to take office - especially as secretary. But these enduring features are balanced by those which must and have changed.

Publishing has changed. The sheer nuts and bolts of committing words on to paper - or disks - and getting them into printed form has changed out of all recognition between the days of the Westaway Press and this age of laser-printed camera-ready copy. The process of getting published has changed too as the old, nostalgic imprints coalesced into the giant publishing houses of today. It is now a truth universally acknowledged that, in the concentration on best sellers, a first-time author will find it harder to become published than in the days when Henry Williamson cheerfully admitted that 'one can sell old rope'. And as with the publishing houses, so with the booksellers, as traditional small bookshops have buckled under the buying power of the big chains. The Association evolved as a response to a problem, the problem of obtaining regular paper supplies after the war, and it has continued to respond to the ever-changing problems with which writers have been faced over the half century.

The WCWA has survived the vicissitudes of fifty years by re-inventing itself in times of crisis, holding on to the things that do matter, but adapting to cope with a changing world. Now we have a website and an e-mail address, and we are on the threshold of our Fiftieth Congress - to be

The West Country Writers' Association

held, suitably enough, at Dartington Hall, the West Country centre for arts and crafts in the heart of Devon. What does the future hold as the millennium turns and we move into the next fifty years of the West Country Writers' Association?

The West Country Writers' Association

Word Processed Letterhead of the 1990s

THE WEST COUNTRY WRITERS' ASSOCIATION
Patron: Lord St. Levan

President: CHRISTOPHER FRY
Vice Presidents: Charles Causley, Bob Cooper, Victor Bonham-Carter, E.V. Thompson

---

From the Secretary:
Anne Double - Malvern View, Garway Hill, HEREFORD HR2 8EZ. Phone & Fax: 01981 580495

And the Latest, customised Letterhead, printed in different colours for different officers.

The West Country Writers' Association
Patron: Lord St. Levan

President: CHRISTOPHER FRY
Vice Presidents: Charles Causley, Bob Cooper, Victor Bonham-Carter, E.V. Thompson
Rachel Billington, Geraldine Kaye, Joanna Trollope, John Rowe.

From the Secretary : Anne Double - Malvern View, Garway Hill, Hereford HR2 8EZ

The West Country Writers' Association

WCWA Rules

ASSOCIATION RULES ! O.K. !

AFTER "CHARIOTS OF FIRE", "LOCAL HERO" AND "GANDHI" THERE NOW FOLLOWS THE LONG AWAITED WEST COUNTRY EPIC: "REVISED RULES OF W.C.W.A. 1984" BRILLIANTLY SCRIPTED AND EDITED, PRODUCED AND DIRECTED, IT COMES FROM THE CUTTING ROOM (OF A.G.M.STUDIOS, TORQUAY) JUST AS BELOW :
CAST OF HUNDREDS OF MEMBERS PLEASE NOTE: THIS ONE LIKELY TO RUN AND RUN..

THE WEST COUNTRY WRITERS' ASSOCIATION : RULES 1984

1. The name of the Association shall be The West Country Writers' Association.

2. The object of the Association is, by the interchange of ideas, to foster the love of literature in the West Country.

3. Admission to membership of the Association shall be by invitation of the Committee. A full member shall be any adult who was born in or is living, working or studying in, or writing about, or for a reasonable period has lived, worked or studied in or written of the West Country, and is the author of at least one full-length published book or has had a substantial body of work published or produced in one or more of the other Media.

    An associate member may be any adult living, working or studying in, or doing work about the West Country, who for at least five years has been engaged in an occupation involved directly with writers and their profession, or who can show evidence that he or she is an aspiring and practising writer who expects to be able within a reasonable period to qualify for full membership, and so far has been published or produced to only a limited extent. Associate members shall have the same rights and privileges as full members, except that they shall not be entitled to vote at any Meeting or in any Ballot.

4. The annual subscription shall be agreed by the Annual General Meeting, and shall be paid by 1st. October, by Bankers Order where possible. Any member whose subscription has not been paid by 1st. January may be deemed to have resigned.

5. The Association shall have: A President and Vice-Presidents, who shall be members of the literary profession, and shall be chosen for their services thereto, and there shall be the following
                                                                Officers:
    A Chairman, to serve for one year, and then be eligible for re-election for no more than two further years.
    A Vice-Chairman, to serve in the same manner as the Chairman.
    An Honorary Secretary and an Honorary Treasurer, both to serve for one year, and to be eligible for re-election without limit.

6. There shall be a Committee, elected at the Annual General Meeting, consisting of the Officers, the immediate past-Chairman, and not less than eight nor more than fifteen full members of the Association. The Quorum shall be six members of the Committee, including at least two Officers. A bare majority of the members actually voting shall be sufficient to pass any resolution of the Committee. In the event of a tie the Chairman of the Meeting shall have a casting vote.

Rules 7 to 12 overleaf.......................

The West Country Writers' Association

...... Rules 7 to 12......

THE WEST COUNTRY WRITERS' ASSOCIATION : RULES 1984

Continued from page 3 ......

7. A General Meeting of the Association shall be held at least once in each calendar year. The Secretary shall give to the members of the Association at least thirty days notice in writing of the time and place at which the General Meeting is to be held.

8. The Treasurer shall keep the Accounts of the Association, and shall present a Balance Sheet and Statement of Accounts up to 31st.December of the previous year, at the Annual General Meeting.

9. A resolution affecting the affairs of the Association may be moved by any full member at a General Meeting, and will be considered carried if a majority of those present shall vote in favour, provided that the Committee shall have an overriding discretion to refer any resolution so moved to Postal Ballot of all the full members of the Association, if they consider this to be in the best interests of the members. If fewer than one quarter of the full members of the Association vote against the resolution on the Ballot it shall be considered to be carried.

10. An Extraordinary General Meeting may be convened at any time on the discretion of the Committee, or at the written request of not fewer than twenty full members of the Association. Not less than twentyone days notice of an Extraordinary General Meeting shall be given in writing to all members of the Association, together with the Agenda for the Meeting.

11. These Rules may be altered at any Annual General Meeting or Extraordinary General Meeting, provided that due notice has been given of the wording of the proposed alterations. Any alter-ation of the Rules shall be put into effect only if carried by the votes of at least two-thirds of the full members present and voting.

12. By a decision made in writing, and signed by not fewer than sixty percent of all paid-up full members, the Association may be wound up. In this event its assets shall be distributed in accordance with the directions of the Committee.

During the years 1982, 1983 and 1984 a great deal of thought and hard work on these Rules has been done by Charles Owen, David Keep, Simon Rocksborough Smith and others, and we are grateful that a clear and workable revision has now emerged. Even our President made a gracious concession on membership, and we should now try to implement the new possibilities to the full extent that they can be implemented in Rule Three.

PART V

THE NEW MILLENNIUM

> *But Westward, look, the land is bright.*
> Arthur Hugh Clough

With this epigraph, culled from Clough's *Say not the Struggle Nought Availeth*, John Trewin customarily opened his editorial prefaces for *The West Country Magazine*. For him, the concept of region was the most important thing about his magazine and the Association which grew from it.

Looking back from a distance of fifty years it is possible to evaluate the motives of the founding fathers when they started *this* Association and no other. Why a *West Country* writers' association, rather than just a writers' association? The situation in publishing at that postwar period was crucial, but if it had just been a question of getting paper and getting going again, then *any* magazine and association would have done. What we see, though, is men - and they were mostly men - driven by the concept of the West Country rather than just by the desire to write and to publish. The West Country connection was by far the more important of the two membership criteria - even if Waveney Girvan did joke that he would have recruited Gilbert & Sullivan on the strength of *The Pirates of Penzance*.

What drove them was something to do with the qualities of the West Country: its landscape and seascape, its gently rolling hills and chequered fields, its romantic moorland crags and wild places, its superb coastline, its rural nature, its distance from big cities and therefore its difference. The West Country, from its geographical position, had kept a distinctive character with its rural population and rich variety of local dialects enhancing the sense of its being a separate kingdom in the south west corner of the island.

Of all the seven ancient British kingdoms, Wessex seemed to have retained its individuality most, to have resisted longest the creeping sameness that spread, inexorably, through the 'influences from Lunnon, other side of Lunnon, up-country, and forren parts'.[1] Hence J. B. Priestley's evocation of the land of knights and enchantresses living on; hence Laurie Lee's confession that for all his flirtation with exotic foreign parts, his 'skin well oiled with wines of the Levant',[2] he was to find his 'heart's keel slide to rest among the meadows' of his home.

It was not just a case of people born and bred in the West Country feeling patriotic. J. B. Priestley was after all a Yorkshireman, and Henry Williamson was brought up in the streets of London before he fell in love with the part of North Devon that he made peculiarly his own. Waveney Girvan the Scot, Eden Phillpotts born in India, and Lady Vyvyan from Australia all came, saw, and were conquered. It was the West Country that caused the founding of the Association, not the generalised need for a writers' get-together.

How does today's WCWA measure up to this? Have we strayed too far from our roots? Would it still be true that our writings 'could not possibly have come from anywhere else',[3] as Lewis Wilshire said of his *West Country Short Stories* all those years ago; or have we, in evolving to survive and prosper, changed out of all recognition and become just another writers' association?

Broadening our interests and our member base has led to change in what we do. The basics of congress are still remarkably similar to what was on the programme in 1951: the congress is the central event, the lectures and the book exhibition are still important features, and at its core is still the annual luncheon with its civic guests and notable speakers. Within that outline there has been much adaptation and innovation, and since the historic session on word processors in 1984 it has become common to devote at least one session of the congress to what we call a 'subject of professional interest'. These have tended to be very practical. In 1995, for example, Kate Pool came from the Society of Authors to give detailed advice on contracts. The following year, when the death of the traditional book was much rumoured, a member of the Electronic Publishing Department at Macmillans came to unfold the mysteries of publishing on CD-ROM. He explained all the jargon and brought members up to date with the developments they were likely to encounter: now, it already seems old hat.

The process of reassurance was continued in 1998 when Peter Macdonald, the first member to publish a novel exclusively on the Internet, shared his expertise on the subject; while our resident high-tech expert, Ken Randall, helped members feel less daunted by the prospect of using the world wide web. At that session, only a handful of members were on the net or had an e-mail address: just three years later it is almost taken for granted. It has indeed been a half century not just of change, but of rapidly increasing change.

Throughout, the two big issues for writers worldwide have been the explosion of IT and the development of publishing conglomerates. Out of both of these has come the rise in self-publishing, as writers rejected from their publishers' lists have found that they had at their fingertips the technology to do it themselves. Accordingly, Barry Turner of Macmillans came in 1998 to outline the changes in publishing houses and their expectations from authors; and as self-publishing shed its vanity image and made it to the short list for the Booker Prize, there was a practical session on the pros and cons of this growing trend. Who knows, in the next fifty years, perhaps a condition of membership will be not three published hardback books, but three self-published books.

Congresses have developed in other ways. Audience participation is enjoyed, whether through panel discussions or readings from members' works. Time for discussing 'writers' problems' - prominent on the 1950 programme - is perennially popular, and though some problems are new in the electronic age, some still seem to be eternal, such as the writer's ongoing love-hate relationship with editors, agents and publishers.

Information technology could even help the undervalued author to fight back. Lately, electronic publishing has completely changed its image and is no longer seen as a threat to writers, as the possibilities offered by the e-book continue to unfold. Any text could be digitised and made available on the net, and once the technology of hand-held reading equipment has been perfected the potential is limitless. Self-publishing straight on to the net could cut out the wicked publisher; 'print on demand' from the net could remove the expense associated with short print runs and mean that no book need ever be out of print. Out-of-copyright books could all be up there, on the net, just waiting to be added to your library free of charge - a sobering thought for the big book chains, as has been the success of online bookselling with its ability to cut prices and find books from all over the world.

No doubt these confusing new issues will find their way onto WCWA congress programmes in coming years. But these are all worldwide writers' problems, not specifically West Country writers' problems, and while younger members in particular ask for more of these professional sessions and criticize the traditional civic reception as 'a waste of conference time', other members like to point out that it is not a conference or a workshop but a congress - a meeting place of friends and colleagues, united by a professional interest in writing certainly, but also rooted in the West Country and existing for social relaxation and 'the interchange of ideas'. Any writers' association can offer practical support with the business of writing - some have the resources to do it far better - so where does our special value lie?

The more we live in a global village dominated by multinationals, with a McDonalds in Moscow or a Tesco in Prague, the more we need to counter blandness with creative individuality. We must have newer, younger members in order to survive at all, and their expectations have to be accommodated, but always in balance with our rootedness in the West Country and its particular character. The new members who do not stay are the ones who joined because they wanted to be in an authors' club but have no great allegiance to the West Country; they just happen to have an address there. Members do not have to live in the West Country

The West Country Writers' Association

but they need to have a strong feeling for it: it is not just an accommodation address. That is why the congress venue moves around the area to inconvenient locations as well as easily accessible ones; that is why the civic reception lives on as our courteous nod to our hosts in the place where we are meeting; that is why the principal toast at every congress has always been *not* 'The West Country Writers' Association' but simply 'The West Country'. When people find these things tedious or a waste of conference time, we know they have come to the wrong association.

It is difficult to hold in balance the needs of old and new members, the social and professional aspects, the entertaining and the useful items at congress. Certainly we must not stand still as the Association did in the sixties and nearly died; the committee must always be considering new ways to respond to new developments.

It may well be that the structure of congress is due for a radical overhaul and, as the cost of good hotels continues to soar, we may need to reconsider the residential weekend 'all under one roof' and see if there is now a more flexible way of doing things. When the Gang of Four introduced the residential congress it was a complete innovation; it must not be allowed to become, in its turn, a sacred cow that blocks further progressive innovation.

One aspect of the Association which is crying out for development is the provision of regional lunches - informal meetings either at a member's home or in local pubs in all parts of the West. This is what members, especially new members, ask for repeatedly, because they want to get to know the other members who live near them. Congress, quite apart from the fact that it is expensive and it often involves a long journey however much the venue is rotated, only happens once a year, and members often express the desire for more frequent and informal opportunities to meet and talk locally. In some areas this happens on a regular basis but at present the coverage of the region is very patchy and the lunches only happen now and again. The original structure of the WCWA made provision for regional co-ordinators in each of the counties, to keep members in touch on a local basis. If volunteers could only be found to take on this role again, the future might well profit from that old idea.

There is a lot more we can learn from our past. It is worth looking back for a moment to the recruiting letter written by the first secretary, John Nance, in 1951:

> Now, whilst your Committee gets down to its side of the business, which is... to put the Association on the map, there is a task for you to do. That task is to fan into a flame the spark of regional enthusiasm which so unexpectedly yet so unquestioningly was lit at the Congress. Many of us have the feeling that something immensely important and significant may come out of our Association, something much larger than a mere gathering together of a few people united by a common love of a particular part of the English countryside or a particular way of life. We have in the Association a living thing; we want it to be courted and respected, but above all we want it to lead. We have stumbled upon a great opportunity to be of service not only to ourselves but equally to the communities we represent. Do not let us pass it by.[4]

There are few people left who remember John Nance and we can only know him now through his writings, the occasional poems scattered through the volumes of *The West Country Magazine*. They reveal a man of quirky humour who looked at things from a quizzical point of view and found it impossible to stay serious. Yet this letter is serious stuff. It is certainly the ultimate answer to potential recruits who ask 'What is the Association going to do for me?' It is over the top to an extent, yet undeniably it comes from the heart. John Nance is not talking about founding a club, he is on a crusade: he is talking about service, not self-interest. He goes beyond asking 'not what the Association can do for you but what you can do for the Association': he is asking what the Association can then do for its eponymous region.

At early congresses there was talk of campaigning on regional issues and Waveney Girvan used examples like protesting against excessive tree-felling, starting West Country exiles' clubs in London, and - perennial favourite - restoring the name of GWR. Not a lot ever came of his proposals. Antony Hippisley Coxe encouraged campaigning over literary concerns like the Theatre Museum or PLR, but bodies like the Society of Authors can do that with a much more powerful voice. If WCWA is to have a unique role, it is to do with perpetuating that spirit of the West which, as Waveney Girvan once warned, 'needs no popularisers but may need friends and protectors'.[5]

The application for Arts Council funding made the same point twenty years later:

> In these days of mass media and technological processes [when] there are many tendencies to produce uniformity in all walks of life, the preservation of West Country thought and expression is more vital than ever, particularly as the part the West Country is now called upon to take as a play or leisure area for the nation is increasing. This has developed in so many ways that it leads to a destruction of the traditions and customs of the area in pursuit of contemporary pleasures, sometimes out of keeping with the West Country environment.[6]

It was a fear that Daphne du Maurier shared when she looked at her much-loved Cornwall in the days shortly before her death. But how *is* a writer supposed to be the befriender and protector of the West Country?

Waveney Girvan believed that, 'men or women of letters, owing allegiance to their region, should be able, when united, to serve the West Country in many ways, either by the pen or through the force of their personalities. Their means may be literary though the ends sought could reach into many other fields of activity.'[7]

For Daphne du Maurier the means was literary. Her last book, *Rule Britannia*, was set in a fantasy future where Britain has capitulated entirely to America and is occupied by the US Army, who promptly designate the whole of the West Country and Wales to be one vast, themed leisure park. Cornwall in particular was to become the national holiday camp, its spirit and its solitude destroyed for ever... but with full employment in the heritage industry. It is an exaggerated satire of course, but the fear rings true: what else is there but tourism for Cornwall without its traditional means of making a living? - the tin mines long gone, the fishing industry increasingly threatened. The summer visitors are very welcome and Cornish people would be lost without them: they have to be practical and make a living. Daphne du Maurier's concern was that Cornwall should not sell its soul in the process of making that living, and through her book she could alert people to the dangers so that perhaps a balance could be maintained. As one of its greatest popularisers she tried also to be Cornwall's friend and protector. One hopes she would have been gratified to witness the success with which the four-year-old Daphne du Maurier Festival has taken off, bringing a special sort of appreciative tourism and much-needed local income to her favourite places.

Once in a while, the pen really is mightier than the planner, as in the case of the Slad Valley, where it is firmly believed that the area was saved from being swamped by disproportionate development only by the power of Laurie Lee's reputation. The greatest fear of locals was that the planners would pounce again the moment that Laurie was dead: he truly was their protector.

'Protection' is a loaded word and can have connotations of reactionary attitudes and exclusivity. Waveney Girvan, who expressly reached out to those who knew the West Country only through holidays as well as to its residents, would not have intended West Country writers to draw up the barriers and try to stop progress. Change will happen. What writers can do is write about it, expressing the values involved, keeping issues in the public eye, questioning, interpreting, helping people to see and evaluate what is going on and whether it is the right move. Often, it happens indirectly, not because they are writing on behalf of a campaign, but simply because they are doing what they do best. In an indirect way, Margaret Drabble probably did more to alert people to the horrid things happening in West Country agriculture through her novel, *The Witch of Exmoor,* than a hundred propaganda pamphlets could have done. Who could look a beefburger in the face again after reading her description of Butler's Bumperburgers?

Indirectly, Henry Williamson has helped the economy of North Devon - an area where it is not hard to see why the locals historically took to wrecking as there are precious few other ways of making a living on that inhospitable coastline. Now, though, it has a flourishing tourist trade linked to 'the Tarka Trail', with its own Tarka Railway Line. It was quite unconscious on the author's part: he did not set out to drum up tourism; he just did what he did best, expressing his sympathy with the place and its people. At the end of his story *Billy Goldsworthy's Cow* he puts it most humbly - 'I went away, feeling this man knew that harmony which I aspired to, but could not yet attain.' He made people interested in the place, and made them respect its special quality - as, for example, the Poldark novels of Winston Graham have fostered people's interest in Cornwall and help them respect and grow to love its specialness. Sometimes writers are able to popularize and protect just by writing.

Sometimes the means can be actual conservation, as was the case with another WCWA member, Rita Tregellas Pope, whose death was announced recently. A Cornish Bard whose writings included many guide books to 'the delectable duchy', she spent a large proportion of her time setting up 'The Tregellas Foundation'. This was a conscious effort to preserve and foster the continuance of Cornish identity by funding a Cornish Cultural Centre based at Baldhu Church near Truro. The church itself had been threatened with demolition as it was built to serve the mining community and it had become, like them, redundant. Rita's idea was to make it an education centre for courses on Cornish history, culture, arts and crafts, where she could also have housed the Tregellas Tapestry which portrays in fifty-eight panels the milestones of Cornish history. To create it, ancient skills had to be passed on to new people, so that the project 'links the past with the present and carries it into the future', in the words of the Foundation's objective.

Language is always a concern for writers. The variety of West Country dialects relished by Lewis Wilshire cannot be heard any more. The development of transport, education and broadcasting have all contributed to this, as mass media now reach the rural corners of the region that were difficult to penetrate in earlier generations. Judith Stinton, of the Dorset Writers' Galleries, knows that the Dorset speech of William Barnes is now unheard in any Dorset school playground. The other growth industry of the West, retirement, has also been partly responsible for this. In the Devon village where my husband's family have lived for thirty years there are now far more London accents than local dialects heard in the pub and the pew. There is no point in bemoaning it. No-one can artificially revive a language that has reached the end of its living currency, and preservation in aspic is not the answer - John Trewin long ago warned against 'pixy whimsies' or 'Mummerset folkweave'. What the writer can do is see that language remains rich and lively - as Laurie Lee has done in prose and poetry.

For Laurie, the world he describes in *Cider with Rosie* was the world we have sacrificed to the motor car. 'I belonged to a generation which saw, by chance, the end of a thousand years' life', he says:

> ...myself, my family, my generation were born in a world of silence... then, to the scream of the horse, the change began. The brass-lamped motor car came coughing up the road, followed by the clamorous charabanc... soon the village would break, dissolve and scatter, become no more than a place for pensioners.[8]

We can no more un-invent the motor car than we can go back to childhood and it would be wrong to try: the WCWA has flourished by accepting change and adapting to it. But Laurie's Slad will live for ever because he wrote about it, passing on to succeeding generations his delight in the odd and eccentric character of that special place and its people.

What the writers of the WCWA can uniquely offer is the continuing expression of that West Country spirit. To give the last word to our first President,

'the great man of Devon', Eden Phillpotts -

> *Let us in good will strive to enrich, with our West Country happiness and wisdom, a backward, cranky little planet still far too short of both.*[10]

The West Country Writers' Association

APPENDIX I

PATRON - Lord St Levan

PRESIDENTS

1951 - 1960 Eden Phillpotts
1960 - 1965 Henry Williamson
1965 -   Christopher Fry

VICE PRESIDENTS
29 to date

Founder Vice Presidents:

A.J. Coles (Jan Stewer)
St. John Ervine
Christopher Fry
Frederick Grisewood
John Moore
A.L. Rowse
Marguerite Steen
H.A. Vachell
Brian Vesey-Fitzgerald
Lady Vyvyan

Elected 1950-1960:

H.M. Tomlinson

Elected 1960-1970:

L.P. Hartley
Henry Williamson

Elected 1970-1980:

Charles Causley
Laurie Lee
J.C. Trewin
William Kean Seymour
Rosalind Wade
Bryan Little

Elected 1980-1990:

Daphne du Maurier
Frank Littlewood
Bob Cooper

Elected 1990-2000:

Ralph Whitlock
E.V. Thompson
Victor Bonham-Carter
Rachel Billington
Geraldine Kaye
Joanna Trollope
John Rowe

-217-

The West Country Writers' Association

CHAIRMEN		VICE-CHAIRMEN
1951-1964	Waveney Girvan	Lady Mander
1965-1972	John Trewin	William Kean Seymour
1972-1974	William Kean Seymour	John Rowland
1974-1976	John Rowland	John Brooks
1976-1978	John Brooks	Bryan Little
1978-1980	Bryan Little	Jacynth Hope-Simpson
1980-1982	Jacynth Hope-Simpson	Antony Hippisley Coxe
1982-1983	Antony Hippisley Coxe	Charles Owen
1983-1984	Antony Hippisley Coxe/ Charles Owen	Nancy Tregenna Piggott
1984-1985	Nancy Tregenna Piggott	Rosemary Jeffery
1985-1986	Rosemary Jeffery	Bob Cooper
1986-1987	Rosemary Jeffery	Simon Rocksborough Smith
1987-1989	Simon Rocksborough Smith	David Keep
1989-1991	David Keep	Dorothy Stiffe
1991-1993	Dorothy Stiffe	John Paxton
1993-1995	John Paxton	Bob Cooper
1995-1996	Bob Cooper	Gloria Cottesloe
1996-1997	Gloria Cottesloe/ Bob Cooper	Frances Brown
1997-1998	Bob Cooper	Frances Brown
1998-1999	Frances Brown	John Harcup
1999-2001	John Harcup	Margaret Bacon

The West Country Writers' Association

SECRETARIES

1951-1952	John Nance
1952-1959	John Keast
1959-1960	John Nance
1960-1965	Honor Carr
1966-1972	Frank Littlewood
1972-1975	Bob Cooper
1975	Ann Manning
1976-1978	Honor Butler
1978-1981	Doris Hodges
1982	Elizabeth Churcher
1983	Nancy Tregenna Piggott
1984-1989	Dorothy Stiffe
1990-1997	Anne Double
1998	Caroline Stickland
1999-	Anne Double

TREASURERS

1951-1952	A.G. Findlay
1952-1959	John Keast
1960-1965	Honor Carr
1966-1972	Frank Littlewood
1973-1976	John Brooks
1976-1979	Meryl Macdonald Bendle
1980-1988	David Keep
1989	Joan Purgold
1990-1994	Ken Randall
1995-1998	John Harcup
1999-	Marina Oliver

PUBLIC RELATIONS OFFICERS

1973-1977	Meryl Macdonald Bendle
1978	John Rowland
1979-1981	Jean Harding
1981-1984	Rosemary Jeffery
1985-1987	Elizabeth Churcher
1987 -	Janet Green

MEMBERSHIP SECRETARIES

1970 Wendy Trewin helped the Secretary with Membership matters
1973-1976 Geraldine Kaye - first full Membership Secretary
1977 Jacynth Hope-Simpson
1978-1990 Olwen Reed
1991-1994 Jean Brain (later Jean Steward)
1994-1999 Gillian Lindsay
2000- Margaret Bacon

NEWSLETTER EDITORS

1968, 69, 71	Frank Littlewood
1973-77	Meryl Macdonald Bendle
1978	John Rowland/Frank Littlewood
1979	Jean Harding (2 issues),
1980	(2 issues)
1981	(1 issue)
1981	Doris Hodges (1 issue),
1982	(2 issues)
1983	(1 issue)
1983	Jacynth Hope-Simpson (1 issue)
1984	Bill Pickard (2 issues)
1985	John Rowe (2 issues)
1986	(2 issues)
1987	(2 issues)
1988	(2 issues)
1989	(2 issues)
1990	(2 issues)
1991	(2 issues)
1992	(2 issues)
1993	(1 issue)
1993	David Keep (1 issue)
1994	(2 issues)
1995	(1 issue)
1995	Anne Double (1 issue)
1996	(2 issues)
1997	(2 issues)
1998	(2 issues)
1999	Jane Tatam (2 issues)
2000	(2 issues)

To the end of the Year 2000 there have been 53 editions of the Newsletter.

The West Country Writers' Association

The West Country Writers' Association

APPENDIX II

CONGRESS SPEAKERS

Date	Venue	Guest of Honour	Other Speakers	Book Exhibition Opener
1950	Bath	J.B. Priestley	Bryan Little	
1951	Bath	Compton Mackenzie	L.A.G. Strong (on poets of Devon & Cornwall)	
1952	Plymouth	Frank Swinnerton	St. John Ervine	J.C. Trewin
1953	Salisbury	Eric Linklater	Angela Thirkell	Lady Mander
1954	Weymouth	G.B. Stern	Marguerite Steen, C.Day Lewis, L.A.G. Strong	John Garrett
1955	Torquay	Robert Gibbings	L.A.G. Strong (on Eden Phillpotts)	Elephant Bill
1956	Bath	St. John Ervine	Sir Charles Petrie	
1957	Exeter	J.E. Morpurgo	A.L. Rowse	A.J. Coles
1958	Bournemouth	Richard Church	L.A.G. Strong (on Hardy's prose)	Kenneth Hopkins
1959	Bristol	C.S. Forrester	L.P. Hartley	Bryan Little
1960	Barnstaple	John Pudney	Coleman Cooke (on Exmoor)	Ronald Duncan
1961	Falmouth	Val Gielgud	Waveney Girvan (on Eden Phillpotts)	Wendy Monk
1962	Taunton	Vera Brittain	William Kean Seymour	Rosalind Wade
1963	Lyme Regis	Jerome Tickell	Bryan Little	
1964	Bath	J.B. Priestley	Jacquetta Hawkes	
1965	Exeter	W.A. Darlington	University - discussion on Henry Williamson with Ted Hughes & E.W. Martin, to mark the presentation of HW's manuscripts to Exeter University	W.A. Darlington
1966	Bristol	James Laver	Visit to Theatre Royal (Bicentenary)	
1967	Cheltenham	Francis Warner	Gwen Hart (on mediaeval Cheltenham)	F.E. Halliday
1968	Plymouth	Lord Goodman	Charles Causley	William Kean Seymour
1969	Bath	Stella Gibbons	Rosalind Wade (on George Eliot)	Kenneth Macleod
1970	Salisbury	E. Martin Browne	Moelwyn Merchant (on George Herbert)	Bryan Little
1971	Torquay	Agatha Christie & Max Mallowan (non-speaking) Robert Speaight (speaking)	Ian Watson (SW Arts Association)	Dean of Salisbury
1972	Bath	Robert Gittings	(Discussion on future of Association)	R.F. Delderfield

-222-

The West Country Writers' Association

CONGRESS DETAILS

Year	Location	Speaker	Others
1976	Bristol		Christopher Fry
1977	Plymouth	Yvonne Mitchell	Christopher Milne
1978	Bath	Lord Caradon	
1979	Bournemouth	J.H.B. Peel	
1980	Exeter	John Elsom	Victor Bonham-Carter
1981	Truro	Winston Graham	E.V. Thompson
		Colin Wilson	
1982	Cheltenham	Penelope Lively	Ion Trewin, Francis King	Frank Littlewood
1983	Taunton	Celia Fremlin	G. Wilson Knight, Tom Salmon	Robert Wolseley
1984	Torquay	Rachel Billington	Christopher Fry	Ralph Whitlock
			Tom Sharpe, Nona Bowring, Gerald Pollinger	
1985	Weston-super-Mare	Victoria Glendinning	Richard Parkinson, Frank Delaney	Antony Hippisley Coxe
1986	Plymouth	John Braine	Mark le Fanu, H.L. Douch,	John Braine
1987	Weymouth	Terry Lloyd-Jones	Bob Cooper, John Brunner, Peter Redgrove	Rachel Billington
1988	Torquay	John Elsom	Sarah Harrison, Nancy & John Sawyer	Christopher Milne
			Bryan Little, Martial Rose	
1989	Barnstaple	Peter Cousins	H.R.F. Keating, Bryan Little, Roger Busby	Araminta Hippisley Coxe
1990	Exeter	David St. John Thomas	Keith Salter, Jean Stubbs, Terry Tapp	Webb & Bower
1991	Salisbury	Michael Gough	Marc & Kim Millon	Ralph Whitlock
1992	Penzance	Eric Quayle	Ruth Hayden, Leslie Grinsell, Bryan Little	Bob Cooper
1993	Bournemouth	George Baker	Maeve Binchy, Helen Rowett	Bob Rigby
1994	Cheltenham	Diana Hendry	Christopher Fry, Meryl Macdonald Bendle	Joanna Trollope
1995	Torquay	Victor Bonham-Carter (read in absentia by Bob Cooper)	Sheila Hardaway (on Agatha Christie)	Geraldine Kaye
			David Keep, Bryan Little	
1996	Bristol	John Mortimer	Christopher Fry, Geraldine Kaye, Ranee Clark	Deborah Moggach
			Charles Bonham-Carter	
			Christopher Fry, Jim Palmer, John Rowe	
			E.V. Thompson, Peter Hawkins, Judith Cook	
			Christopher Fry, Raymond Allen, Bob Rigby	
			Tricia Henry, David Godwin	
			Penelope Tremayne, Brian Carter, Kate Pool	
			Melvyn Bragg, Christopher Fry,	
			Deborah Moggach	
1997	Plymouth	Christopher Fry	Francis King, Edward Murch, John Harcup,	Mollie Hince
			Mary Wesley	
1998	Weymouth	Margaret Drabble	Barry Turner, Christopher Somerville,	Gerald Pollinger
			Peter Macdonald,	
			Judith Stinton, Anne Ashurst	
1999	Exeter	Terence Frisby	Christopher Fry, Michael Holroyd	Gene Kemp,

-223-

The West Country Writers' Association

APPENDIX III - MEMBERS 2001

Michael Abbot
Peter Ackroyd
Rosemary Aitken
Jenny Alexander
Raymond Allen
Dr Christine Allison
Reuth Ambre
Mark Andresen
Audrey Andrews
Jeffrey Archer
Anne Ashurst
Eileen Atkinson
Margaret Bacon
Eva Bailey
Graham Baines
George Baker
Julia Barnes
Paul Barnett
Susan Barrett
Gary Bartholomew
John C Bayliss OBE
Heather Beer
Peter Beere
Jean Bellamy
Lady Rachel Billington
Hon Charlotte Bingham
Sheila Bird
Sheila Bishop
Jane Bolitho
Victor Bonham-Carter
Barbara Boote
Ann Born
Terence Brady
Isabel Briggs
John Brooks
Frances Brown
Barbara Brown
Chris Bryant
William John Burley
Robin Bush
Enid Byford
Ian Campbell Thomson
Hilary Cannock
Charles Causley
Dawn Cawley

Merle Chacksfield
Mack Chahin
Judy Chard
Jan Clark
Rosemary Clinch
Judith Cook
Nigel Coombes
Dr Robert Cooper
Lady Gloria Cottesloe
Peter Cowlam
Diana Crighton
Jean Crowcroft
Sheila Cutts
Patricia Daly
Sheila Danton
Jo Darke
Marjorie Darke
Nick Darke
Angela Davies
Betty Donaldson
Anne Double
W Douthwaite
Margaret Drabble
Jane Dunn
Karen Eberhardt-Shelton
Lesley Eldred
Rosemary Ellerbeck
Peter Epps
Barbara Fenton
Patricia Ferguson
RM Flemington
Sarah Foot
Pamela Forrest Taylor
Vivien Foster
John Fowles
Terence Frisby
Christopher Fry
Andrew Fry
David Gamon
Jamila Gavin
Pamela Gillilan
Winston Graham
Janet Green
Ms Beverley Grey
Paul Groves

Harry B Guest
Dr John Harcup
Melissa Hardie-Budden
Paula Hare
Frida Harris
Sarah Harrison
Michael Hartland
Jane Hatton
Aileen Hawkins
Peter Hawkins
Suzi Hawkins
Karen Hayes
Michael D Henderson
Diana Hendry
Dr Brian Hick
Evelyn Hilary-Szydlowska
Mollie Hince
Joanna Hines
Mark Holloway
Pat Holness
Michael Holroyd
Mavis Hooper
Jacynth Hope-Simpson
Jeanne Hopkins
Jenery Howard
Ann Hutton
Paul Hyland
David Ingham
H J Ingrey
William G Jackman
Florence E Jackson
Valerie Jacob
Alan Jefferson
Rosemary Jeffery
Catherine R John
Jenny Jones
Phyllis Jones
Roger Jones
Anna Kalnars
Eleanor Kaye
Geraldine Kaye
Kate Keenan
Revd Dr David Keep
Brian Kellock
Alan Kent

The West Country Writers' Association

Gene Kemp
Julia Killingback
Jocelyn Kingsnorth
Astrid Klemz
Dr. Penny Kline
Lois Lamplugh
Berta Lawrence
Peter Lawrence
Philippa Lawrence
Brian Le Messurier
Julian Lea-Jones
Kathy Lee
Richard Lee
Lornie Leete-Hodge
Gillian Lindsay
Joan Lowry
Meryl Macdonald Bendle
Peter Macdonald
Jon Mackley
Molly Martin
John Mayled Porter
Maria McCarthy
Sheila McCullagh
Corinne Mellor
Greg Morse
Dr T W Mowl
Edward Murch
Dr Nora Naish
David Needham
P E M Nesbitt
R H Nesham
Revd Dr John Newton
Jill Nice
D E S Nutt
Geoffrey Nuttall
Jean Oliver
Marina Oliver
Gordon Ottewell
Charles Owen
G O W Paice
Sue Palmer
Jean Paton
John Paxton
Lesley Pearse
Shirley Peckham
Elizabeth Pewsey
Dee Phillips
Ann Pickard
Bill Pickard

Barrie Pitt
Frances Pitt
Valerie Pitt Hall
Gerald Pollinger
Anne Powell
Jeremy Powell
Margaret Powling
Eric Quayle
Vivienne Rae-Ellis
Ken Randall
Avis Randall
Peter Redgrove
Olwen Reed
Joyce Richell
Simon Rocksborough Smith
John Rossiter
Dr John Rowe
E Helen Rowe
Helen Rowett
Jeremy Rowett-Johns
Betty Rowlands
Penelope Ruddock
Jill S Salkeld
Fay Sampson
Jean Saunders
Michael Scanes
M Schneider
Tim Scott
Belinda Seaward
Geoffrey Shrives
Jenny Smedley
Frederick Smith
Godfrey Smith
Chris Smith
Hon G R St Aubyn
Lord St Levan
Andrew Stacey
Peter Stacey
Aline Stackhouse
Robin Stanes
Margaret Starks
Roger Steer
Dr Derek Steinberg
Jean Steward
Jill Stewart-Rattray
Caroline Stickland
Dorothy Stiffe
Judith Stinton
Pamela Street

Colin Style
Eugenie Summerfield
Dee Sutherland
Pamela Sykes
Janet Tanner
Terry Tapp
Revd Beverley Tasker
Jane Tatam
David Templar
Judith Thomas
E V Thompson
Andrew Thomson
Willow Tickell
Michael Tod
Raymond Tong
Marcia Treece
Joanna Trollope
Margaret Trump
Angela Tuckett
Margaret Turner
Barbara Twigg
Nadine Vokins
Victoria Wakefield
Joan Wakelin
Sir Robert Wall OBE
B H Warmington
Thelma Wax
Jane Welch
Noel Welch
Dr James Whetter
B C White
C White
Katie Whittal-Williams
Prof G W Wickham
Valerie Wilding
Malcolm Williams
Merrilyn Williams
Katie Williams
Richard Williamson
Penelope Willis
Michael Willmott
Colin Wilson
Frank Wintle
Sally Withnall
Christina Wood
Dr John Wroughton
Roy York
Dr Robert Youngeson

Notes

Abbreviations

BC - Bob Cooper
BL - Bryan Little
DS - Diana Stephenson
FL - Frank Littlewood
HW - Henry Williamson
JCT - J.C. Trewin
JN - John Nance
LL - Laurie Lee
MMB - Meryl Macdonald Bendle
NL - Newsletter of the WCWA
TWCM - *The West Country Magazine*
VB-C - Victor Bonham-Carter
WCSS - *West Country Short Stories*
WG - Waveney Girvan
WKS - William Kean Seymour

PART I

1. Victor Bonham-Carter, address to WCWA luncheon, Torquay 1995.
2. Henry Williamson, open letter to WCWA, November 1964.
3. *The West Country Magazine*, Vol. I, No. i, p.3
4. HW, op. cit.
5. VB-C, op.cit.
6. HW, op. cit.
7. HW, op. cit.
8. HW, diary entry 6 March 1934 ff.
9. JC Trewin, letter to Meryl Macdonald Bendle, 1977
10. Kenneth Hopkins, *Poems: English and American,1968*
11. TCWM: I (i) 5
12. S.E. Crisp
13. Jo Darke (monuments), Frances Pitt (jumble sales), Merle Chacksfield (postcards), Vivien Foster (aphorisms), Geoffrey Nuttall (G&S), Frances Brown (fairground folk)
14. Authors: G.O.W. Paice, Jean Crowcroft, Jan Clark, Nigel Coombes
15. TWCM: VI (iii) 165
16. Ibid., p.167
17. Ibid., p. 168
18. Ibid., pp. 170-1
19. Florence Hardy, *Life of Thomas Hardy*, Ch. IX
20. Ibid., Ch.XXI
21. *West Country Short Stories*, ed. Lewis Wilshire (Faber & Faber, 1949), p.11
22. Ibid., p.11
23. TWCM: I (i) 4
24. Bryan Little, 'Bath & Literature' Bath Assembly 1950
25. A.L. Rowse, *The West in English History* (Hodder & Stoughton 1950)
26. TWCM: II (i) 9
27. Ibid. V (ii) 87
28. Ibid. V (iii) 172-3
29. Newsletter, May 1991, p. 19
30. NL, May 1981, p.5
31. E.M.Forster, *Aspects of the Novel* (Penguin 1964) p.30

PART II

1. Letter, Waveney Girvan to Bryan Little, 06.07.49 - WCWA archive

2. WG to BL, 08.07.49, archive
3. Ibid.
4. WCWA 40th anniversary booklet
5. TWCM: V (iii) 168
6. Ibid. V (ii) 87
7. Ibid. V (i) 7
8. Programme 1950
9. JC T, 40th anniversary booklet
10. Bryan Little's diary, 1950
11. TWCM: V (iii) 167-8
12. JC T, letter to MMB 1977
13. Ibid.
14. TWCM: V (ii) 87-8
15. Ibid. III (i) 59
16. Ibid. III (ii) 96
17. BL, 'Bath & Literature' 1950
18. WG, letter to BL 14.12.50 - archive
19. Ibid.
20. Ibid.
21. Ibid.
22. Ibid.
23. TWCM: VI (i) 5
24. JCT, op.cit.
25. TWCM: VI (iii) 167-8
26. Ibid. VI (iii) 168
27. Ibid. VI (iii)166
28. John Nance, TWCM: VI (ii) 154
29. JN, TWCM: VI (iii) 172
30. JN, open letter, June 1951
31. Ibid.
32. TWCM: VII (iii) 166
33. Ibid. VII (ii) 85-6
34. Ibid. VII (iii) 165
35. Ibid. VII (iii) 165
36. VB-C, op. cit.
37. TWCM: VII (iii) 223
38. Ibid. VII (iii) 223
39. Ibid. VII (iii) 166
40. Edna Manning, WCWA Scrapbook, 1953

PART III

1. WCWA 40th anniversary booklet
2. JCT to MMB, 1977
3. 40th anniversary booklet
4. Ibid.
5. Ibid.
6. Ibid.
7. Ibid.
8. NL January 1994, p.6
9. TWCM: I (i) 39
10. 40th anniversary booklet
11. Frank Littlewood to Charles Irving, 15.09.67 - archives
12. NL 1968, p.1
13. Anthony Rye to FL, 06.03.69
14. NL 1969, p. 14
15. William Kean Seymour to FL, March 1969
16. FL to JL, 21.05.70
17. 40th anniversary booklet
18. WKS to Bob Cooper, 17.05.72
19. WKS to BC, July 1972
20. WKS to FL, 11.05.71
21. FL to WKS, 20.10.71
22. WKS to FL, 19.10.71
23. FL to WKS, 20.10.71
24. Minutes, 16.11.71
25. Ibid.
26. Ibid.
27. FL, letter to members, 02.01.72
28. Ibid.
29. Ibid.
30. Ibid.
31. FL to WKS, 19.04.72
32. WKS to FL, 21.04.72
33. WKS to FL, 28.04.72

34. NL 1973, p.2
35. Ibid.
36. Ibid., p.3
37. NL May 1992, p.13
38. NL July 1998, p.26
39. FL to BC, 16.05.72
40. BC to WKS, 09.05.72
41. WKS to BC, 17.05.72
42. 40th anniversary booklet
43. NL May 1990, pp.14-5
44. Ibid., p. 15
45. 40th anniversary booklet
46. Ibid.
47. NL 1973, p. 2
48. NL 1977, p.5
49. NL 1973, p. 3
50. NL 1976, p. 1
51. BC to WKS, June 1972
52. BC to WKS, July 1972
53. BC to WKS, July 1972
54. BC to WKS, 17.08.72
55. BC to WKS, 10.10 72
56. BC to WKS, August 1972
57. WKS to BC, 10.10.72
58. WKS to BC, 15.10.72
59. 40th anniversary booklet
60. NL 1978, p.2
61. BC to WKS, 09.05.72
62. FL, draft application to Arts Council, 1974
63. Diana Stephenson to BC, 22.12.74 - archives
64. DS to BC, 05.01.75
65. BC to DS, 22.03.75
66. Minutes, 12.12.75
67. Minutes, 09.02.76
68. NL January 1987, p.9
69. Ibid.
70. 40th anniversary booklet

71. NL 1978, p.1
72. HW to BC, 28.05.74 - see after Pt III

PART IV

1. NL 1976, p.1
2. NL 1976, p.5
3. NL 'Congress News' 1980, p. 8
4. NL1975, p.8
5. NL, 'CN' 1980, p. 8
6. NL, 'CN' 1982, p.2
7. NL 1983 p. 3
8. NL January 1989, p. 11
9. NL, 'CN' 1982, p.2
10. Ibid.
11. Ibid.
12. WKS to BC, 15.10.72
13. NL, 'CN' 1983, pp. 7-8
14. BC to WKS, 20.10.72
15. NL July 1998, p. 26
16. Rules 1984, NL May 1984
17. NL May 1984, p.9
18. NL January 1984, pp. 5-6
19. NL January 1988, pp. 7-9
20. 'Looking for a Language' (Kings College, London 1992), p. 11
21. NL 1978, p.1
22. *Cyrano de Bergerac*, Oxford World's Classics, p. 80
23. *One Thing More or Caedmon Construed*, Kings College, London (1986), pp. 41-2
24. NL January 1996, pp. 10-11
25. Minutes, AGM 1969
26. VB-C, *What Countryman, Sir?* (1996) p. 268
27. Valerie Grove, *Laurie Lee: the Well-Loved Stranger'* (1999), p. 502

PART V

1. TWCM: V (iii) 171
2. Laurie Lee, 'Home from Abroad'
3. WCSS p. 11
4. JN, open letter, June 1951
5. WG, TWCM: VI (iii) 167
6. FL, draft application to Arts Council, 1974
7. WG, TWCM: VI (iii) 167
8. LL, *Cider with Rosie*, 'Last Days'
9. From Eden Phillpotts' letter, read by L.A.G. Strong at the 1952 Civic Luncheon at Buckland Abbey, quoted in the 26th and last issue of TWCM: VII (iii) 165

Index of Names

Allen, Raymond 199
Allingham - see Butler
Allsop, Kenneth 148
Andrews, Audrey 200
Arkell, Reg 44, 52
Ashurst, Anne 200
Bacon, Margaret 200
Bailey, Eva 200
Baker, Denys Val 20, 22
Baker, George 183, 185
Bath Assembly 39, 41, 42, 44, 49-58, 61, 71, 72, 82, 110
Bayliss, John 66, 185, 199
Billington, Rachel 127, 198
Boddington, J.E. 41, 42, 46, 56, 57, 76
Bonham-Carter, Victor 21, 22, 24, 66, 72, 188
Bromhead, Freda 126, 192
Brooks, John 110, 112, 122, 128, 130, 132, 136, 139, 150, 162, 164, 170
Brown, Frances 198, 199
Butler, Honor 123, 126, 133, 143, 150, 159, 164, 200
Carr, Honor 96, 97, 100, 157
Causley, Charles 52, 66, 102, 103, 188
Churcher, Elizabeth 145, 165, 187
Coles, A.J. 52, 64
Cooper, Bob ... 21, 101, 107, 108, 110, 119-124, 127, 130-134, 136-138, 140, 146, 150, 155, 157, 164, 172, 182, 185, 188, 194, 198, 199
Cottesloe, Gloria 198
Daly, Pat 199
de Selincourt, Aubrey 56
Double, Anne 145
Drabble, Margaret 198, 214

du Maurier, Daphne 28, 127, 132, 167, 213, 214
Ellerbeck, Rosemary 200
Elwin, Malcolm 22, 23, 33, 34, 71
Ervine, St John 62, 64, 65, 70, 71
Faunthorpe, Bertram 106
Fenton, Barbara 200
Findlay, A.G. 65, 96
Flying Saucer Review, The 25
Fry, Christopher 28, 65, 66, 99, 104, 113, 119, 147, 168, 178-186,
194-196, 198, 200
Garrett, John 56, 57, 62
Gill, Crispin 133
Gillilan, Pamela 200
Girvan, Waveney . . . 19-26, 29, 32, 33, 39, 41, 42, 45, 47-49, 51, 53, 54,
56, 58, 59, 61, 63, 64, 71, 74, 82, 87, 95, 96, 98, 99, 105, 118,
136, 150, 152, 162, 166, 207, 208, 212, 213
Graham, Winston 66, 215
Green, Janet 103, 162, 183, 187, 190, 199
Grigson, Geoffrey 47
Grinsell, Leslie 200
Grisewood, F.H. 44, 49, 65
Guest, Harry 183, 184
Harcup, John 167, 198, 199
Harding, Jean 165, 166
Hare, Kenneth 47
Harris, Frida 167
Hartland, Michael 175
Hartley, L.P. 95, 188
Hilary-Szydlowska, Evelyn 126
Hince, Mollie 199
Hinton, Phyllis 38
Hippisley Coxe, Antony 161, 166, 167, 169, 170, 186, 212
Hippisley Coxe, Araminta 166
Hodges, Doris 140, 144, 164, 165, 171
Hollis, Christopher 62

Holroyd, Michael 198
Hope-Simpson, Jacynth 38, 47, 126, 164, 165, 171
Hopkins, Kenneth 27, 30, 31, 49, 56
Howard, Jenery 200
Irving, Catherine 101, 106, 109, 111
Jackson, Florence 200
Jeffery, Rosemary 178, 199
John O'London - see Swinnerton
Jones, Peggy Loosemore 190, 191
Kaye, Geraldine ... 95, 110, 122, 124-126, 130, 133, 136, 137, 164, 166, 173, 198, 200
Kean Seymour, William 99, 106, 107, 109, 111, 119-121, 124, 125, 130-135, 147, 150, 162, 170, 172
Keast, John 66, 70, 96, 186
Keep, David 22, 32, 37, 146, 165, 172, 173, 178, 183, 193, 199
Lamplugh, Lois 66, 149
Lawrence, Berta 119, 120
le Messurier, Brian 200
Lee, Laurie ... 28, 29, 105, 178, 185, 186, 188, 195, 196, 198, 214, 216
Lindsay, Gillian 200
Little, Bryan .. 34, 40-42, 44, 47, 48, 50-56, 58, 66, 74, 76, 82, 83, 143, 150, 164, 165, 170, 186-188
Littlewood, Frank ... 96, 99, 100, 102-113, 115, 118, 119, 121-123, 131, 137, 142, 143, 158, 163, 164, 168, 186, 188
Lowry, Joan 99, 106, 146, 147
Macdonald Bendle, Meryl 39, 50, 110, 122, 127, 130, 136, 140, 147, 164, 186, 200
Macdonald, Peter 200, 209
Mackenzie, Compton 29, 60-62, 66, 87
Mander, Lady 44, 45, 47, 52, 56, 62, 96, 99, 136, 162, 165
Manning, Ann 140, 142-144, 150, 157
Manning, Edna 72, 133
McClintock, Mary 56
Mellersh, H.E.L. 134
Milne, Christopher 193

Monk, Wendy 102, 108, 110, 119
Moore, John 32, 62, 65, 104
Nance, John 62, 65-69, 95, 96, 212
National Book League 50, 57, 61
Oliver, Marina 200
Owen, Charles 173
Paton, Jean 126, 199
Paxton, Joan 194, 199
Paxton, John 178, 193, 194, 199
Phelps, Gilbert 56
Phillpotts, Adelaide 44
Phillpotts, Eden 20, 32, 64, 71, 96, 151, 168, 208, 216
Pickard, Bill 173, 200
Pollinger, Gerald 199
Pope, Rita Tregellas 215
Powys, J.C. 66
Priestley, J.B. 34, 45, 47, 50, 52, 96, 208
Purgold, Joan 186
Randall, Ken 199, 209
Reed, Olwen 164, 165, 200
Richell, Joyce 200
Rocksborough Smith, Simon 123, 127, 172, 173, 178, 199
Roseveare, Sue 100, 186
Rowe, John 198, 199
Rowett, Helen 200
Rowland, John 112, 119, 136, 143, 163, 164
Rowse, A.L. 32, 34, 49, 65, 66, 87, 95, 137, 198
Rye, Anthony 103, 105
Sampson, Fay 200
St. Levan, Lord 189, 190
Steen, Marguerite 65
Stephenson, Diana 140, 142
Steward, Jean 200
Stewer, Jan 44, 47, 50, 52, 64, 71
Stickland, Caroline 145, 200

Stiffe, Dorothy 72, 142, 145, 168, 190, 193, 199
Stinton, Judith 215
Street, A.G. 49, 66
Strong, L.A.G. 32, 49, 56, 57, 62, 70, 71, 87, 95
Stubbs, Jean 175, 178
Swinnerton, Frank 71
Sykes, Pam 200
Szydlowska, Evelyn Hilary 200
Tapp, Terry 174, 175
Thomas, David St John 172
Thompson, E.V. 188, 189
Tomlinson, H.M. 66
Tong, Raymond 126
Tregenna-Piggott, Nancy 145, 178
Treneer, Anne 44
Trewin, John ... 24, 26, 34, 39, 41, 46-51, 53, 56, 57, 61, 64, 66, 69, 71,
    72, 87, 98-103, 107-110, 112, 118, 119, 121, 124, 132, 135, 136,
        150, 166, 168, 169, 180, 181, 186, 207, 215
Trewin, Wendy - see Monk
Tuckett, Angela 126, 200
Uglow, Sam 35, 49
Vachell, H.A. 45, 47, 50, 52, 62, 65, 87, 96
Val Baker, Denys 72, 106
Vesey-Fitzgerald, Brian 65, 66
Vyvyan, Lady 32, 65, 208
Wade, Rosalind 108-111, 120, 124, 135, 186
West Country Magazine 20-24, 27, 30, 32-35, 39-42, 45, 48, 51, 53-
        55, 60, 63, 66, 70-72, 99, 103, 105, 140, 207, 212
Westaway Books 21
Westaway Press 22
Whitlock, Ralph 174, 187
Williamson, Anne 25, 149
Williamson, Henry ... 20-24, 32, 66, 96, 97, 99, 105, 146-151, 155, 158,
        162, 163, 179, 196, 201, 208, 214
Wilshire, Lewis 32, 48, 208, 215

Wroughton, John 199
York, Roy 200
Ziolkowska, Adele 185, 195, 200

The West Country Writers' Association

SUBSCRIPTION LIST

Raymond Allen	Ryde, Isle of Wight
Margaret Bacon	Highworth, Wiltshire
Graham Baines	Clifton, Bristol
John Clifford Bayliss	London
Frances Brown	Lydeard St Lawrence, Somerset
Penelope Byrde	Bath
Bob Cooper	Abingdon, Oxford
Patricia Daly	Bath
Betty Donaldson	Oxford
Anthony Double	Hereford
Katy Double	Herefordshire
Margaret Double	Hereford
Rosemary Ellerbeck	Sturminster Newton, Dorset
Barbara Fenton	Plymouth, Devon
M. Flemington	Barnstaple, Devonshire
Christopher Fry	Chichester
Pamela Gillilan	Clifton, Bristol
Janet Green	Bristol
John Winsor Harcup	Malvern, Worcs
F. Joy Harcup	Chew Magna, Somerset
S. Claire Harcup	London
Michael Hartland	Branscombe, Devon
Michael D. Henderson, MCIJ	Westward Ho! N. Devon
Mollie Hince (Elizabeth Daish)	Seaview, Isle of Wight
Charles and Kay Holland	Bootle, Merseyside
Rosemary Jeffery	Saltash, Cornwall
Geraldine Kaye	Bristol

David Keep	Exeter, Devon
Lois Lamplugh	Barnstaple, Devon
Philippa Lawrence	Salisbury, Wiltshire
Joan Lowry	Devon
Peter Macdonald	Bristol
Meryl Macdonald Bendle	Stoke Bishop, Bristol
Brian Le Messurier	Exeter, Devon
Edward Murch	Dousland, Devon
Nora Naish	Chipping Sodbury
David E. S. Nutt	Bristol
Marina Oliver	Bledlow, Bucks
Jean Paton	Probus, Cornwall
John Paxton	Bruton, Somerset
Bill Pickard	Weston-super-Mare, Somerset
Gerald J. Pollinger	Walton-on-Thames, Surrey
Simon Rocksborough Smith	Wimbledon, London
John Rowe	Par, Cornwall
Helen Rowett	Dousland, Devon
Dorothy Stiffe	Llandrindod Wells, Powys
Chris Smith	Payhembury, Devon
Caroline Stickland	Bridport, Dorset
David Templar	Bournemouth, Dorset
Christine Thomas	London
Ion Trewin	London
Angela Tuckett	Stoke, Plymouth, Devon
Henry Williamson Literary Estate	North Devon
Dr John Wroughton	Bath